ADVENTURES OF A FLYING DUTCHMAN

First published in 2006 by

WOODFIELD PUBLISHING
Bognor Regis, West Sussex, England
www.woodfieldpublishing.com

© Rudolf Idzerda, 2006

ISBN 1-84683-014-1

Adventures of a Flying Dutchman

RUDOLF IDZERDA

Rear Admiral (ret.) Royal Netherlands Navy

Translated by Antoinette Idzerda

Woodfield

For my grandsons Jeremy and Thomas

Contents

Presenting the first copy of the first [Dutch] edition to HRH Prince Bernhard of the Netherlands at Soestdijk Palace.

Preface

When my daughter Françoise asked me many years ago to write my memoirs, I said I would do so if and when she produced a future generation.

When this condition had been fulfilled and I had to keep my promise, I was faced with the problem that although I still had my pilot logs, I had never kept a diary. This was forbidden during the war in any case. The memoirs had therefore literally to come from memory, so I apologise for any inaccuracies.

I can say, however, that this work would have been considerably shorter and less complete were it not for the excellent memory and unceasing help and inspiration of my wife, Toni, who also translated the book.

We are both grateful to my brother-in-law, David Da Silva, and his wife Carole, for going through the translation so thoroughly.

Foreword

Paleis Soestdijk, september 2001

Rudi Idzerda is eigenlijk "per ongeluk" in het voormalig Nederlands-Indië vlieger bij de MLD geworden. Ik weet zeker dat hij daar nooit spijt van heeft gehad. Gezien zijn rijke ervaring is Rudi de aangewezen man om in deze autobiografie een persoonlijk beeld te geven van de vele facetten van de Nederlandse militaire luchtvaart.

Toen Rudi in 1975 de Koninklijke Marine als Schout-bij-nacht verliet, heeft hij mij laten weten niet stil te willen zitten en nog wat werkzaamheden voor het WWF te willen verrichten. Gelet op hetgeen hij tot dusver als persoon had gepresteerd konden we Rudi bij het WWF prima gebruiken. Hij heeft zich dan ook tot zijn vertrek in 1984 op bijzonder goede wijze van zijn taak gekweten. Ik ben hem daar zeer erkentelijk voor. Een man die én bij de Koninklijke Marine, in het bijzonder de Marine Luchtvaartdienst, én bij het WWF zijn sporen verdiend heeft.

Prins der Nederlanden

Soestdijk Palace, September 2001

Rudi Idzerda actually became a pilot in the former Dutch East Indies 'by accident'. I am sure he has never regretted it. In view of his rich experience, Rudi is the obvious man to give his personal impressions of the many facets of Dutch military aviation.

When Rudi left the Royal Navy in 1975 as Rear Admiral, he told me that he did not wish to remain idle and would like to do something for the WWF. In view of what he had achieved thus far as a person, we could make good use of him in the WWF. He carried out his task in an outstanding manner until he left in 1984, and for this I am very grateful to him. He is a man who, both in the Royal Navy, in particular the Naval Air Service, and with the WWF has earned his spurs.

Bernhard

Prince of the Netherlands

Prologue

Bandung, Netherlands East Indies, September 1941.

A sun-drenched drilling ground at the barracks of the 5th Battalion of the Royal Netherlands Indies Army (KNIL).

A group of conscripts from class '23, just out of High School, dressed in ill-fitting Army khaki, standing stiffly at attention.

In front of the troop, in immaculate white uniforms, are two naval officers and a corporal-clerk, haughtily regarding the sloppy-looking lot. After the command 'At ease', one of the officers explains that in view of the increasing threat from Japan, the Royal Netherlands Navy has ordered forty new flying boats, for which new crews will have to be trained at short notice. There is especially a need for Officer-Navigators and it has been arranged with the KNIL that a number of volunteers can be transferred to the Naval Air Service (MLD) for immediate training, following which, promotion to officer rank is possible.

'And will volunteers take one step forward?'

Nobody makes a move. I have my doubts, as I suspect that such a training course, followed by a posting in an air-crew, will last much longer than the conscription year I have been called up for, after which I intend to go to university in Batavia to study medicine. So I put up my hand.

'Yes, young man?'

'Sir, may I ask you something?'

'Take one step forward! What is your name and date of birth?'

'Idzerda. October 30th 1923, Sir, but I ...'

'Corporal, write that down. And what is it you wanted to know, young man?'

That's how I got shanghai'd. The Netherlands Royal Navy had clearly not lost any tricks since the seventeenth century. I could not then foresee that this commitment was going to last almost 34 years and would lead to a career that I had never contemplated.

But for that, I have to go back to the beginning...

1.   The beginning

I was born in Surabaya, Java, Netherlands East Indies. My mother, Jeanette Philippus, came from a Rotterdam family and was the eldest of eight children, three sons and five daughters, one of whom had died at an early age. Actually her real Christian name was 'Jannigje', not Jeanette. On the way to the register office my grandfather met a friend with whom he decided to have a drink to celebrate the birth of his first child. Perhaps it was more than one drink for by the time he arrived at the register office he had already forgotten the name for the newly born. He remembered that the name my grandmother had given him began with something like 'Jan' so the Registrar helpfully suggested that it could be 'Jannigje' (a very old-fashioned Dutch name). I can imagine what my grandmother's reaction was, and 'Jannigje' remained a well-guarded family secret.

When she was about twenty years old, my mother met a businessman, and they got engaged shortly before he was sent out to the Dutch East Indies.

She followed him as soon as he was installed at his new post in Surabaya. However it did not work out and so my mother found employment as a secretary with a trading company. She soon met Wieger Sybrand Idzerda, the man she was to marry in 1922 at the age of 22 and who would become my father. They were married in Singapore where the honeymoon was spent at the Raffles Hotel.

My father was the second son of Aurelius Idzerda, descendant of an old Fresian clan that had left East-Friesland (now in northern Germany) at the beginning of the fifteenth century to go to Friesland in the Low Countries.

As a young man Aurelius had been sent to Australia by his father, a gentleman farmer, with a small breeding herd of Fresian cattle that had been ordered there. On the return voyage via the Indies, Aurelius met a beautiful, petite and slender Indo-European girl, Petronella Retel, for whom he apparently fell immediately, and they were married in 1893. He decided to settle in Java, much to the initial dismay of his family in Friesland (although they did receive the money for the cattle…)

Petronella had a Dutch father and a Javanese mother; she was to give her fair-haired, blue-eyed giant of a husband four sons and one daughter (who died at an early age).

Soon after I was born I was packed off to Holland to be shown off as the first grandchild to my grandparents in Rotterdam.

In the sling of the gendoh (nursemaid)

This procedure would be repeated every three years; my mother did not take very well to the tropical climate and returned regularly to Holland to recuperate. My father, who had set up a successful import and export car business together with a partner, 'De Bont and Idzerda', eventually sold out to a large Dutch firm, Lindetevis Stokvis, where he was offered a position as a Director. This gave him the right to three months so-called European leave every three years which suited my mother very well. My father, however, only made sporadic use of his European leave as he preferred to go hunting in Sumatra, Java or Bali. One consequence of this arrangement was that I have attended a total of five different schools.

Naturally I remember little about my early school years, but I do recall that I was always very glad to get back to my beloved Indies after staying in Holland. Compared to the Dutch climate, stolid Dutch food and the rather narrow-minded life style, life in the Indies, with its freedom and beautiful nature, was paradise on earth, certainly for youngsters.

Always been a car buff.

My most pleasant early memories go back to the time when we lived in Bandung in West Java. The climate in Bandung, which is situated at a height of about 700 meters, and is surrounded by mountains with several volcanoes, is relatively cool and mild.

We lived in a new neighbourhood on the outskirts of town in a new house, surrounded by a garden. Unfortunately there were no large trees in it as yet which I sorely missed in view of my early developed passion for climbing trees. However this defect was easily compensated, as far as I was concerned, by the fact that our house bordered on extensive sawahs (rice fields), where there was so much to do, like sloshing around in the mud with bare feet, catching fish and moreover … snakes! At the age of 8 or 9 years old I had become very adept at catching snakes. I grabbed them quickly behind the head so they could not bite, completely unbothered by (and unaware of) the fact that some snakes are poisonous, and are certainly not uncommon in the Indies. One day, however, this was brought home to me very clearly by my father when I ran all excited into the house, shouting: 'Look what a beautiful snake, bright green with a red tail!' Papa turned pale and quietly said: 'Hand it to me, son'. He very carefully took the reptile away from me, went outside and threw it as far away as he could into the sawah.

Then he came back and explained with admirable calm that I had just caught one of the most poisonous snakes that existed. From that moment on I knew that green snakes with a triangular head and wide jaws, due to the poison glands, should be left strictly alone.

My father was an ardent hunter and possessed an impressive collection of rifles. He had a Mauser 10.75 mm that you could down an elephant with, a Mauser 9mm carbine, a Winchester .22 'slide action' with which he taught me to shoot, and his greatest pride, a so-called triple-barrel Sauer which had been specially made to measure for him. This was a double-barrel 12 gauge with a Mauser 7.6 mm barrel mounted underneath. It was a magnificent gun, with hunting scenes engraved on it in silver.

One of his most precious trophies was a giant crocodile measuring more than six meters, at the time the largest crocodile ever shot in Asia. He had been hunting the animal for a long time because it was known to be a man-eater. A crocodile hunt always takes place at night as these animals never show themselves in daytime, certainly not in inhabited areas. The technique was to let yourself be taken downstream by boat while shining a strong light on the river banks. The eye of a crocodile reflects red in the light of a torch, and that is exactly the spot to aim at. After the shot, it is crucial to jump into the water immediately in order to grab a leg before the crocodile vanishes into the deep with one last desperate swish of its tail. Needless to say that the men who were hired for the job would only dare to do this if they knew the 'Tuan' (the boss) and his shooting proficiency well!

This monster, which was a real danger in the river Brantas in the vicinity of Modjekerto in East Java, had once again seized a Javanese woman who was doing her washing at the edge of the kali (river). My father was informed, and he went after the crocodile the following weekend, and this time he was lucky. After skinning and cutting the crocodile open, a number of silver bracelets were found inside ...

My father with the giant crocodile.

I was about three years old at the time and was fetched from home, and made to sit on the head of the crocodile for a photo, which promptly won a prize. (His gift for photography ran in the family: a relative in Holland, also an Idzerda, had written a book on photography at the end of the 19th century that was recognised as a standard work until well after the war.) My father later sold the prepared crocodile skin to an Australian travelling circus.

My father kept two other trophies at home in his study. One was the enormous horns of a 'banteng', the Asiatic wild buffalo, which he shot in Bantam, West Java. He corresponded for a while with the publisher in England of Rowland Ward's 'Records of Big Game'. My father claimed that the horns of 'his' buffalo were wider than those of the buffalo shot in Cochin China, the present-day South Vietnam by the record holder at that time, the Duc de Montpensier. Unfortunately I do not know how it ended.

The other special trophy was the skin of a Balinese tiger, prepared in the traditional manner which included the head with fierce wide-open jaws. My father had shot tigers before in Sumatra and Java (in those days they were still plentiful and considered to be dangerous and harmful) but what was so special about this tiger was that a black 'B' was by chance clearly visible on its head between the ears.

Teluk-Trima, Bali. August 12 1925. The Balinese tiger shot by my father (in the middle of the photo with a cap). It is the only photo in the world showing this extinct species.

Highlights of the Bandung period after my tenth birthday were the camping trips with my father and two friends of mine with their father to what was then the still unspoilt and wild south coast of West Java. The most memorable event took place during the last trip, alone with my father.

As usual the first priority after setting up the tent was to ensure our food supply. My father was very Spartan in his ways: if you wanted to eat in the wilds, you had to shoot something to eat yourself. We only took oatmeal, salt and sugar with us as emergency rations. Wild pigeons were usually first on the menu.

But early one fine morning we were walking along the edge of a clearing in the forest, when all at once a herd of wild pigs digging for food came into view, at a distance of a couple of hundred meters. Without saying a word my father unexpectedly held out his very heavy Sauer triple-barrel rifle to me, and nodded in the direction of the pigs. With my heart pounding, and as in a dream, I crept up to the herd while seeking cover among the bushes. Finally I arrived at shooting distance, lifted the heavy weapon with difficulty, took aim and shot at the largest animal. A loud bang, and I was knocked over backwards by the force of the recoil. The herd scattered in all directions, but – one remained, lying on its side! I had just turned eleven, and I believe that from that moment on my father looked at me with different eyes: I was somewhat more than a spoilt little brat.

The annual crate with presents (mainly books) from my grandparents in Holland. In the background the sawah's and a karbauw (water buffalo).

My first driving lessons date from around the same period. My father had a special hunting vehicle, an old open Hupmobil, equipped with enormous wheels with wooden spokes, large fenders and wide running boards. These boards were ideal for carrying the game, pigs and deer that had been shot. After a while they began to sag with the weight of the load, and were often stained with blood. To drive the car you needed a certain amount of skill and muscle power. Changing gears was heavy work and you had to double clutch in all three gears. Accelerating was combined with manipulating the ignition handles on the large wooden steering wheel, which itself was strenuous to turn.

It will be clear that the car was a sight and my mother refused to set foot in it. Until one unfortunate day when my parents had arranged to visit their friends, Doctor Hammacher and his wife, who lived in a smart and prosperous neighbourhood in Surabaya. As luck would have it, the 'normal' car refused to start but the old Hupmobil was still standing outside, covered in mud and blood after Papa's last hunting trip a couple of days earlier. My mother resigned herself to the inevitable, and my father, never bothered by outward appearances, drove unperturbed to the Hammacher's house, where he was intending to park the car on the driveway in front of the house. However Doctor Hammacher, alerted by the sudden loud noise of the engine of the Hupmobil, and not immediately recognising my parents, came out gesticulating, in an unmistakable way, that the car should be moved around the corner out of sight. My mother's mood was predictable.

The Hammacher family, for that matter, had gone through worse things in life. Years before Mrs. Hammacher had been staying with their two small children in a holiday resort close to the Gunung Lawu volcano, at 3300 meters one of the highest mountains in Java. The crater of this volcano, which had been dormant for as long as people could remember, was filled with rainwater, as was often the case, so that a lake had been formed in the crater. When the volcano unexpectedly erupted, a boiling hot cloud of steam rolled down the mountain, followed by a flood wave of boiling lake water, and finally by the all- destroying flow of lava. The cloud of steam and the flow of lava had missed the house of the Hammachers, but Mrs. Hammacher was taken by surprise by the approaching wave of water, and just managed to escape with one child under the arm. It was too late to reach the baby in the cradle. While fleeing she was overtaken by the flood, lost her child and was herself seriously injured. Later on it appeared that the baby in the cradle had been miraculously carried along by the flow of water, like baby Moses in his basket, and had landed somewhere safe … and unharmed!

My own experience with craters was limited to a descent in the crater of the Tankoeban Prahoe, one of the most active volcanoes of the Preanger Plain on which Bandung is situated. Lava was escaping through cracks and bubbling in small pools everywhere, clouds of steam were spouting up high, and it smelt strongly of sulphur. Shortly afterwards a dreadful fatal accident occurred during a similar school outing. One of the boys stumbled and to the dismay of the others remained lying on the ground. Luckily the person in charge was immediately aware of the cause and forbade everyone to bend down to help their schoolmate get up. A deadly blanket of poisonous gas, hydrogen sulphide, was hanging about one meter above the bottom of the crater. After this, no more expeditions to the bottom of the crater were allowed.

The years of innocent youth were drawing to a close when my father was transferred to Semarang on the North coast of central Java, and my mother, myself and my recently born brother Peter travelled once more to Holland. My father made a business trip to the United States and visited a number of car factories there. After several weeks he joined us at my grandparent's house where we were staying, dressed like a gangster, complete with hat and long coat with turned-up collar. Moreover, his face had a few scars where he had had some birthmarks removed. My mother nearly fainted when she saw him. Not so my grandmother and aunts who all adored him with his dark curly hair.

A hard time lay ahead of me: I was by now twelve years old and had to do entrance exams for High School. Curiously enough, tuition in the primary schools in the Indies did not properly correspond with that in the Netherlands, which was a handicap when having to pass the entrance examination. To increase my chances of success I was first sent to a boarding school in The Hague for a few months for more preparation.

This was probably a salutary experience for a doubtless quite spoilt young boy who had been an only child for eleven years. The discipline was strict and I was initially looked upon as an outsider by the other boys, all 'cheese-heads' (born in Holland), of course, and this sometimes led to a fight. However, I soon settled down and it was with regret that I had to leave the school and the many new friends I had made to concentrate on the entrance exam. In order to reduce the risk of failure, my parents had registered me at two different schools: the Grammar School in The Hague, and the High School in Rotterdam.

Luckily, I passed both examinations, but the choice fell on the High School because Semarang, where we were moving to, did not have a Grammar School.

And so I spent my first year of secondary education at the Municipal High School in Rotterdam.

The journey back to the Indies on the m.s. Dempo went smoothly with the exception of one frustrating incident. We spent a day in Naples, and made use of the opportunity to visit the excavation of the ruins of Pompei, which were then in full swing. Very interesting, especially when we arrived at the entrance to what I seem to remember was a bath house, which was said to have erotic mural paintings. So I was very annoyed and disappointed when my mother would not allow me to accompany her and my father, and made me wait outside for them.

However my vexation quickly changed to glee when it appeared that my mother was not allowed in either! In those days it was apparently considered that such sights were not suitable for ladies.

2. High School 1936-41

When we arrived back in the Indies just before I was due to move up into the second class of High School, I was again confronted with the poor coordination between schools. In the end I was conditionally accepted in the second class of the High School in Semarang. To catch up I spent the Summer holidays with a teacher's family in the mountains at Sarangan in Central Java so that I could benefit from extra tuition.

Sarangan had a special meaning for me because some years before my father had carried out a stunt that made the newspapers. It was a popular holiday resort situated next to a beautiful mountain lake, but it was difficult to reach as the last couple of kilometres were extremely steep and moreover it was a gravel road. It was finally decided to asphalt the road, but the fact that the road was actually too steep for most of the cars at that time was overlooked. When the festive opening took place in the presence of the Governor and other dignitaries, as well as the press, virtually only the larger eight and twelve cylinder cars, such as Cadillacs, Packards and Fords V8 were presented for the start. At that moment Papa suddenly turned up in a small 4 cylinder Peugeot. His firm imported this make, as well as other more popular cars of the time such as Hudson, GMC's Terraplane, and Opel. When it was his turn to start the climb, he got in the car under the derisive looks and comments of his contenders, who were naturally well represented at the event in order to display the qualities of their respective makes. Papa turned his car around, put it in reverse gear, and speeded up the hill backwards without any problem! He knew that reverse gear of the Peugeot was much lower than first gear …

Notwithstanding the daily lessons and tasks, it turned out to be an enjoyable holiday. The oldest son of the teacher, Bob Ronteltap, was to become my best friend and classmate at Semarang High School. Bob was an enthusiastic athlete, and so every morning before breakfast we jogged around Sarangan lake, and at least twice a day we swam the whole length of the lake, which was about one kilometre. We also watched with admiration and some envy the training of Piet

Stam, an older boy from our school, who not only had a marvellous swimming style, but had also won just about every prize there was to be had in the Indies at that time. Furthermore he was the first in the Indies to swim the 100 meter free style in less than a minute. He was therefore chosen to participate in the Olympic Games of 1936 in Berlin. Alas … because of the poor coaching in those days, he was not sufficiently prepared for the temperature of the European swimming water, and was almost paralysed – as he told us later on with his customary humour – when he first dived into the water at the sound of the starting shot.

Our second passion at the time (we had not yet developed an interest in girls) was casting molten lead into moulds to form toy soldiers, which we then painted, and used to enact complete battle scenes.

In Semarang we lived in a lovely house in the hills of New Tjandi, where it was considerably cooler than lower down in town. I had a spacious room with double doors opening on to the beautiful garden surrounding the house, in which a number of huge mango trees were growing. One of these was especially inviting to climb, since it had a comfortable fork between branches at the top, where I liked to sit and do my homework.

On weekdays the day began early with the 'mandi' bath, which is how you bathed in the Indies. The 'mandi room' contained a large tiled basin filled with cold water. A 'gajoeng', a small pan with the handle on the inside, was kept on the edge of the basin, and with this you scooped water out of the basin and poured it over your head; very cool and refreshing, and at tropical temperatures of around 30° C, even early in the morning, the best way to wake up properly. This was followed by breakfast, which for me always consisted of porridge because I could gobble that down quickly, and just make it to school on time, which started at seven o'clock. Punctuality was my father's department where my upbringing was concerned. Every now and again I found a note, containing encouraging incentives, pinned to the inside of the door of my clothes cupboard. One that I remember in particular is: 'Make haste when you have time, then you will have time when you are in haste.'

The school was at the foot of the hills. At a quarter to seven I raced down the hill on my bicycle in the (relative) coolness of the early morning, in sharp contrast with the return journey at half past twelve, uphill in the heat, often on foot pushing the bicycle because some parts were too steep to ride.

We had our warm meal at midday, usually soup and a main course, followed by dessert. We only ate my favourite food, rice with assorted spicy dishes of the Indies, the so-called 'rijsttafel', on Sundays. The bread meal in the evening was occasionally substituted by a Chinese dish, which was delivered to the house. If there was something special to be celebrated, we went down into town to the well-known Chinese restaurant Kit Wang Kie. There was always a surplus of fruit: mangoes in at least three different varieties, depending on the season, bananas, also in several varieties, papayas and hairy leechees. I bought the more exotic fruits like salaks, doekoes (kind of leechee) and djamboes (guavas) which my mother, being a 'totok' (born in Holland) did not fancy, from vendors on the street.

I was quite happy at school. The curriculum was demanding, especially in the fourth and fifth year, but we were free in the afternoon, apart from home work, which was strictly supervised by my mother. After that we usually got together in the swimming pool, on the tennis court or at Boy Scouts to which I also belonged.

My classmates were made up of three different ethnic groups: (Indo)European, Chinese and Indonesian. The first group was hardly in the majority, certainly not in the higher classes, which I naturally remember best. The Indonesians, many of whom were Javanese of aristocratic descent, so-called 'Radens', kept mostly to themselves out of school, although contact in the classroom was relaxed. It was easier to communicate with the Chinese, especially on the sport fields.

I remember getting on well with one Chinese boy in particular, not in the least because he sat next to me in the classroom, and was much better at mathematics than I was. This contact led to my being invited to his home one afternoon to do our homework together. In exchange for his assistance with mathematical problems, I could help him with Dutch composition. He lived in a large house with green glazed roof tiles (green is a lucky colour for the Chinese) in the Chinese neighbourhood of town, and I remember the large white-washed lion statues, and the enormous vases containing flowering plants along the driveway. I was received in a formal yet friendly manner by his parents on the large front verandah. We sat down on beautifully carved dark wooden chairs, inlaid with mother of pearl, around a marble table, where we first drank tea and I was soon asked what my father did. When my host had correctly understood my name he gave a broad smile; it appeared that he knew my father well and they had apparently done good business together. After this we were able te retreat and get down to our homework. When I told my parents about this visit, my father was surprised because such contact at home was unusual, although there were often good business relations with the Chinese men, who sometimes also took part in hunting expeditions with Europeans. It was much later that I became more aware of these different social relationships, which I had automatically taken for granted when I was young. I now realize that, at least in my experience, there was no (or hardly any) question of a colour bar in that colonial era as was the case in the British colonies; it was more a social/ cultural barrier.

Class 5C, Semarang: European-Asiatic mix!

Back to school. One of the teachers I particularly remember was the mathematics teacher – mathematics were certainly not my best subject, but that was not his fault for he was an excellent teacher and very popular. His wife had the reputation of making a fantastic 'rijsttafel ', to which his girth bore witness. One day he invited our class for 'rijsttafel' on Sunday at his home – provided we went there on our bicycles. The catch was that he lived in the mountains about 40 kilometers away. Four of us were not put off and accepted the challenge. I am still not sure why I went along; was it the prospect of a delicious 'rijsttafel' or the chance for better marks ? Several times we had to dismount and walk in the burning hot sun because the road was too steep. We finally arrived on time and the friendly reception, and especially the 'rijsttafel', which surpassed all our expectations, made the effort well worthwhile. Alas, it had no noticeable effect on my marks.

My passion for 'rijsttafel' had been developing for some time. Since we only ate rice on Sundays, and always had potatoes, meat and vegetables during the week (couldn't be more Dutch), I sometimes used to still my craving for something more spicy by secretly sending out the 'kebon' (gardener) in the afternoon when my mother was resting, and my father was at work, to buy something to eat from the nearest 'warong' (small open-air restaurant). It was often 'gado gado', a mixed vegetable dish eaten cold with a warm, spicy peanut sauce.

At the time there was a lot of typhus and dysentery about, so that it was strictly forbidden to eat food from places like that, but I still think that this is how I managed to increase my natural resistance, and the fact remains that I never caught anything.

The servants, especially our 'kokkie' (cook) were quite amused by my obvious preference for their cuisine. The kokkie even taught me the basic principles of cooking, from which I am still benefitting today. The relationship with the servants was pleasant, and from my experiences at that time I found Indonesians in general friendly, cheerful and gentle people. The 'djongos' (butler), a rather reserved and dignified man, always wearing his distictive head cloth which showed that he originated from Central Java, was in charge of the staff. The second in line was clearly the kokkie. I still remember her friendly, grinning blood-red mouth with the eternal sirih/betel nut-wad in her cheek. My mother had trouble with this custom and the accompanying spitting-out of a bright red stream, but my father was able to reassure her that kokkie would only spit into the garden through the kitchen window, and impressed upon her not to say anything about it. Then came the 'babus', the maids, one for the house and one for the washing and ironing, and the 'gendoh', a young nursemaid. I still remember how sweet and patient these young girls were with the babies and young children entrusted to their care. When the parents went out at night, the gendoh often slept on a 'tiker', a mat of woven palm leaves, in front of the door of the nursery. Finally there was the 'kebon', the gardener, and the 'supir', chauffeur, who was actually in the service of my father's firm, Lindetevis Stokvis.

Some of the servants slept in the servants' quarters behind the house.There they had the customary water well which they also used for bathing. The little bucket for taking water from the well was the same type of 'gajung' that was used by us in the mandi room in the main house. Even when showers were later installed in the more modern houses, many people, including myself, still preferred that exhilarating and breathtaking splash of cold water from the gajung.

Holidays were spent in the mountains. My parents had a holiday bungalow in Bandungan, a village some distance away in the mountains behind Semarang, where especially my mother spent a lot of time to escape the often oppressive heat and humidity on the coast. Occasionally I also spent a holiday at the home of my uncle Theo, who was manager of a coffee plantation in East Java on the slopes of the Semeru volcano, at 3776 meters the highest mountain in Java. The coffee beans were picked by hand by the native women, sorted out according to quality, and then spread out to dry in the sun on large round dishes made of woven bamboo bark. The quality was largely determined by the ripeness: dark red berries produced the best coffee. However, the best coffee of all was the so-called 'loewak coffee'. A loewak is a large member of the civet cat family, and feeds partly on a vegetarian diet of fruit and berries. One of its favourite foods is apparently the coffee bean, or rather the fruity pulp around it, and then only the very ripe ones, which are carefully selected by the animals at night. In the early morning the undigested coffee beans, the remains of their nocturnal banquet, spread all over the ground in their droppings, were collected separately and kept as superior 'loewak coffee', exclusively for personal use!

I also enjoyed the hunting trips in the area with my cousin, Wim, who was one year older than me, and a passionate woodsman. We were only allowed to hunt with a caliber .22, and yet we both managed to shoot an Asiatic wild chicken (which is an extremely shy and elusive bird, the ancestor of our domestic chicken), which was good for our reputation as aspiring hunters.

My uncle's home, the traditional-style manager's house, built on poles for coolness, was situated on the edge of the jungle, and was surrounded by a large garden which bordered on the coffee bushes. As was customary, the house included an enormous verandah at the front where most meals and other activities in the home took place. There was no electricity so that at night the verandah and living quarters were lit by large carbide lamps, which spread a bright white light. When you went to your bedroom, you had to carry a so-called 'lampoe templek', an oil lamp with a long glass funnel which gave a pleasant soft yellow light, and which was hung on a special hook on the wall. You also needed to take this lamp with you when you went to the toilet in the evening which was behind the house at the end of a long, dark, roof-covered tiled path. I remember that I tried to avoid these trips in the dark as much as possible as it was known that panthers were in the habit of sneaking around the house at night. The family had a number of dogs and, aware of the fact that panthers specially fancy dog meat, these were carefully locked up in the house at night since they had already lost several. Panthers supposedly hardly ever attack human beings – but you never know …

From an early age I was extremely interested in everything that walked, crawled, flew or swam. I devoured my father's hunting books, which filled a whole bookcase, including the well-known standard work *Brehms Thierleben*, although, at least in the beginning, this was confined to looking at the illustrations, not yet being proficient in German. I still remember, among others, the beautiful copper engravings by Albrecht Dürer.

When I was twelve I started on my first aquarium, and it was not long before I had three of them, plus a terrarium. I caught the fish and reptiles myself, and sometimes if I had enough pocket money I would buy imported tropical fish from the Chinese shop. Years later I met a colleague in the Navy, Theo Vlothuizen, whom I recognised straight away as an old school friend with whom I had often gone hunting for reptiles in an old fort on the outskirts of Semarang. The instant recognition was mutual, and we both called out simultaneously, 'kadals!' – which is Malaysian for lizards.

'Snort' as a baby.

I was also greatly interested in mammals. When I was much younger my father had once brought home after a pig hunt a very young piglet that had been abandoned by its mother during the flight. This little pig, with attractive stripes along its rump, was promptly given the rather unoriginal name of 'Snort', and soon settled in as our house pet. He was fondled by everyone and I can still hear the clicking of his little hooves on the tile floor when he was tripping along behind me; he was really an adorable and intelligent pet.

However as time went by Snort was growing like anything without us really noticing that he was slowly acquiring quite a ferocious appearance. On one memorable day my parents had organised a dinner party at home for the managing director of Lindetevis Stokvis who had just arrived in The Indies from Holland with his wife on an official visit. My mother had gone to great trouble to ensure a stylish reception, since in effect it concerned my father's boss.

Next to the dining room there was a separate scullery, where the dishes to be served were kept warm, and the connecting doors between the dining room and the scullery were swinging doors so that the 'djongos' had his hands free to carry the dishes.

The animated conversation around the table was suddenly interrupted by a strange clicking noise (Snort's tusks against the swinging doors), and a loud 'GRUNT!', and then, to the amazement and horror of the guests, an enormous wild boar came charging into the dining room. Pandemonium!

Shortly afterwards when the gardener threatened Snort with his broom because he was again caught digging up the plants, Snort chased the gardener up a tree where he stayed the whole afternoon because he didn't dare to come down, and that was the final straw. Snort was banished to the Zoo to be with his own kind, where we visited him several times and he always recognised us. We could pick him out from the others because of his tail, which had apparently been partly bitten off before he came to us as a baby.

'Jacob' drinking milk.

Another animal, that was easier to handle, was a civet cat, a kind of marten, which I had once bought at the 'pasar' (market) as a very young hairy little ball, for fifty cents. He was given the name 'Jacob' and slept in my room in a basket. He rapidly grew into a very attractive, striped and lively pet. A bit too lively for my mother's angora cat because Jacob had a habit of quickly pulling out tufts of the cat's fur whenever their paths crossed. However, as is really always the case with wild animals, it is fine while they are still young but problems arise once they are fully grown. So it was with Jacob. Before he chose freedom of his own accord, he had even bitten my big toe. Soon after he disappeared, we were driving home late one evening after the cinema, when we suddenly saw his eyes lighting up in the beam of the headlights. He was standing on his hind legs as usual, and was making that typical clicking sound that these animals are known for (vide Rikketik in Rudyard Kipling's classic 'The Jungle Book'). I got out of the car and tried to touch him, but he would have none of it, and vanished into the night – and quite rightly so.

For my birthday I was once given a large birdcage, which was constructed around an immense mango tree in the back garden. Unfortunately the holes in the wire turned out to be a little on the large size, for the smaller birds soon managed to escape. However there was enough choice of bigger birds to be had at the weekly bird market in Semarang, all equally beautiful and colourful.

I had a somewhat sadder experience with my tame 'badjing', an Asiatic squirrel, which I had also bought at the pasar. It became very tame, and liked to sit on my shoulder where he would sometimes chew on my ear, which was less appreciated. But one unfortunate day I was walking in the room with the badjing on my shoulder, followed by my little brother Peter, who was then about three years old. The little squirrel suddenly jumped off my shoulder on to the floor, probably to climb up Peter, with the sad consequence that my little brother stepped on it by accident – and that was the end of the badjing.

And then there was the Beo, a beautiful, shiny, black bird, belonging to the starling family, and adorned with large bright yellow ear lobes and beak. He possessed a melodious singing voice, but more importantly, he was gifted with a talent for almost perfectly imitating people's voices, better than any parrot. But not only people's *voices*. Our Beo had been given to my father by a Chinese business associate, who had kept the bird in a cage in the passage next to the toilet, and we were quickly entertained with a unique imitation. First the squeaking of a door, then the grinding of a key in the lock, followed by the bang of the toilet seat being let down (the reader will be spared the rest …). Then came the flushing of the water closet, and once more the grinding key and the squeaking door. Luckily we were, in time, able to teach Beo a more refined repertoire. For instance he could whistle the first few bars of the national anthem perfectly with his marvellous high-pitched tones. He also unfailingly greeted us with: 'Hello, how did it go?' or 'Would you like a cup of tea?' when you approached his cage. In short, Beo was a delightful companion who was allowed to flutter about freely in my room, and would come and sit on my shoulder when I was home. But alas also Beo came to a tragic end.

When my mother travelled once more to Holland with my brother and me, my father stayed behind for a couple of months alone with Beo, who became noticeably more and more subdued. Being a natural performer, he was missing the attention he was accustomed to. My father told me later that Beo would suddenly burst out in the middle of the night and sing his whole repertoire; he had clearly become neurotic. When my father also had to leave, Beo was left with friends, and after a couple of weeks, and refusing to eat, Beo was found dead in his cage. This was apparently not a unique case: Beos are very sensitive birds, and they not only need a lot of attention but also get attached to people.

Notwithstanding my love of animals, I had no problem with hunting. My father had impressed upon me at an early age that it was acceptable to kill animals as long as it was done for food, or for a worthwhile trophy, and as long as it was done skilfully, without unnecessary suffering. Hunting and fishing expeditions were therefore unforgettable adventures for me.

One fishing trip in particular is still fresh in my memory. My father and I, together with the Idzerda clan, two uncles and cousin Wim, went camping on the south coast of East Java. There was a large cliff just under the surface of the sea, barely visible in the surf when a wave broke against it. It was known that there was always a lot of fish around that rock. We had rented five outrigger canoes from native fishermen, one for each of us, complete with skipper and fishing tackle. This consisted of a heavy line of woven palm fibers with a huge hook at the end to which a cock's tail feather was attached. The idea was that this feather would start spinning because of the current, and this was apparently an irresistible bait for fish. However I was beginning to wonder how reliable this theory was when, after bobbing about on the strong swell of the Indian Ocean for more than an hour, I still had no bite, and neither had the others. But then something happened. A strong tug, and the line was running out with a hissing sound at great speed. My skipper shouted 'indjek!' (step on it) and pointed to my – naturally – bare foot, but I thought it was more sensible to grab a bamboo stick, that was lying on the bottom of the boat, to put a brake on the line. After a hard struggle we managed to pull the fish aboard, and it turned out to be a monster of more than a meter (no fisherman's tale). It was apparently one of a shoal of tunny that had been hunting other fish, and it just happened that we were in the middle of one of those hungry shoals, because within a quarter of an hour, with the help of my skipper, I caught two more, one of which was even larger than the first, while my companions jealously looked on. But then it was over, and after the excitement had died down, the constant swell was making me feel squeamish. Luckily the others had also had enough, so it was decided to go back on land.

That evening we had an unforgettable feast. My youngest uncle, the fair-haired Aaldert, turned out to be a natural born cook. The fish was first cleaned, then rubbed with a mixture of tamarind, soya sauce and fresh 'lomboks' (red peppers) and wrapped in banana leaves. While the fish was marinating, a big camp fire was prepared on the beach to cook the rice. As dusk began to fall, the fish was placed on the hot ashes – that aroma! And then the taste, the fun, and the teasing back and forth – of course, being the youngest, they had let me have the best spot to fish to avoid disappointment…

At the time it was possible at sixteen to obtain a temporary driving licence, with certain limitations. My father gave me a very small Opel for my birthday, an early version of the Mini. I was allowed to practise driving in the back garden where there was a large lawn with several trees, around which I could practise manoeuvring. I once made a trip to Bandungan in the mountains with three friends crammed into the car. Although my passengers had to get out and push on the steep parts, the journey went a lot quicker than our bicycle trip before.

Unfortunately a fatal accident occurred, caused by a minor, whereupon the Governor promptly withdrew all temporary driving licences, and the little Opel passed on to a new owner.

The German occupation of The Netherlands in May 1940 caused a lot of upset, especially when some time afterwards we received a letter via the Red Cross informing us that my grandparents' house in Rotterdam had been totally destroyed in the infamous air raid. Luckily the whole family had survived the attack. A direct result of the German agression was the internment of all German nationals living in the Indies, and the decision to stop German lessons in the High Schools. Looking back, this last measure seems rather foolish, although I myself had no real objections at the time being as German was my weakest foreign language subject.

My last hunting party was the most unforgettable of all, although I could not know then that it would be the last time with my father.

Now that I had turned sixteen, my father decided that I was old enough to handle a real gun, his Mauser 9mm carbine. That made me feel quite grown-up already, and this feeling was only enhanced by what was still to come.

The Idzerda clan had organised a hunting expedition to the island of Bali, and cousin Wim and I were allowed to go along. In those days the west coast of Bali was practically uninhabited; there were even tigers roaming about. The starting place for the crossing was Banjuwangi, a fishing village at the farthest point of East Java. There we rented a number of outrigger boats to take us to the coast of Bali. However, the crossing had to be postponed because of unfavourable winds, so we had to spend the night there. The Kepala Kampong (village head) offered us hospitality, and somewhat to my surprise this was accepted, instead of looking for hotel accommodation in Banjuwangi. It was a special experience for me: the natural dignity and culture of these very simple villagers and the way they received us, was for me, a city boy, whose contact with Javanese had in fact only been with servants, quite a revelation. Equally so was the respectful manner of my father, who conversed with our host in fluent high- Javanese, of which, for that matter, I did not understand a word. (Malay was the 'Lingua Franca' between Europeans and natives in those days).

The crossing took place the next day without any further setbacks. (little did I know then of the drama that was to take place in that very area a year and a half later, when our Royal Navy battled with the Japanese Imperial Navy and suffered heavy losses)

We landed late in the afternoon on a narrow beach with the jungle right behind. The tents were set up, and Wim and I were sent off with our light caliber .22's, to forage for food, which would most likely be pigeons. We split up, and after a while I suddenly sighted a 'kidang', an Asiatic roe deer, near a small pool of salt water, which was filled by the sea at tide. That was rather too big a target for a .22, but luckily I had put a couple of loose 'Extra Long' cartridges in my pocket, so I decided to try anyway. No way Wim could match that with his measly pigeons.

I crept up as close as I could, and aimed at a spot just above the animal's front leg, for the so called heart-shot. It worked! The deer fell over and just to make sure, I gave him a mercy shot behind the ear. The catch was too heavy for me to carry by myself, so I returned triumphantly to camp to report, and to get help. That evening we ate 'sateh' (meat marinated in soya sauce and spices, and roasted on skewers), together with Wim's roasted pigeons. Such hardship …

I had noticed on my way back to the camp a very strong wild animal odour, the kind you smell at the cages of wild animals in zoos. I was apparently taken seriously because the next day we retraced my path in the company of a native guide, and indeed, he discovered fresh tiger tracks. I had thus probably been followed by a curious tiger, although I didn't understand why he had not been more interested in my left behind kidang. I did have to swallow a few times though, despite the fact that I knew a normal tiger is not supposed to attack an upright person. Still, you never know for sure whether the tiger knows that tale too!

The big event, however, took place a few days later, when I went out to reconnoitre alone with my father very early in the morning, and we saw in the distance a large deer with beautiful antlers. And again, just like five years earlier, my father looked at me and without a word nodded in the direction of the deer. This time I had my 'own' Mauser, and I was able to down the animal with a single shot in the region of the heart. Nothing could spoil my holiday after that.

Another time we suddenly saw, at quite some distance away, a large deer with handsome antlers, grazing on the mountain slope on the other side of a ravine. We looked for cover, and my father brought his large Mauser 10.75 with telescope into position. The distance was easily several hundred meters and I held my breath in anticipation. After carefully and lengthily taking aim, his finger finally curled around the trigger. Then a dry click followed instead of the loud bang I was expecting, and I looked at him in astonishment. He grinned, and said:

'We've already got one of these, haven't we?' He was right, of course, we already had a beautiful trophy, and for the meat it would be better to shoot a young, tender animal.

With my father and guide at my trophy.

After this wonderful summer holiday, the last school year began, at the end of which, if the final examinations went well, I would be in possession of my diploma, necessary for entering University. However this was by no means certain since my schoolwork had suffered greatly under all sorts of other, more pleasurable, activities, which usually had higher priority, notwithstanding my mother's admonishments and my father's threats, one of which was to send me to a strict boarding school.

My intention was to study medicine, and so it was high time to do something about my marks. I did indeed work very hard that final year, and even girl friends dropped out of the picture. Luckily I made it, and I was entered at Batavia University since Leiden, in Holland, where I had originally planned to study, was no longer attainable because of the German occupation. A room was found for me at the home of friends in Batavia., the capital of the Netherlands East Indies. The diplomas were celebrated in style; first with a fancy dress ball in the gymnasium, followed – with no sleep in between – by a nocturnal climb to the top of the Merbabu, a nearby volcano. Six school friends, led by Ulco van Wijck (a student who throughout his whole school period had earned the highest average marks in the history of the school) participated in the climb. Ulco was a budding genius, and an amateur astronomer, who would later be awarded a scholarship in the United States, followed by an appointment at the famous Mount Palomar Observatory in California. I was to meet him again under the most unlikely circumstances, but that will come later.

Ulco had pagan tendencies and wanted to watch the sunrise from the top of the mountain. Although on the way up I kept wondering how I could have been so crazy as to go along, it turned out to be a very special experience.

With Bob Ronteltap.

I was given a motorbike as a present for passing the final exams, as was my friend Bob Ronteltap. My mother, who was not at all enthusiastic about the idea of a motorbike, made a pact with me that she would pay for my petrol as long as I was accident-free. I managed to keep it up for a few weeks until one day, in a sharp bend on a mountain road, I suddenly came across a peanut vendor, carrying two large baskets of peanuts attached to the ends of a yoke on his shoulders. Moreover, he was walking in the middle of the road. He was not hurt, and I had nothing more than a scare and a few scratches, and I would have probably been able to keep the whole thing quiet were it not for the fact that when I arrived home and was greeted by my mother, while dismounting the peanuts rolled out of my clothes.

I made a wonderful trip with Bob on our motorbikes from Semarang via Surabaya to Nongodjadjar, a holiday resort in the mountains, where my mother was newly installed after my father had been transferred to Surabaya. This journey of about 500 km brought to mind a feat that my father had accomplished in his younger days. He had participated in a long-distance motorbike race from Batavia to Surabaya, a distance of more than 1000 km, which in those days would easily take up to twenty-four hours. Towards the end of the race he was in the lead, but was suddenly overcome by fatigue and fell off his bike . He clambered on again, and managed to stay awake for the rest of the distance by now and again touching the spark plug of the engine. The electric shocks were effective and he won the race.

This marked the end of the last carefree holiday of my youth, because the Army was now calling, but that is another story.

3.   The Dutch Royal Navy 1941-42

It all began when I was called up for military service at the end of August 1941.

As was to be expected, I was conscripted for the Royal Netherlands Indies Army, which meant that I would have to walk around in army uniform for a whole year before I could start on my studies. I was assigned to the 5th Battalion in Bandung, together with my fellow schoolmates for the training course for reserve officer. The soldier's life did not agree with me at all. We all slept in a large hall on wooden cots with coarse mattresses filled with straw (and cockroaches), with grubby covers. The food was abominable, and the drilling exercises were exhausting and mind-dulling. I had never felt so awful and humiliated in my life.

My parents had sent me some money – or rather my mother, for Papa didn't think it was all that bad, it makes a MAN out of you – so I could stuff myself on Sundays at a Chinese restaurant when we were allowed out of barracks.

This episode did not last long because within a few weeks our class '23 had to fall in for the confrontation with the Royal Navy, as I have already described.

In retrospect I have never regretted the 'voluntary' transfer to the Navy. We – apart from me, a number of other 'volunteers' had also been assigned – were stationed at the Naval Air Base Morokrembangan near Surabaya, at the time the largest Naval Air Base in the Southern Hemisphere. We were quartered in a spotlessly clean building with separate dormitories and proper beds with real sheets. Breakfast was at six-thirty and at ten o'clock there was a second breakfast. The lunch was excellent, and in the evening an extensive bread meal was provided. Moreover, we could change our detested sloppy green outfits and the puttees, which were continually coming loose, for a light white sailor's uniform, delightfully cool in the hot tropical sun of Surabaya. Working and flying uniforms were khaki with a bamboo hat and gym shoes.

The course began with a military basic training with the Marine Corps at the Oedjoeng Barracks in Surabaya. There we were traditionally handled roughly, and yet I had no trouble with the extremely strict discipline. The Marines were a special kind of people, a class apart. I remember one incident when we were being drilled by a Marine corporal, and the man in front of me, my school friend Jan Adriaanse, made an awkward movement with his rifle and nearly stabbed my eye out with the mounted bayonet.

The four sailor boys. From left to right: Jan Adriaanse, Rudi Idzerda, Luc Oldhoff and Leo van der Graaf, October 1941.

'What the hell do you think you are doing, asshole?'

'I got perspiration in my eyes, Corporal'.

'Perspiration? Perspiration? *Officers* perspire ... Petty Officers sweat ... and you lot ... you...you only fester!'

Yet we couldn't help liking the tough little corporal, and we were full of admiration for his prowess on the obstacle course. We did our utmost, healthy chaps at least twenty years younger, to beat him, but never really succeeded. Ultimately, I and another school friend of mine, Bram Kruit, managed to keep up with him (after some hard training in our spare time), perhaps we were even a centimeter ahead of him, which elicited an approving grunt. After that he treated us almost like human beings.

The theoretical lessons in navigation, aeronautics, meteorology, aerial gunnery, etc. were partly given in the Royal Institute of the Navy in Surabaya, sometimes together with the Naval Cadets, and partly on the Naval Air Base. I was surprised and relieved to discover that mathematics made much more sense to me than at school now that I had to apply it in practice.

We thought that our simple sailor uniform did not compare very favourably with the smart dress of the cadets with their traditional silver dagger hanging on a chain. One time some of us attempted to compensate this by veering out our jack-knife (traditional issue for sailors, carried in a black sheath on the belt) with the cord that was normally tied around the hilt, so that the jack-knife was dangling at knee-height, just like the dagger of the Cadets. This was not appreciated at all: it was 'an insult to the Cadet Corps', and a severe reprimand was the result.

We were further instructed in Morse code, and in shooting with pistol, rifle and aerial machine gun. It became really interesting when we had to put theory into practice on board a real aircraft. Years before in Semarang my parents had once treated me to a short air trip over the town, but this was quite different. To begin with we were taken by sloop to the plane, a twin-engined Fokker T IVa on floats, and the first flight was much less comfortable. However I soon got used to it, and flying began to fascinate me. Only I would have preferred to sit in the pilot's seat at the controls instead of in the uncomfortable nose dome, where I was expected to pass on the correct course to the pilots.

Communication with the pilots was very primitive. There was a kind of intercom, consisting of a funnel connected by a rubber tube to the pilot's head phone, but you usually indicated changes in the course by sticking your hand outside the nose turret, showing the number of degrees by the number of fingers you held up, while pointing to port or starboard as required. If a message had more substance, you wrote a note and tapped on the shoe – gym shoe as leather shoes were forbidden on account of the vulnerable linen fuselage covering of the Fokker – of the pilot who was sitting in the cockpit above you, and whose feet you could see on the rudder pedals behind you.

The navigator also had a drift meter at his disposal. This consisted of a hole in the floor that was fitted with a rotatable bronze ring marked in degrees, with three steel wires on the diameter which you had to line up with the wind stripes or the wave crests which you saw below you; we seldom flew higher than 1000 meters. You also learned how to estimate the wind velocity at sea level with the help of these wind stripes and wave crests, which together with the drift angle were needed for calculating the ground speed, with the aid of a plastic calculator disc.

In the front turret a 7.7 mm machine gun was mounted which you had to operate standing up, in the breeze. Shooting exercises were carried out exclusively on ground targets.

I made up my mind that I would apply for pilot training as soon as I had a chance, but for the time being this was out of question. The Japanese war machine was slowly but surely rolling our way, and the training was speeded up. We received our navigator's licence with the accompanying gold wing on our sergeant's uniform, as we were simultaneously promoted, just when the first air raid attacks on Java began in February 1942.

The Naval Air Base Morokrembangan was an obvious and frequent target, and an attacking bomber formation arrived every morning at exactly ten o'clock, when we had to rush to the bunkers. These bunkers were rather exceptional, and to my knowledge they have not been used anywhere else in the world. They were heavy egg-shaped concrete constructions, and the bottom of the 'egg' fitted into a concrete basin. The idea was that a direct hit would bounce off the top of the 'egg', and the subsequent explosion right next to it would then be absorbed by the bunker being able to sway in its basin, and thus yield to the pressure. When the first air raid occurred, my class was in the Navigator School building and as soon as the siren sounded, we were directed to the nearest bunker. Indeed all we noticed during the heavy air raid were muffled rumblings, and a slight swaying motion if a bomb dropped close by. However I did not like the feeling of being locked in, and I decided that the next time it was necessary I would shelter outside in the trenches that were also available for that purpose.

Naval Air Base Morokrembangan 1941. With Jan Adriaanse,
and Leo van der Graaf (with bamboo hat and gym shoes).
Left in the background is the egg-shaped bunker.

The first attack on Morokrembangan took place on the third of February, 1942, with 36 'Bettys' (twin-engined bombers) and an escort of about the same number of Mitsubitshi 'Zero' fighters. At a height of 4000 meters, the 'Bettys' accurately hit the base, and after a couple of days of daily attacks, 'Moro' was practically demolished, and all the float planes and flying boats that were moored in the basin were reduced to smoking and half-sunken wrecks. What the bombers had overlooked, was finished off by the fighters. We were completely taken aback, as we had been led to believe that the Japs, with their poor eyesight (didn't they all wear glasses?) and their rickety aircraft, were nothing to worry about.

Just promoted to Sergeant-Navigator, with my mother and brother.

A few of us once tried to hit back at them after we had succeeded in dismantling a machine gun from one of the flying boat wrecks. We set it up on a pole, and emptied a cartridge belt at the low-flying Japanese fighter planes. We nearly had to pay dearly for this, because one of the Zeros, having seen our pathetic attempt, turned back and treated us to a lengthy burst from his 7.6 mm machine guns. The heroes plunged into the water to hide under a concrete slope, used for pulling the flying boats onto the shore. But there we discovered, to our horror, a large sea snake, which had apparently also looked for shelter. Reminded of my snake escapades as a child, I knew that all sea snakes are poisonous (wide jaws), so better to face the Japanese bullets, but luckily the fighters had by then disappeared.

This was a bad blow to our morale since it was clear that our forces were no match for the Japanese superior power. This conviction was further strengthened when one day I watched how a lone P40 fighter (either American or Australian) over Surabaya lost out in a dog fight against a number of Zeros. A steep dive and a long smoke trail behind the fighter announced the end of an unequal battle.

With this in mind, I was feeling quite tense when I was placed in an operational crew as Sergeant ARO (Aspirant Reserve Officer) Navigator, although, having just turned eighteen, I was also very proud of my new status. The patrols with our Fokker T-IV were mainly over the Java Sea and the entrance to the Straits of Madura. Flights further away in the Archipelago were considered too risky for the slow and fragile T-IVs. We flew distant reconnaissance for the Allied fleet under the command of Rear Admiral Karel Doorman, and we also escorted the US cruiser *Marblehead* and its escort of four destroyers for a while, but fortunately we never met any Japanese fighters – otherwise this story would never have been told.

I did once observe a submarine under water. The Java Sea that day was very clear, and moreover I could see the wake of a periscope just disappearing. When I reported this to the plane captain, he had his doubts (after all, he was saddled with an eighteen year old boy-navigator) and moreover, the position of our own submarines was not certain, so it was decided to do no more than drop a marker, consisting of a kind of paper bag, filled with aluminium powder.

Upon our return to base I was summoned by the Chief of Staff at 'Moro' to report on the incident. He looked me up and down doubtfully, and asked how I could be sure that it hadn't been a whale, to which I replied that I had never seen a whale with a periscope. I was promptly reprimanded for being cheeky!

My plane captain told me later that none of our own submarines had been reported in that area at the time …

Alas we were not all lucky. A navigator colleague and a very good friend of mine, Koos Kuiken, was shot down with the rest of his crew off the coast of Bali, close to where a year and a half earlier the Idzerda clan had happily embarked on their hunting expedition.

The situation soon became hopeless, and at the end of February 1942 the Navy High Command decided that all remaining aeroplanes were to be evacuated to Colombo in Ceylon, and to

Australia. My Group had already been evacuated in February to an emergency base on the River Brantas, close to the village Modjekerto, the very place where my father had shot his world record giant crocodile fifteen years before.

This emergency base, which was given the codename Leeuwarden (the name of a town in the north of Holland), was ordered to be destroyed on 1st March and our Fokker T-IVs, which did not have sufficient range to reach Australia, were scuttled in the river. The crews went over to Dornier Do24s and Catalina flying boats. With pain in my heart, I gave my motorbike away to someone who was staying behind, and made him promise to call my parents as soon as we had taken off, to inform them that I had left the country.

The Fokker T-IV.

Our Dornier, the X23, had engine trouble, so we could not leave at the same time as the others. A hasty repair was made and night had already fallen by the time we were finally able to take off – quite a feat for the pilots on that rather narrow, winding river in the pitch dark.

It would be more than three and a half years before I would return to the country of my birth.

Our destination was Broome, a small pearl-fishing village on Roebuck Bay on the west coast of Australia. The flying distance was about 2000 kilometres, and this could only be attained with the Dornier by taking along a large amount of gasoline in tins. We had to pour the fuel from the inside of the aeroplane, during the flight, into the outboard tanks, so-called 'stummels' which in the Dornier also served as floats.

We escaped to Australia with a Dornier DO-24

The stench of fuel in the cabin was not very conducive to a pleasant flight – obviously there was no smoking – not to mention the constant fear of Japanese fighters. Apart from that I had other things on my mind for I was responsible for the navigation, which I had to do with the help of a page torn out of a small school atlas. On this map Java was in the top left corner and Australia at the bottom on the right. I drew a straight line connecting the two, and it was up to me to get there. Well, I could hardly miss Australia, but when after more than ten hours flying we finally reached the coast, the pilot asked me:

'Port or starboard'?

A fair question, but I had not the faintest idea, since there were no recognisable landmarks. So I gambled with fifty percent chance:

'Starboard, Sir.'

Wrong. Although this mistake probably saved the lives of our crew, as would appear later.

So we followed the coastline in a south-westerly direction, and arrived with the last drop of fuel at a place which I was able to identify as Port Hedland. We landed on the sea, and taxied into the little harbour in the hope of finding some fuel, because by now we realised that Broome was in the opposite direction. However the village looked deserted. I was sent ashore with the wireless operator in a rubber dinghy to investigate. Suddenly we saw a weather-beaten face under a wide-brimmed hat peering round the corner of a building, followed by the rest of the Aussie when he realised that we were not Japanese. Our Dornier, with its red, white and blue roundels on the fuselage and wings, had been mistaken for a Japanese aircraft with red 'sun' markings.

After refuelling, we took off again and just made it to Broome before dark, where we landed and anchored in the large bay. The next morning the wireless operator and I were again sent ashore. In the meantime we had noticed that the bay was filled with our flying boats, nine Dorniers and Catalinas, all that was left of the Naval Air Service, apart from the few that had got away to Colombo.

We had only just gone ashore when we heard the drone of aircraft engines high up in the sky. We looked up and saw a perfect formation of nine fighters, which first went into 'line astern' followed by a dive, one by one. I was about to comment on what modern aircraft the Australians had, when all of a sudden I recognised them: The much feared Zeros!

Then all hell broke loose with a deafening din. First a burst with their 7.6's to get properly in range, followed by the muffled 'pom-pom-pom' of their 20 mm cannon. They certainly were good shots, those 'short-sighted' Japanese. Our flying boats burst into flames, one after the other. We noticed how the Catalinas burnt much more fiercely than the Dorniers: allegedly the American aluminium alloy contained more magnesium.

Our own Dornier, which as latecomer was lying somewhat apart, seemed at first to have escaped attention since it was partly concealed by the heavy smoke. This is probably what saved our crew, since they had time to jump overboard. Unfortunately that was not the case with the other flying boat crews, some of whom in desperation had even found the courage to shoot back with their machine guns. It was only years later, after the war, that I read in a Japanese report that one of the Zeros had been hit and had to ditch in the Timor Sea, whilst some of the others had several bullet holes.

As opposed to our aircraft, the others were crammed with the wives and children of navy personnel. This was against all regulations, but who would blame them if it were a choice between that and leaving them behind under Japanese occupation.

The ensuing disaster was terrible. Forty-eight people were killed, including thirty-two women and children, and another thirty-two were wounded, during the few minutes that the attack lasted.

We were watching from the shore, unaware of the fact that there were women and children on board. We more or less assumed that the crews, fit as they were, would be able to save themselves and swim to safety. All of a sudden I saw something dropping from one of the fighters and heading straight for us, and at that moment I really thought my time had come – you could not survive a bomb at such a short distance away. I threw myself flat on the ground, clamped the peak of my cap between my teeth, and stuck my fingers in my ears, to protect against the air pressure, as we had been instructed. However, there was no explosion, so I slowly opened my eyes and saw the 'bomb' lying in front of me with a big dint in it. It was a discarded drop tank! At that time we had never heard of such a tank that was used for taking extra fuel along, but I did realise that a bomb would not have a dint in it after being dropped.

Somewhat recovered from the scare, we set off in our dinghy to see if we could be of help to our mates. At a given moment I saw the round, bald and black head of someone who was obviously in trouble (for a moment I thought it was an Indonesian), so I jumped into the water to help him into our boat, and saw to my amazement that it was a European woman. Her face was terribly burnt and scorched black and she had lost all her hair. She carried a dead baby under one arm, and crying she told us that she had had another child with her, but we never found it. Later on it appeared that this was Mrs. Amsterdam, the wife of Lieutenant-Commander Amsterdam. They had lost all three of their children, and were themselves both badly burnt.

I heard later from the wireless operator that prior to the raid, he had been surprised and irritated by the constant chatter he had heard over the radio from apparently American aircraft on and around Broome airfield, whereas we had to adhere to strict radio silence! It was obvious that the Japanese had picked up and homed in on this radio contact (a Japanese reconnaissance plane had flown over Broome only the day before the air raid) and the result was evident.

The attack was soon over, but panic and chaos remained. Everyone expected a Japanese invasion shortly, or more air raids. Moreover there was no one in charge. The senior survivor, a commander, was completely demoralised, and not up to his task. Everyone, also the Australian inhabitants of Broome – women and children had already been evacuated – was convinced that it was time to head for the south of Australia, where it was safer, as soon as possible.

I myself and two of my colleagues from the Navigator course, Van Lienden and Mooyaart, had lost all confidence in the leadership, and decided to save our own skins. In retrospect, this was very unwise, of course, we should have stayed with the others, or at any rate informed someone of our plans. Some Australians, who had given us hospitality in their home, offered us a lift in their lorries through the desert to a safe get-away.

'You blokes know all about airplanes, so you can watch out for the Japs.'

This appealed to us a lot more than joining the others on ex-Japanese pearl-fishing boats, abandoned in the harbour, which is what had ultimately been decided upon. The Japanese attack was still fresh in our minds, and those little boats looked to us like too easy a target.

The immediate result of our action was that we were promptly reported as deserters, and we would later be confronted with the consequences.

It turned out to be an unforgettable trip. The West-Australian desert, actually more like a savannah, with here and there a few eucalyptus trees among large rocks, seemed endless, but our Australian companions were obviously used to it. We travelled with the aid of a compass and by the sun, and there were plenty of provisions: flour, with which a special kind of bread, 'tampe', was baked in a hole in the sand, and numerous tins of fruit. Together with a kangaroo that was shot, and once a large monitor lizard, especially its fleshy tail, it was all quite edible. Fresh water was carried in special canvas bags, which were slightly porous, thus always damp on the outside, and through evaporation the water stayed fairly cool. We got on well with the Aussies and my school

English was quickly supplemented with a profusion of new expressions, like 'bloody', at least twice in every sentence. They were rough, hearty and uncomplicated chaps and we trusted them completely.

It was a very special experience when, after a couple of days of rain and bad weather, something went wrong with the navigation. This was very unfortunate since we were also getting short of petrol. Suddenly out of nowhere a figure from the Stone Age appeared, a black man, all by himself, standing on one, very thin leg like a stork, and leaning on a stick or spear. He was completely naked and adorned with long, wavy, dark brown hair and a full beard. But he was not too primitive to understand where we wanted to go. After some deliberation using gestures, he started to trot in front of us – he refused to get on board! After an hour or so he suddenly stopped and pointed to a telegraph pole that suddenly loomed. It was clear that as long as we followed those telegraph poles, we would end up at a place that was inhabited. To thank our Aboriginal – for that is who he was, of course – we gave him some tobacco and a knife. When I looked back after a while, he was still watching us, standing on one leg and leaning on his spear, the first 'real' Australian I had met!

The journey came to an end, for the time being, at an isolated sheep farm on the coast called Anna Plains. There was a primitive radio transmitter there, for which the current had to be generated by pedalling a mounted bicycle. There we met the crew of a Douglas DC3, belonging to the Royal Netherlands Indies Airline, under the command of a well-known pilot, Ivan Smirnoff, famous for his pioneering flight with the Fokker 'Pelican' in 1933 to and from the Indies and the Netherlands. We heard that he had escaped from Java with his DC3 on the same day that the Broome drama took place, and on the way to Australia had been attacked by those same Zeros on their way back from Broome. He had had to make use of all his skills as an ex-fighter pilot and Ace (he served with the Russian Air Force during the First World War) to elude the Zeros, but notwithstanding all his tactics, he was eventually shot down and forced to make a belly-landing on the beach of Anna Plains. Years later I heard that he had been handed a parcel of diamonds in Java to be picked up in Australia, but this was missing after the crash. Later there were rumours that a beachcomber had found a few diamonds, and handed them in to the police, and also that he had suddenly shown signs of prosperity …

When we were once having a meal together at the sheep farm, the owner asked if any of us could ride horse back. I had taken a few riding lessons years before in Bandung and so once more I 'missed a chance to keep my mouth shut'. (Quote from my father).

I immediately realised the blunder I'd made when I was confronted with the snorting steed, foaming at the mouth, which first had to be caught with a lasso. However the embarrassment of backing out seemed worse than falling off a horse, so I clambered on. Luckily it did not last long; after we had been launched like a rocket into the savannah, I could see that he was going to get rid of me by scouring me against the trunk of a tree – this was my chance. At breakneck speed I grabbed an overhanging branch, and we were delivered from each others company.

Soon after, we were picked up by a plane and taken to Adelaide. There we were temporarily housed in a girls school (without girls) yet under strict arrest for we were, after all, deserters. Then we were taken to Flinders Naval Base near Melbourne, the capital of the State of Victoria, where our fate would be decided. We slept in hammocks, which was for me a new and not unpleasant experience, but the food was awful. The Australian Navy folk were not unfriendly; they knew that no one in their right mind would ever desert in the outback of Australia.

One day an officer even asked us if we would like to go sailing. The other two were not interested, but I immediately agreed, even though I had never sailed before – anything to relieve the boredom! I was directed to a small harbour that belonged to the base, where a number of dinghies were berthed, about the size of an Optimist I would say, and I was left to my own devices. I had plenty of time to find out how to rig a boat and to teach myself the rudiments of sailing. Until now, I had only watched it being done. Luckily there was not much wind and moreover I had all the space I needed because everyone was at work, so I could mess about with no one to get in my way, until I had more or less mastered the principles of sailing.

Still, I was beginning to fear that I would have to spend the rest of the war there, when one fine day a Dutch naval officer happened to visit the base and heard about the Dutch detainees. When he saw me there, he asked in surprise: 'What are *you* doing here?'

It was Lieutenant-Commander Amsterdam, his face still bandaged up for the burns.

Within twenty-four hours we were free, accommodated in a choice hotel and told to report to the most senior Dutch naval officer in Melbourne, Rear-Admiral Coster. While we stood stiffly at attention in front of his desk, he started off by giving us a severe dressing down for about fifteen minutes. When he was finished, he cleared his throat, pulled open a drawer, threw a number of coupons on the desk and said gruffly:

'Use these to get your officers uniforms from the clothing store and come back tomorrow to be sworn in.'

Unnecessary to describe how I felt. Promoted as from the second of March 1942, my career as Officer-Navigator in the rank of sub-lieutenant in the Royal Navy Reserve had begun, and would last somewhat longer than I anticipated at that time.

After recovering from all the emotions, I filed a request for pilot training. This was granted and soon I was shipped to the United States with a few other latecomers.

The training of Air Cadets of both the Naval Air Service and the Military Air Force (of the Royal Netherlands Indies Army), who had been transferred earlier from Java via Australia to the United States in February, had already begun.

It was an uneventful journey, in spite of the constant threat of Japanese submarines, and later in the Gulf of Mexico, of German submarines. Our ship was the brand-new SS America, which had been rechristened USS *WestPoint* as a troopship. At twenty-eight knots, it had the Blue Ribbon as the fastest passenger liner in the world, and much too fast for the submarines of those days. There had been no time to transform it into a troop transport ship, so that all the luxury cabins were still intact. It didn't take us long to find out, and soon everyone had exchanged his berth in the dormitory, which had been assigned to us, for a luxurious private cabin.

There were very few people on board, a curious sensation on such an enormous ship. Apart from our group of six, there were a few American officers and civilians, and five American nurses. These were the so-called 'Nurses from Bataan', who became famous later on through the film about the last days of the hopeless fight of the

Americans against the Japanese on the Bataan peninsula in the Philippines. These nurses, who had apparently conducted themselves very courageously, were said to have been evacuated at the last moment in April 1942 by submarine on General McArthur's orders, before the total surrender of the American Forces in the Philippines was a fact. They were traumatised by their experiences, and we saw very little of them. Once I was woken up in the night by screaming. When I rushed out into the corridor, I bumped into one of them, who said: 'Just a nightmare, mister, Go back to bed...'

Due to a lack of Dutch naval uniforms, my friend Leo van der Graaf and I had to wear uniforms of the Royal Australian Air Force.

We sailed to our destination, New York, via the Panama Canal and the Gulf of Mexico. We were in New York just long enough to be taken out by a couple of Americans (we were regarded as war heroes!) to the most famous nightclub of the time, the Stork Club. A young, slender, black woman sang wonderful blues: Ella Fitzgerald. And I had never heard of her.

Within a few days we were on the train to Fort Leavenworth, Kansas, and a new and important phase in my navy career was about to begin.

During the four-day journey we heard that the famous jazz musician, Fats Waller, who was also on board, had died on the train, and this caused some consternation. And I had never heard of him either …

4. Royal Netherlands Military Flying School 1942-43

As well as being a military prison and an Infantry barracks of the U.S. Army, Fort Leavenworth was also an Air Base for the elementary flying training, the so-called Primary Training, and had been assigned to the Dutch by the American authorities. In the meantime the training of the Naval Air Service and of the Military Air Force of the Royal Netherlands Indies Army had been combined.

We were not exactly enthusiastically received by the Dutch Commanding Officer, Lieutenant Colonel 'Max' van Haselen. He began by informing us that the flying course, which had begun a couple of months earlier, had an over-capacity, so that about 30% of the students would have to be transferred to other training courses, such as navigator and air gunner (ultimately it was 47%!) Therefore he didn't give us much chance, especially as some of us, like myself, already had a Navigator's licence.

The instructor to whom I had been allotted, did not help to raise my morale either. Lieutenant Commander Hans Holtz, nicknamed 'Handsome Hans', was admittedly an excellent pilot, and probably also a good instructor, but unfortunately he was one of the old school, who believed that it was necessary first to belittle and humiliate a new student, so as to prevent him from growing too self-confident which could lead to dangerous stunts. However this kind of treatment was the last thing I needed after the encouraging welcome by Lt Col van Haselen. One incident I shall never forget. I had really tried very hard to do my best, and after the last more or less smooth landing, I was hoping for at least an approving nod or something. But Holtz climbed down from the cockpit with a big sigh, shaking his head at me as he slowly pulled off his gloves, and finally said in a pitying tone:

'No Ids, (that's how I was called in those days), no my boy, you're never going to make it!'

I was close to tears and walked away dejectedly. Until a bit later I saw one of his other students leaning against the tail of his airplane, and indeed crying, and that is when my fear of

'Handsome Hans' suddenly switched to anger because I saw through him.

But this didn't help me much until one lucky day when Holtz had a cold and I was passed on to another instructor, Lieutenant Willem van den Bosch, also a Navy man, but an amiable, jolly fellow. Nevertheless he really put me through it and made me do everything that I was supposed to have learned, and then after the last landing said with a grin:

'Alright, Ids, for Christ's sake let me out, now you are on your own, get on with it!'

And I was SOLO! For every pilot an unforgettable milestone.

The PT-19a (Primary Trainer) above Kansas, the aeroplane I went solo on.

This was not at all to the liking of Holtz when, with concealed glee, I informed him of this on his return, and I had to take off with him straight away so that he could check me out again. In the meantime I had done a few more solo flights and regained so much self-confidence that I was no longer afraid of him. However my final satisfaction didn't come until more than a year later during the advanced fighter training. After having had various other instructors, I again had Holtz for the so-called dog-fight. The procedure was that you first had a lesson with the instructor sitting in the back, and subsequently brought into practice what you had just learned by flying solo against your own instructor. This was the chance I had been waiting for, and I made up my mind that I was going to get him, at all costs. And sure enough, after many wild manoeuvres I got on his tail and had him in the gun sight, which I announced by calling 'pop-pop-pop' over the radio, as was customary. He could not shake me off and called an end to the exercise. When I reported to him after landing, he growled something and actually gave a nod of approval.

But I am running ahead of things. We were flying the Fairchild PT 19a, a light low-wing plane with two open cockpits in tandem which, coming from the tropics, took some getting used to in the winter. It was at this time that a phenomenon occurred that I was only able to explain much later, which was the daredevil recklessness. Such behaviour is not uncommon among young men who are trying to prove themselves, but in our case it went beyond all bounds. Even after a thunderous lecture by the C.O., who threatened us with expulsion from the course for the slightest violation (there were too many of us anyway), the extreme low flying continued. The story went around that when Colonel Van Haselen opened his newspaper one morning at the breakfast table, he was confronted with a photo taken from the highest diving board at the local swimming pool *into* the cockpit of a PT 19a … Luckily the pilot was not recognisable.

Also later when we moved on to the Advanced Training with the AT 6 it was a 'must' to fly under the railway bridge over the Mississippi river at Vicksburg – at night, because it was too easy in daytime and moreover your number could be spotted and reported. Naturally I could not be outdone, but I did get a shock when I heard, the morning after, that the bridge was being painted, and steel cables had been suspended for the painters' platforms.

I think the explanation for this recklessness lies in the fact that in the Indies there was a 'macho' culture among schoolboys, who tried to outdo each other in activities like sports, camping and hunting, the climate in the Indies of course also contributing. Possibly, be it subconsciously, the humiliating idea of being kicked out of one's country by the Japanese, had also something to do with it. Years after the war I read reports in which American authorities expressed their amazement over those 'wild Dutchmen', who had a much higher percentage of fatal accidents during training than their American counterparts.

The training proceeded smoothly and we were then transferred to Jackson, Mississippi for the Basic and subsequent Advanced Training. The journey of several hundred kilometres to Jackson, was done by car, since everyone had by now managed to get hold of a second-hand vehicle. We drove in a convoy of about ten cars, and being an officer, I was put in charge of one of these convoys . This brings me to the rather unique position I held during training. Through the special speeded-up course with the Naval Air Service, I was one of the very few officers of my age, then not quite nineteen years old. Almost all the fellow students of my age, who would normally have belonged to my circle of friends (some were even ex-classmates from High School) were at most Sergeant-ARO, and had to address me as 'Sir'! This often caused me some embarrassment, and a few times I was given a reprimand by superior Instructor-Officers for being too familiar and not keeping enough distance. Naturally social contact was much more formal sixty years ago, compared to present day behaviour when school pupils are often allowed to call their teachers by their first name.

Another consequence of my junior officership was that I was always being charged with special tasks, such as leading a delegation to funerals of student pilots killed in flying accidents, which alas happened far too often. I must have done this at least six times.

Furthermore, when there was a shortage of teachers, I was sometimes called upon to give lessons in aerodynamics,. This meant that I first had to study the material myself the evening before so as to be well prepared the following day.

We were billeted at Jackson Airbase in comfortable barracks, although without air conditioning which would not have been a luxury in the sweltering hot Mississippi summers, but in those days we didn't know any better. It took some time for the inhabitants of Jackson to get used to us. We all came from the Indies and some of us were quite dark, and this initially caused some resistance among the local population until they had been convinced that they were not 'niggers', as blacks were then called in the deep South …

Next step was the Basic Training on the Vultee BT 13a, nicknamed the 'Vibrator', more of a 'real' aeroplane with its 450 hp engine. We were usually taken by lorry in the morning to a small grass airfield nearby so as not to hinder the more advanced air traffic on Jackson Air Base.

I remember one incident there very well. My instructor had just got out of the plane, so that I could practise the last lessons by myself, and he left his parachute behind in the rear cockpit ready for his next instruction flight. I took off, and after dutifully carrying out the prescribed steep turns for a while, I thought it was time to develop my flying talent some more, naturally out of sight of the airfield. However, after the very first loop and half roll, I had a real problem for I had completely forgotten the parachute in the back, and it had slid from the seat during my anything but perfect roll, and got caught between the rudder pedals. With more luck than skill, I managed to get the plane sufficiently under control to make a more or less normal landing, after which I was admonished for the 'sloppy landing' and the too short exercise. Needless to say, I never mentioned the real reason.

After the Basic Training was completed, a selection took place for fighter pilots and bomber pilots. Luckily my wish was fulfilled and I was assigned to the Advance Training for fighter pilot on the AT6, which is called the Harvard in Europe.

Attaching the parachute for a training flight with the AT 6. The metal D-ring, with which the parachute is pulled open, is shining on the left side of my chest, and the primitive gun sight can be seen in the cockpit.

With its 600 hp this was almost a real fighter and required careful handling to avoid problems when landing because of the narrow track landing gear, so you had to watch out for ground loops – but therefore a joy to fly.

By this time it was 1943 and we began to give serious thought to getting into the war. But we first had to spend many hours on shooting exercises, dive-bombing and dog-fights.

The shooting exercises, on a target towed by another aeroplane, took place from a base in Florida, Tyndall Field. The 7.7 bullets of the individual aeroplanes were painted in different colours, so that after the exercise it could be ascertained to whom the bullet holes in the target banner (if any) could be attributed.

In order to gain more practice for estimating the required angle-off for aiming at a moving target, i.e. an enemy aircraft, we practised skeet shooting with shot guns at clay pigeons. This was done some distance from the camp at a facility in a wooded area. One late afternoon our group was returning from a shooting exercise, and two of us were walking in front carrying the shotguns, 12-gauge repeat slide-action Winchesters. All of a sudden, a huge wild boar crossed over in front of us. The two in front, both from the Indies of course, reacted automatically by immediately sliding a couple of cartridges into the magazine of their guns and opening fire at short distance. What they had not counted on was that the 12 gauge cartridges were filled with very fine pellets intended for clay pigeons and not for the thick hide of a wild boar! The result was that the infuriated animal went straight into the attack; every time he nearly got one of the two Nimrods, the other one fired a load into its body at literally a few centimetres away. After at least four or five of these shots, the fine pellets began to take effect and the beast fell over. It all caused quite some excitement and in no time a strong branch was cut to hang the trophy on, which was then carried by two men. When we marched into camp with the wild boar, our American colleagues couldn't believe their eyes: 'Those crazy Dutchmen!'

That evening we organised a barbecue and treated our camp to *sateh 'tjelleng'* (wild boar meat roasted on skewers). It tasted good, only you did have to spit out a few pellets now and again.

Soon after, in June 1943, we received our pilot's wing in a ceremony on the Air Base, and it was with great satisfaction that I pinned it on my uniform in place of the old navigator's wing.

It was a real experience to fly the Curtis P40 Kittyhawk fighter, which had been allotted to us, for the first time. There was no two-seater version, which meant that you went solo straight away. Naturally you first had to practise extensively letting down and retracting landing gear and flaps, and under supervision of an instructor, identify all the cockpit instruments and point them out blindfolded. This was done in a plane that had been raised off the ground on jacks.

That first take-off with the P40 was also one of those milestones that as a pilot you never forget. The 1100 hp engine gave a strong torque that you had to counteract with lots of rudder and trim so as not to leave the runway – this was a real fighter!

Day after day we were darting around the sky in our P40s: navigation flights, formation flying, stunting, dog-fights and bombing exercises all had to be practised. The P40s that had been put at our disposal by the Americans were a collection of used planes of at least three different models: the P40-E, the –M and the –N. Especially the 'E' differed from the later versions through the shorter tail, and through its dangerous flat-spin, from which it was almost impossible to recover. For this reason the later versions were equipped with a longer tail that resulted in more docile flying characteristics. The 'M' was an interesting experiment. Since the experiences of the American volunteer squadron, the 'Flying Tigers' in China under the command of General Chennault in 1941 and 1942, it had been established that the P40 was no match for the super-light, manoeuvrable, Japanese Mitsubishi 'O' fighters or 'Zeros', which were given the code name 'Zeke' by the Americans. The P40 was a typical American product, solid and heavy like their cars, at least in those days. (The life of at least one of our pilots was saved thanks to that robustness; after a very bad crash he literally shook off the fragments, and was able to walk away unharmed). Attempts were made to improve the P40M by removing one fuel tank, two machine guns and the armour plate behind the pilot's seat, all of which made the fighter several hundred pounds lighter. The 'M' was indeed a revelation; she climbed like 'a homesick angel', as the Yanks could so aptly put it. However the price for this was not acceptable: too little fire power, and increased vulnerability of the pilot.

We had been told that ultimately we would hopefully be equipped with the modern two-engined Lockheed P 38, a very welcome prospect, since it was clear that the P40 was becoming obsolete. For this reason we were given auxiliary training on a twin-engined trainer, the Beechcraft AT 11, and our departure to the front was postponed.

We made fairly long navigation flights with the AT 11. For these exercises, two fighter pilots took turns at doing the navigation during the flight. On one of these trips I was assigned together with Hans Knoop, who was already a first lieutenant in the Army Air Force, and thus had two silver stars on his shoulder pads. One of the places where we had to land was Robins Field, an American Army Air Force Base, where we were also planning to have lunch. We gave instructions to the ground crew for filling up the plane with gasoline, and I noticed that the mechanics were very respectful towards Hans and even addressed him as 'General'. (In his twenties Hans looked older than he was). Then we realised why: as opposed to the Dutch, only generals have stars in the U.S. Army! (The independent Air Force did not then yet exist in the United States). We decided to play along, and so I carried the navigation case and walked one step behind Hans as his aide-de-camp. In the Officers Mess we were immediately led to the reserved corner for General Officers, and contrary to the other officers, we were served at the table. A signal occasion, especially in view of the fact that Hans would end his career many years later as lieutenant-general and Commander in Chief of the Netherlands Royal Air Force.

Later it became known that the P 38's would not be available in time for the Dutch, so that we would have to go into action with P40s after all, albeit with the latest version, the P40 N.

In September 1943 I was again sent to Tyndall Field, Florida, together with other colleagues, this time to tow the target with an AT 6 for the other students who were following the shooting course. This course ended unexpectedly and dramatically, at least for me and two others.

As so often happens in those regions, a hurricane was approaching from the sea, and all aircraft had to be evacuated. Since it was impossible to tell which direction the storm would take (there were no satellites in those days…), we were all sent in different directions to airfields at a safe distance away. I was given a navigator in the back,

Jan Broekhuyzen, and another pilot, Charlie Uiterelst, was instructed to follow us in formation. Our designated destination was Columbus, Mississippi. However, that turned out to be a bad choice for it soon appeared that the storm was ahead of us, and in no time we were in the middle of the hurricane. Although luckily I had had plenty of instruction in instrument flying, this was something quite different.

The plane was tossed back and forth like a ping pong ball, and now and again was flipped on its back by the strong vertical air currents in the storm, and once we even got into the dreaded flat-spin, but my predilection for aerobatics now came in useful and I managed to recover. All these manoeuvres in the dark, flying on instruments, certainly amounted to a crash course in instrument flying. But I quickly realised that I couldn't keep it up; we had no idea where we were, and trying to land was also out of question. Moreover I was running out of fuel.

We had already lost our companion plane for some time, and I tried to reach him on the radio to advise him to bail out. However I couldn't get contact, so he had probably already crashed and been killed, as would appear later. So I turned our AT 6 on its back, and told my navigator to bail out, which he promptly did. Then it was my turn, and strangely enough I was not at all afraid because there was obviously no choice, and anything was better than being thrown about in that tossing and bucking aircraft. Alas, the hood of the cockpit had closed again, so that after unfastening my seat belts, I found myself lying on the hood and struggling while the aeroplane was flying on its back. How I finally got out, I don't remember.

The sensation of the jump was one of relief, suddenly the engine noise was gone. First count to three as we had been taught so as to fall free of the aeroplane, then a tug at the ring and the parachute opened. The jolt was as expected quite severe, but floating in the dark was definitely not unpleasant. Although now and again air currents got hold of my parachute so that I began to swing about wildly, and several times the canopy closed up, which was not so pleasant. Yet every time the canopy opened out again of its own accord, to my great relief. I tried to call my colleague a few times to make sure that he had also made it, and I shouted at the top of my voice: 'JAAAN – JAAAN', with unexpected consequences, but that only appeared later.

After a few minutes I landed in pitch darkness, in the top of a tree, at least that's what I thought. For after I had finally loosened myself with much difficulty from the parachute harness, and started to climb carefully out of the tree, I bumped straight away against the harness – I had been hanging a few feet above the ground.

In spite of the darkness I found Jan almost immediately; he had landed very close by. I took off my tie, which we held in between us so as not to lose each other in the dark, and we set off to look for some kind of habitation. We soon arrived at a Negro village which was in commotion. They had of course heard the eerie sound of my calling out to Jan in the sky, and that, coupled with the terrible storm, could only mean the coming of the Messiah. The Preacher started ringing the bell, and the entire parish hastened to church to welcome the Redeemer. Alas it was only Jan and Ids...

None the less, they quickly recovered from their disappointment and we were received with warm hospitality. The next morning we were picked up by ambulance, somewhat exaggerated as we had nothing more than a few scratches, and taken to Jackson.

This emergency jump with a parachute made us eligible for the traditional membership of the international 'Caterpillar Club', founded early in the twentieth century by an American, Irvin, as a tribute to the silkworm, which at the time provided the material for parachutes. Irvin was the founder of the Irvin Parachute Company, which supplied parachutes to the Air Force in the United States. The badge is a little gold caterpillar with two tiny rubies for eyes, to be pinned on the lapel, and I have always worn it with pleasure.

An unexpected turn of events then occurred. As a navy pilot I was initially destined to serve on aircraft carriers operating in European waters against the Germans. But since I had left my parents and brother behind in the Indies, I was far more motivated to fight against the Japanese. I filed a request, and quite to my surprise, this was granted. I later heard from my parents that Commander Van der Kroeff, the most senior naval officer in Jackson who had to handle my request, was a friend of theirs years before in Surabaya – whether that had anything to do with it? In any case I ended up as the only naval officer detached with the newly formed 120 Fighter squadron of the Netherlands Indies Air Force. The only other navy man was Sergeant-Pilot Hirdes, who was tragically killed in action not long before the end of the war.

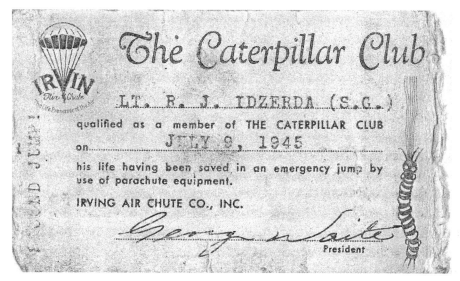

This proof of membership of the Caterpillar Club was presented to me for my second jump on July 9, 1945. I lost the card for my first jump, and I never bothered to ask for one for my third emergency jump on August 31, 1951.

At the end of 1943, we left San Francisco with a C 54 Skymaster-DC 4 for Australia, where our home base would be Canberra. The aircraft had been converted for troop transport, and was equipped with metal bucket seats on either side, which became all the more hard to sit on as we progressed. It was the most uncomfortable air trip I have ever made.

5.   120 Squadron 1944-45

Our squadron was attached administratively to the Royal Australian Air Force, the RAAF, and was stationed at Merauke in New Guinea, the only part of the Dutch East Indies that the Japanese have never conquered. The home base was Canberra where the reserve aircraft were kept and where the pilots were based after being relieved for an exercise and leave period. We were organised in two flights of about fifteen pilots each, who were in turn sent to the operational base for a period of three months.

I can't say much more about Canberra than that I had never seen so many flies in my life, partly due to the enormous flocks of sheep grazing all around. The town itself – *nota bene* the capital of Australia – did not then amount to much, and was actually still in the course of building after an American architect had won the international prize for a design for the new capital.

The camp at Canberra was primitive and the food, which included a lot of mutton, was downright poor, especially after what we had been used to in the United States.

The camp at Merauke was naturally not much better, but you didn't expect it to be. Furthermore our meals (Australian rations of tinned vegetables and so-called bully beef (corned beef) were regularly supplemented with game from hunting. There were plenty of deer around (they had once been imported by colonists) and thousands of geese and duck in the marshes nearby. One less agreeable member of the fauna was the mosquito, of which there were literally millions. We were of course used to mosquitoes in the tropics, but this beat everything. One unusual sport we had was a competition of how many mosquitoes you could kill in one go with a slap on the lower arm – six or seven was a good average. Moreover malaria was rampant so that we had to swallow Atebrine tablets daily, which made your skin turn yellow.

The single landing strip was made of so-called PSP, perforated steel plates, a typical American invention, which allowed a landing strip to be constructed on practically any level surface in a very short time. However the taxi strips were very narrow and this presented problems when you had to zigzag during taxiing (necessary to be able to see past the long nose of the P40). Some of us therefore preferred to stand up in the 'stirrups', that is unstrapped and standing up in the cockpit with the control stick between the knees, while peering over the nose, until arriving at the landing strip where you quickly strapped yourself in for the take-off.

We slept on camp beds in tents, two men to each tent, and meals were eaten in the mess, a fairly dilapidated barrack. There was hardly any diversion; it was too swelteringly hot for intensive sports, and swimming in the sea or in the Merauke river was not recommended in view of the many crocodiles.

When I had just arrived from Canberra, I was given an assignment to make a short reconnaissance flight in order to familiarize myself with the new surroundings, as was customary. I was also given a parcel containing post to be delivered to Digoel, an inland settlement on the River Digoel. I noticed a long ribbon that was tied around the parcel, but didn't give it a second thought. On arrival at Digoel looking down on an extremely short landing strip in the jungle, I was somewhat taken aback that my mates would actually dare to perform the feat of landing there with P40s. Naturally I could not be outdone, and fortunately, before my carrier-destination had been changed, I had practised the so-called dummy deck landings at Jackson, just like the other navy fighter pilots. This entailed the technique of flying at extremely slow speed, which you would normally never attempt. These lessons were in preparation for the real aircraft carrier training that would follow later. But now it came in handy. I lowered the landing gear and selected full flaps, cut back on the throttle, and pulled up the nose as prescribed to reduce the speed to just before stalling. Then I again opened the throttle a little to maintain flying speed in the nose-up position, and aimed for the very edge of the landing strip, which now looked even shorter than before. 'But hell, if they can do it, so can I, right?' Anyhow, I touched down properly, and with full brakes stopped just in time at the end of the strip, with the nose of the plane almost in the forest. By now a crowd had gathered to watch, and an Army Officer climbed on to the wing and shouted excitedly:

'Wonderful. Nobody has ever done this before!'

It was then brought home to me what the purpose was of that ribbon around the parcel: you were supposed to throw it out of the cockpit and with the help of the fluttering ribbon, the parcel could easily be spotted and located on the ground.

After recovering with a glass of coconut milk, I turned the fighter around and had it pushed backwards as far as possible into the jungle by some of the spectators, by now a few hundred soldiers, Papuans, women and children, to extend my run as far as possible. Then full flaps again, full throttle on the brakes, brakes off, and the old trusty P40 became airborne after an incredibly short run, shuddering with exertion, with the wheels just skimming the tops of the coconut palm trees.

Waved off by the whole community of Digoel who had not enjoyed such entertainment in ages, I set off for Merauke.

My feeling of relief was soon replaced by one of uneasiness: how was I going to talk myself out of this one to the CO? But luckily Major Maurenbrecher was quite sporting about it all: I was obviously not one of the brightest, but at least I could handle my P40 reasonably well. The howling laughter of my colleagues was more difficult to live down.

120 Fighter Squadron in Merauke 1944. Two divisions on stand-by. Second from the left my only naval colleague, Sergeant-Pilot Hirdes, later killed in action; fifth from the right Hans Knoop, later Commander in Chief of the Air Force.

Major Maurenbrecher was rather aloof, very sportsmanlike, and respected by all. Apart from flying his true passion was hunting. While others went on leave to Australia, he preferred to stay behind in Merauke so as to be able to devote himself entirely to hunting. I remember one day that one of the colleagues, who had also been out hunting, mentioned that he had sighted a deer as big as a horse, but he couldn't go after it because it was getting dark. So early next morning, he and the Major set off, full of expectations, only to return dejectedly after several hours. And the deer? It *was* a horse…

There were several feral cows and horses roaming around Merauke, that had been left behind by unsuccessful colonists. Deer had also been imported in the past and do not belong to the original New Guinea fauna.

Merauke, playing poker to pass the time away. Paul Verspoor places his bet.

Another peculiarity of Maurenbrecher was that he once had all the camouflage paint removed from his P40, and then had it polished so that the aluminium shone like silver in the sun: 'The Knight in Shining Armour'. He apparently later realised that it was not exactly wise to advertise yourself as leader, and thereby attract special attention from the enemy.

After his retirement as Major-General of the Air Force many years later, he undertook a solo sailing trip around the world. After his departure from Sydney Harbour in Australia, almost halfway round, nothing was ever heard of him again. Later, some wreckage was found, and curiously, he must have gone down not far from the area where we were operating during the war, The Great Barrier Reef.

To my surprise I came across my former high school comrade, Ulco van Wijck, in Merauke. While studying at university in California, he had volunteered for the Dutch Forces – on a patriotic impulse, as he put it. However, he was turned down for military service and sent out to Merauke as a low-ranking civil servant. Fortunately, it soon became apparent that he was more useful behind a telescope at Mount Palomar, and he was sent back.

Two other striking personalities whom I remember from that period were the Doctor and the Intelligence Officer. The Doctor was a jolly Australian, nicknamed 'Pepsodent Jack' because of his perfect white teeth and cheerful wide grin. He once took on a bet with some of the Dutch colleagues that he would be able to speak Dutch in a short time. Months later – everybody had already forgotten all about the bet – he suddenly stood up at the squadron dinner on the Queen's birthday, August 31 1944, ticked on his glass, and without notes gave a speech in faultless Dutch, be it with an Australian accent!

The Intelligence Officer, Igor Hmelninsky, a Dutchman of Polish descent, was a well-known concert pianist from Sydney, and just like Ulco van Wijck, had felt called upon to do his bit for his country. Flying fascinated him, and once one of the colleagues succumbed and secretly took him along, on his lap, in the single-seater P40! It meant first removing the parachute from the bucket seat to make room. The pilot, Rudy Trebels (moreover a giant of a man), thought he had got away with the escapade unnoticed until after landing he was asked over the radio by the Air Traffic Controller: '(Call name), who is your co-pilot?'.

Another stunt ended less favourably. Igor was also a brilliant jazz pianist, and on the Queen's birthday he actually managed to play the national anthem in boogie-woogie style. Notwithstanding the applause he received from the majority of us, it led to him being confined to barracks for one day; Major Maurenbrecher qualified this performance as *lèse majesté*.

The operational activities didn't amount to much. We were scrambled a few times for a Japanese reconnaissance aircraft flying high overhead, but with our primitive radar of that time, we were always too late to catch up with him. We did carry out some attacks on the nearest Japanese base, Timuka, which also had a landing strip. Our standard tactic was a dive-bomb attack from about 4000 meters with as a rule two 500-pounders carried under the wings, followed by a strafing run on the target with our six 50 cal. machine guns.

During one of these attacks the aircraft of Jilles Verspoor was hit by anti-aircraft fire. Luckily he was able to get some distance away, and put his P40 down on the beach with a belly landing.

He soon got company from a number of fierce-looking Papuans, who at first were merely curious, but after a while started behaving in a less friendly manner. Jilles wisely retreated to his cockpit and closed the hood, only just in time before a rain of arrows started to clatter against the perspex. Fortunately he was rescued fairly soon by a Catalina flying boat belonging to the Naval Air Service, which happened to be in the neighbourhood for intelligence purposes (i.e. dropping agents) and Jilles returned to base unharmed, carrying a few arrows as a souvenir. Another colleague had a more favourable experience with the natives. While test flying some distance away from the base over the impenetrable jungle, he encountered engine trouble. He couldn't possibly attempt a landing, so Nick Czismasia de Somogy (of Hungarian aristocratic origin, his father was said to have belonged to the Imperial Guard) bailed out with his parachute. Unfortunately his foot got caught behind the rudder pedals, and that cost him the loss of a boot and a sprained ankle. Hardly an ideal situation for walking through a tropical jungle. Luckily he was soon found by a band of Papuans, who if anything looked even more savage than Jilles' coastal Papuans. We knew this kind, because occasionally an inquisitive bunch of them would come and look around our camp; they were magnificent looking savages with colourful bird of paradise feathers adorning their fuzzy hair, bones or boar tusks pierced through the nose, brightly painted faces, and arrayed with enormous penis sheaths. Although according to a visiting missionary they actually still practised cannibalism, they turned out to be quite friendly. Only if one of these warriors came and visited you in your tent, inquisitive as they were, you had to air everything the rest of the day to get rid of the stench. But perhaps to them Nick didn't smell too good either; at any rate he was not eaten but on the contrary well treated, and was even carried safely to our base.

For that matter this missionary looked almost as wild as the Papuans with his long beard, and holes in his shoes and clothes all torn, but he was a marvellous story-teller, and when he finally took his leave, dressed in new shoes and khakis from our clothing store, to return to his 'parish' in the jungle, we saw him go with regret.

Lieutenant Governor-General van Mook visiting 120 Squadron in Merauke. Behind him our Commanding Officer, Major Hans Maurenbrecher.

The daily routine consisted of one flight of four fighters on stand by, which was relieved around midday by another flight. The rest of the pilots were kept busy with practising shooting on ground targets, dive bombing and dog fights. One dive bombing exercise ended tragically in the death of one of our most experienced fighter pilots, Mulder, nicknamed 'Bels', a former instructor. It was a classical case of target fixation, whereby the pilot is hypnotised by the target below him, and in his eagerness to make a bulls eye, continues too long and too low to be able to pull up in time. Bels pulled up too late and therefore too hard with a high speed stall and a fatal snap roll as a result. He ended up in a deep hole right next to the target. The same thing happened to another pilot not long afterwards. More modern fighters were later fitted with a radio-altimeter that warns the pilot in time by means of a signal in his head phone as soon as the predetermined minimum safety limit has been reached.

A favourite outing occurred when one or more planes had to be flown back to Australia for a major inspection, which could not be done at the operational base, or when a number of new aircraft had to be picked up. On one of those occasions there were about five of us in Brisbane, waiting for the aeroplanes we had come to fetch. 'Iepie' van Olmen, a cheerful, well-liked comrade, had only one fault: he was an awful sponger. He had just got married and probably wanted to save money. Whenever we were at the bar, he always cleverly managed to join a group where someone was just ordering a round. Before it was his turn, he would discretely withdraw to join another group. After a while, of course, this was noticed, and when we were in Brisbane it was decided it was time to teach him a lesson. With Piet Stam (the Olympic swimmer) in charge, we all went to a Chinese restaurant where an elaborate dinner was ordered. When the last bite and drink had been taken, and at a prearranged sign from Piet, everybody grabbed their cap which by way of precaution had been kept under the chair without Iepie noticing, got up and ran out of the restaurant. Pandemonium! Astonished, Iepie tried to run after us, but was grabbed by the collar just in time by the Chinese owner: 'Hee, you must pay for the flied lice, yes?

For days Iepie tried to recover everybody's share, whereupon we would thank him profusely for his generous treat. Poor Iepie, but he had got the message.

Pilots of 120 Squadron with Commanding Officer Maurenbrecher. I am the only one with a shoulder holster, exchanged with an American pilot.

One of those trips to Australia ended dramatically. This time ten colleagues were due to be relieved and they were able to get a lift in a Dakota that had landed in Merauke. But three P40s also had to be flown to Australia for inspection, and fate had to decide which three pilots would fly them over and which would be the seven to go in the Dakota. So lots were drawn to decide who the three would be. One of this threesome, an ardent hunter, stowed his luggage, two rifles and some ammunition in the Dakota for there was no room for that in a P40, which could take at most a weekend bag. On the way to Cairns the Dakota got caught in one of those heavy tropical storms in North Australia for which that area is notorious (the highest Cumulus Nimbus ever observed, about 40.000 feet, was reported at that time in The Northern Territory.) The Dakota never arrived. We spent many hours looking for them, and so did others, but from an aeroplane the tropical jungle below is one green impenetrable mass, and after searching for several days we had to give up.

Forty-five years later an Australian biological expedition was clearing a path through the extremely dense forest on a hillside not far from Cairns. All of a sudden one of the group came across the wreck of an aeroplane – the jungle was so dense that if he had walked two metres further away, he would have passed by without seeing it. The Dakota was finally discovered and the remains of the bodies were still inside.

A memorial ceremony for the colleagues who had perished was later organised by the Air Force at Soesterberg Airfield, in the Netherlands. One of the pilots killed in the Dakota, Bob Salm, had been a schoolmate of mine in Semarang, and I met his much younger sister at the ceremony. She looked just like him; it was very moving. I also met there the 'lucky' one who had drawn the lot to fly the P40, and had put all his luggage in the Dakota. He told me that when the wreck was discovered he went to Australia to witness the salvaging himself. When he was at the wreck, he was amazed and dismayed to discover that one of his guns had been fired; there were two empty cartridges in the barrels, whereas he had obviously unloaded the gun beforehand….

The posting in Merauke was something of a disappointment and a comedown. According to some reports, we were possibly one of the most highly trained fighter pilot units in the Allied Forces, with moreover, at least in the beginning, a very high morale. However, this was being severely taxed by the lack of real action, but that would quickly change once we moved to Biak.

With my P40 Number 562, which I later had to abandon by parachute.

Biak, a sleepy, tropical island in the Geelvink Bay off the north coast of New Guinea, was occupied by the Japanese in 1942, and transformed into a strongly defended base with three runways. It was recaptured by the Americans with very heavy losses in 1944 in their advance on the Philippines. Biak is a coral island that had been pushed up out of the sea over millions of years, so that on the southern edge fairly high cliffs with caves had been formed. The Japanese had dug themselves in these caves with their artillery, so that when the Americans landed they received a very warm reception, notwithstanding the usual preliminary bombardment by ships and aircraft. Ultimately, the Japanese lost out of course, and the few survivors who had not fought to the bitter end, withdrew in a disorderly manner in to the jungle, which covers the northern part of the island. Driven by hunger, some of these would occasionally steal food at night from the American camps.

It was said that the Americans had finally cleaned up the last Japanese soldiers who had retreated into the caves and refused to surrender, with drums of petrol, which were rolled in from above and then ignited with flame throwers. A number of us once visited one of those caves where the remains of pieces of equipment, and even some burnt and decaying bodies, bore witness to what had happened, and we quickly left.

We were transferred with our squadron to Biak at the beginning of 1945, so that from there we could attack various Japanese bases on the north coast of New-Guinea. The most important was Manokwari, which had a large garrison of Marines, Japanese elite troops, who were well equipped with excellent anti-aircraft artillery, said to be of German design.

But we first had to get ourselves installed. In no time everyone had an American tent with a proper wooden floor (the price, if I remember correctly, was three bottles of Australian Corio whiskey), an enormous improvement on our Australian tents with canvas floors that were always damp. This came about because the Americans were suffering under the 'no alcohol rule' of General MacArthur, the Commanding General of the whole Pacific Theatre, whose Headquarters at that time were in Hollandia on the north coast of New Guinea. We, however, fell under Australian Command, and had a monthly ration of either one bottle of spirits or six bottles of beer. It didn't take us long to find out that the Americans would sell their soul for liquor, and we gratefully made use of this. Especially in view of the fact that they had everything in abundance and of much better quality than our Australian issue. Soon we were all dressed in smart American khakis, baseball caps and jungle boots.

We were highly impressed by the American approach. Tens of thousands of Americans were stationed in Biak, spread over various camps, which were all equally luxurious according to our standards. Similarly, there were at least six open-air cinemas with the latest Hollywood films. A remarkable fact was that sometimes Japanese soldiers had been spotted at the edge of the forest, looking at the back side of the screen! Naturally they always managed to get away.

Except one time.

I was driving one day with three other pilots along the edge of the forest when we suddenly saw a jeep standing still in front of us with some agitated and excited Americans in it. We soon heard the reason: they had spotted two armed Japanese soldiers crossing the road, but none of them felt the urge to go after them. One of us however, 'Blum' Soesman, didn't hesitate for a moment, picked up his jungle carbine that we always had with us, and disappeared into the forest. After some hesitation, we decided to follow him when all at once we heard a couple of shots. Then we saw Blum standing and aiming his gun: one dead Jap was lying on the ground, and another was standing with his hands up. We triumphantly took him back to our camp as a prisoner of war, with the Yanks looking on with some admiration. Our prisoner obviously expected to be swiftly beheaded – in accordance with good Japanese custom – but when instead he was actually given a cigarette, he was clearly relieved. Later on he asked to speak to Major Maurenbrecher and told him in broken English/Malay that he was actually an aircraft mechanic, and offered to work on our fighters. His offer was not taken up.

Soon after our arrival in Biak the first serious operations began against the enemy, for which we had been waiting so long. And soon we suffered our first losses. Within a couple of months we lost six aircraft, but luckily three of the pilots could be saved. Two of them, Jerry Fokkinga and Bill Bakhuys Roozeboom, were hit during an attack on Manokwari, and both of them had the misfortune to end up in the sea very close to the coast. Jerry ditched his plane in the sea, and Bill jumped out with his parachute. They were both quick to climb into their dinghies but then had to wait anxiously to see if and when the Japanese would come and pick them up. Luckily their colleagues had seen them go down, and stayed to give cover as long as their fuel lasted. They were both eventually rescued from their critical position by an American Catalina flying boat which was always sent along when we went on an operational flight for that purpose – Air Sea Rescue. Its appropriate radio call-name was 'Playmate'. These Air Sea Rescue crews had the deserved reputation of having 'GUTS', and we often treated them to drinks in our mess.

Our Japanese prisoner of war.

Another spectacular rescue concerned Bob Esser, a former champion hockey player. He also ended up in the sea and in his dinghy, but then came under fire from the coast. The other P40 pilots had seen him ditch, and while circling above him managed to silence the Japanese fire until they had to leave after a short while because of fuel shortage. Bob was nevertheless extremely lucky because by chance an Air Sea Rescue B 17 Flying Fortress was close by, and it carried a newly developed life boat under the fuselage. I believe that Bob had the honour of being the first to get acquainted with this apparatus. The sloop – for that is what it really was – was dropped close to him by three parachutes, and the moment it touched the surface of the water, a number of lines were automatically released on both sides by small rockets, so that Esser only had to swim a few strokes before hoisting himself on board via one of those lines. There he found absolute luxury: an abundance of food, fresh water, fishing tackle, first-aid kit etc. plus a small outboard motor that quickly took him out of firing range from the coast. He was later picked up by Playmate. When he got back, he was questioned by the Americans on his experiences with the lifeboat, and asked if he thought there was anything lacking. He replied:

'Yes, a glass of cognac and a good cigar!'

Jules Scheffer, the benjamin of the squadron (one month younger than me) was more fortunate and managed to bring his crippled plane back home with a belly landing on the airfield.

Another pilot, who was also shot down during that disastrous raid on Manokwari, was not so lucky. Sergeant-Pilot Hirdes, my only navy colleague, was hit after repeated machine gun attacks on an AA battery (courageous but very unwise) and crashed on land. After the war it appeared that the Japanese, out of admiration for his bravery, had buried him with military honours close to the battery that he had hit. Our Commanding Officer, who was one of the party that accepted the official surrender of the Japanese in Manokwari, was handed Hirdes' .45 pistol that the Japanese had kept. They had fastened his identification tags to his grave marker.

A typical example of the surprising Japanese mentality, for as a rule they had little respect for a defeated enemy, on the contrary. (They were Marines, which could be an explanation.) For the rest it should be mentioned that the tactics of this attack, which was led by our C.O., were at the time controversial, to say the least, and led to severe criticism of Major Maurenbrecher.

It should be noted that Manokwari was important because the Japanese had a radio beacon there that transmitted on the same frequency as that of an American station in Biak. Consequently in bad weather American transport aircraft were sometimes misled and ended up above Manokwari, where they were promptly fired at, and a few had actually been shot down.

On July the 9th 1945 it was my turn. On an attack on Manokwari the day before I had only received a couple of bullet holes in the tail of my P40, but during my strafing run on a number of barracks, I had noted the position of the anti-aircraft battery that was firing at me. In my youthful recklessness I resolved to get them the next day when another attack was planned on Manokwari in the morning.

In those days we flew in the usual battle formation of a flight of four fighters, made up of two sections. It was a sacred rule that at least the two in a section always stayed together to give cover to one another, so that if one got into trouble, at least the other would know what had happened to him.

I was a flight leader in the next operation. An attack formation normally consisted of three flights of four, so twelve fighters in total. My number two on that fateful 9th of July was a sub-lieutenant who had been posted to our squadron not long before, thus not a member of the Royal Netherlands Military Flying School (RNMFS) from the U.S. He had already attracted attention during a couple of successive operations by breaking away prematurely because of 'engine trouble' (unthinkable for a RNMFS man).

As usual we started the action from a height of 12.000 feet with a dive-bomb attack, after having first released the drop tank (since Broome no longer unknown to me!) This was the first tank to be emptied because otherwise any remaining petrol and fumes in the drop tank would be fatal in case of a direct hit, and so it was standard procedure to get rid of it before attacking. After the dive, one single strafing run followed; to come back a second time would be asking for trouble, and always in the direction of the sea, so that if you got shot down you could try to end up in the sea where hopefully Playmate would pick you up.

We were greeted high up with anti-aircraft fire, little black clouds which looked threatening, but were not really dangerous for the small and fast fighters. It did increase the tension though, even to a point of fear, but that quickly subsided through the intense concentration needed for the attack, although in fact you then had to face the far more dangerous small calibre rapid fire. This anti-aircraft fire came into action at low height during the strafing run: a rain of bullets that you attempted to evade with quick zigzag manoeuvres. But at the very last minute when you opened fire yourself with the six .50's in the wings, you naturally had to fly straight ahead for a short while so as to be able to aim accurately, and those were literally the most dangerous seconds of the whole operation. And that was also apparent now, most decidedly. Suddenly I felt three heavy blows, the aeroplane began to roll and it took all my strength to turn it upright again. The rudder pedal was also shaking violently – but the engine was still going! Meanwhile safely over sea, I was slowly able to gain some height, and take stock of the situation. I saw that my port aileron had a big hole in it and a piece was sticking straight up, which of course explained the rolling motion.

I used my belt to fasten the control stick in the right-hand corner of the cockpit to a handle so as to unburden my right arm. And so I pottered along with my faithful, solid P40 in the direction of Biak, all the time wondering how I was going to get it safely on the ground. For on the way I passed Playmate, who cheerfully announced: 'Boy, you've gotta hole in yer tail you can drive a f …… coach through!' I couldn't even thank him for the message because it appeared that my radio transmitter had also broken down. But at least somebody could pass on the news that I had survived, for I had not seen my team-mate since the moment I began the attack.

Nearing Biak I saw to my dismay an enormous 'CuNim', a tropical rainstorm, sitting in my path. Impossible to fly through it with my lame duck, so I decided to fly around it and try to reach the base from another direction But a bit later the engine suddenly began to sputter: it was obvious that the fuselage tank had also been hit – so that had been the third blow – and was now empty. My wing tanks were already empty so this was clearly the end of the journey. I realised that a ditch in the sea would be a risky undertaking without engine power, certainly on the Pacific Ocean swell, which was quite considerable off the north coast of Biak where I had now arrived. Another bail out was my only remaining option, which in itself was not a problem were it not for the fact that I was aware that this time there would be no friendly reception in a Negro church awaiting me. However, I had no choice so I carried out the required steps like a true 'routiné': jettison the cockpit hood, loosen oxygen tube and radio connections, roll the plane over on its back (so as not to hit the tail when dropping out), undo the straps and go!

After counting to three as usual, I pulled the ring and the parachute opened with the expected sudden jolt. I just saw my P40 explode against a hillside when I – again – landed in a tree, but this time really high up in a tree, and this time at least in bright daylight. With some difficulty I managed to climb down after loosening my jungle pack which was attached to the parachute like a kind of rucksack This pack was an indispensable attribute for survival in the jungle for it contained all sorts of necessary articles, such as a chocolate emergency ration (90%, terribly bitter), a chopper, water purification tablets, Atebrine (anti-malaria), iodine, fish hooks, a mirror to signal with, a compass etc. The iodine came in useful straight away because my face especially was full of scratches. Setting off on my journey I had to clear my way through the extremely dense jungle with the chopper, the rotan creepers were a particular hindrance with their three-pronged thorns, even worse than barbed wire. In no time I looked like a vagabond in torn clothing. But I had other things to worry about because I had seen that during the parachute descent I had been moved quite some distance inland by the wind and I had to get to the coast as soon as possible for any hope of being rescued; nobody could possibly find you in the jungle.

I progressed very slowly and when dusk began to fall it was time to look about for a bivouac. I had just arrived at a clearing in the forest, where giant elephants-ear plants were growing, and I decided to spend the night there. The evening meal consisted of a piece of the bitter chocolate, indeed an excellent emergency ration because after a few bites I had already had enough. During the day I had drunk water by squeezing rain water into my mouth from moss growing on trees, but now I could take time to disinfect a shallow puddle of water with my purifying tablet and kneel down to suck it up. Suddenly I saw to my amazement a number of freshly chopped tree trunks, and then my surprise turned into horror when I noticed footprints in the mud of Japanese jungle boots, with the typical separate big toe. I quickly hid myself under the enormous elephants-ear plants, and drew my revolver, fully resolved to defend myself to the utmost if I were discovered, knowing only too well how the Japanese treated their prisoners. (A B 25 bomber plane under the command of Captain André de la Porte, which belonged to 'our sister' 18 squadron, operating from 'Bachelor' base close to Darwin, had to make an emergency landing on the beach of one of the Kai islands after being hit by anti-aircraft fire, and the entire crew were taken prisoner and later beheaded by the Japanese.)

And so began an extremely scary night until I suddenly heard loud grunting and snorting. That made me feel better because wild pigs were naturally the best watchdogs I could wish for. They were obviously after the roots of the elephants-ear plants, but luckily they left mine alone. I actually managed to get some sleep. I needed that rest for the next day I had a long, difficult trip ahead of me to reach the coast, where I finally arrived late in the afternoon after crossing a marsh complete with a large water snake. I followed the coast along the beach, cautiously seeking cover at the edge of the forest until I heard the sound of wood chopping. I crept up close with my revolver at the ready, and discovered a Papuan peacefully at work there. Once I had ascertained that he was alone, I called out gingerly: 'Hey!'

The Papuan dropped his axe in fright – I believe he even went a shade paler – and ran off. I probably looked quite frightening with my face painted with iodine and my ragged clothes. As a precaution I hid behind some bushes until I saw four Papuans approaching, without Japs! I tried to reassure them with a few words in Malay, and after a while they took me with them to their village on the coast close by, where a friendly, even enthusiastic reception awaited me. It soon became clear that they wanted no part of the Japanese, they had even managed to kill a couple. I heard this from an 'educated' Papuan, who had been dropped there by the Netherlands Forces Intelligence Service to collect information, and with whom I could converse fairly well in my Malay and a few words of Dutch.

I was comfortably accommodated in a hut on the beach with a view on the Pacific Ocean, and I slept on a so-called 'baleh baleh', a simple bed made from split bamboo. I was better fed than I had been for a long time: fresh fish every day, which was caught before my eyes beyond the coral reef, and a soup made from coconut milk, bamboo shoots, and some kind of vegetable. The fish that had just been caught in the morning was first proudly shown to me for approval, and then I would smilingly gesture: 'Take it to the kitchen!'

Meanwhile I had made a large cross of palm leaves on the beach, a standard procedure, in the hope that someone would see it. Later on I heard that after four days of searching, they had given me up, but at the insistence of my friend and tent-mate, Paul Verspoor, it was decided to do one more search, and this time survey the north coast of Biak, just in case. (Paul told me much later that he had a feeling all along that I was still alive). Well, they spotted my cross, and then me jumping excitedly up and down on the beach, and before long I was picked up by a Catalina belonging to the Dutch Naval Air Service under the command of Lieutenant Landman, who surprisingly happened to be in the neighbourhood for an intelligence operation.

The farewell from my Papuan friends was quite moving and I was overwhelmed with presents: fruit, sea shells, coconuts, and to my surprise my jungle carbine which some of them had managed to retrieve from the wreck of my P40. The barrel was all twisted like a corkscrew, and the butt was completely burnt (unfortunately I lost this souvenir when my cabin trunk was stolen later on).

For the rest I was received with scant enthusiasm by Landman for he had struck a coral reef while taxiing, with a leak in the bottom of the flying boat as a result. He was therefore in a hurry to get started before too much water entered.

Then the reception at the base, Mokmer, awaited me. In those days it was the custom that if a colleague got killed, his possessions were sold by auction for the benefit of his next of kin at a special gathering in the mess, with lots of drinking. To an outsider such a spectacle would probably seem cynical and callous, but in fact of course it was the very opposite. So when I got back I found all my possessions had already been sold. My friend Paul Verspoor – known for his sense of humour at all times – had picked up my expensive Leica camera, and feigned disappointment: 'I finally got hold of a good camera, and now I suppose you want it back!' As he had never really believed that I hadn't survived, the disappointment cannot have been that great.

Paul was the younger brother of the earlier-mentioned Jilles; quite unusual, two brothers in the same squadron.

After a medical examination, I was pronounced to be in very good condition (I had even gained some weight) and four days later I was back in action.

I was told that it had not ended so well for my team-mate, who had abandoned me. After he had made an 'emergency landing' due to so-called engine trouble, on a landing strip available for that purpose on the island of Noemfoor nearby, a team flew out there to check. One of the pilots climbed into the cockpit, started the engine, tested everything thoroughly, and then switched off. After leaving the cockpit, he went up to the 'unlucky' one without saying a word and slapped him full in the face. He then warned him that in future there would always be someone flying behind him, and if he would ever again break off prematurely, he would be shot down! My (ex-) team-mate reported this to the C.O., and the man was immediately transferred to Australia, and I never saw him again. Years later he was killed in an air crash when he was a pilot with KLM.

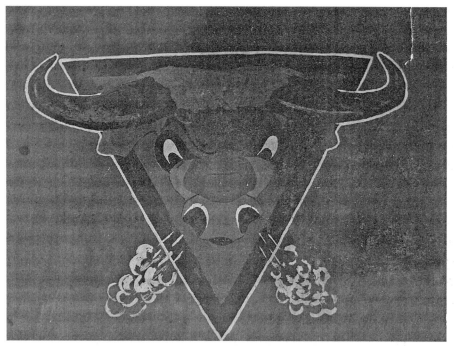

The emblem of 120 Squadron, NEI/RAAF: banteng madjah, a bristling buffalo.

One week later I went back in a P40 to the kampong (village) called Warsa, as I had now found out, to show my gratitude by dropping some packs of cigarettes, wrapped in a discarded old parachute. My next visit would be exactly seventeen years later, but that's still to come.

Meanwhile the war was drawing to a close, although we were then not aware of the fact, and our last loss was therefore all the more tragic. One of the pilots had a date with an American nurse for some kind of party, and changed his turn for an operational mission with a colleague, Iepie van Olmen, who was always willing to help out. This was against all rules, both officially and traditionally, changing missions was taboo. However they both thought it would be an easy one. Alas this was not the case and Iepie was killed on the 11th of August 1945, just four days before the Japanese capitulation. Needless to say that the man who had made the date was treated more or less like a pariah for some time.

The end of the war came as a complete surprise to us. Nobody had ever heard of atom bombs, of course, and the wildest rumours were circulating. The Americans went completely mad: 'Home for Christmas' was in the air. Celebration parties were going on all the time, and everyone emptied his rifle or pistol by shooting in the air like fireworks.

After one wild party a man heard somebody in the tent next to him say: 'I finally saw my chance and I shot the son of a bitch!' This was immediately reported to the Military Police of course, who promptly started an investigation. It soon came out that the 'son of a bitch' had been a parrot, that in his neighbour's opinion had made too much of a noise with its screeching.

For the rest this unexpected end to the war was felt as an anti-climax by many of us. We could look back on a period in which boredom and frustration alternated with moments of fear during dangerous missions, and sorrow at the loss of comrades. Through accidents and enemy action we had lost thirteen pilots, about thirty per cent of the squadron complement. And now a period of waiting and uncertainty had begun.

For me it meant the end of my detachment with 120 Squadron, because suddenly the Navy remembered that a lone Navy pilot was still out there with the Air Force fighter pilots. For that matter the only maritime aspect of the military operations of this Naval pilot was that he was shot down by an anti-aircraft battery manned by Japanese Marines …

I was called back on the sixth of September to report to the Netherlands Naval Headquarters in Melbourne, where I was informed that I was posted to the Netherlands Naval Air Service at Rose Bay, Sydney, a seaplane base. I was back in the Navy.

6. Naval Air Service, Australia and Netherlands Indies 1945-48

Back in the Naval Air Service (MLD) I was immediately assigned to a Catalina flying boat crew as co-pilot/navigator as I had naturally no experience on flying boats. First my knowledge of navigation was thoroughly tested since they did not expect too much from a fighter pilot. I was assigned to the crew of a very experienced pilot, Wim Landman (in the beginning I had to address him as 'Sir', of course), whom I had already met! The crew further consisted of a wireless operator and two mechanics. The task of the MLD-detachment 'Rose Bay' was the evacuation to Australia of ex-prisoners of war of the Dutch Royal Navy and others who had been interned in Japanese camps in the Indies, Thailand and Japan. Sometimes when you saw those walking skeletons, you almost had a guilty feeling that you had got off so well yourself.

Landman was admittedly a good pilot who taught me a lot, but he was also an arrogant fellow. I recall one incident with great pleasure. We were on the way back to Rose Bay with a plane full of passengers, one of whom was a tall, emaciated, middle-aged man, his skin all yellow from atebrine, but he had a certain charisma about him. We made a fuel-stop landing in the bay of Townsville on the east coast of Northern Australia, and after refuelling, Landman wanted to take off straight away although it was already dark. Bad weather was expected, and we knew only too well how violent storms could be in the north of Australia. When starting up the engines, however, it appeared that the starboard engine showed a severe magneto-drop, and that had to be dealt with first. There are folding seats on the engine nacelles of the Catalina, somewhat like those used by window cleaners and painters, on which the mechanic can sit to work on the engines. In the meantime a thunderstorm had developed, and nobody felt very much at ease. At that moment, the tall man came up to the cockpit and said:

'Isn't this a strange time to be painting the engines?'

It cleared the air, and everyone burst out laughing, all except Landman.

By the time the repair was finished, it would have been ill advised to take off in the worsening storm, so we went ashore to get something to eat in a small restaurant. The tall man joined Landman and me at our table, which was clearly not to the liking of Landman as he started behaving even more arrogantly than usual. I, on the other hand, thought that the man was very entertaining and obviously erudite. In the course of the conversation, he asked Landman about his background, and Landman answered gruffly:

'Second mate with the Koninklijke Paketvaart Maatschappij. (KPM, a freight and passenger shipping company), what about you?

'Oh', said the man, I am the President-Director of the KPM …

Shortly afterwards I was transferred to the crew of Peter de Groot (who later became Flag Officer Naval Air), with whom I could get along better, although he clearly did not have the qualities of Landman as a pilot, and I was soon to bear the consequences. The reason for my being assigned to his crew was that a number of civil servants and soldiers had to be transported to Biak, New-Guinea, and my familiarity with that area could come in useful. During the very first landing on the Darling River, near Brisbane, it was obvious that Peter had some difficulty. Although there still hadn't been time to give me instruction on the Catalina, I did by then have some idea how things were done. However the next landing on the River Merauke went reasonably well, so I was somewhat reassured when we headed for Biak.

It soon became apparent that my optimism had been premature. We had to land on the roadstead off the coast at Biak, where the 'wambrau', as the local wind was called, had increased and caused a strong swell. This turned out to be a bit too much for Peter's flying capacities. At the first attempt he held the 'Cat' back at too great an angle, and was knocked out of the water by the very first wave. This is risky for a 'Cat' and it called for full throttle to go around and try again, which he did. Meanwhile it became clear to me that Peter had problems and I was prepared for the worst. The next attempt was indeed disastrous; he landed this time too flat which caused the plane to dig its nose in the water, with a so-called 'sea-loop' as a result, and the violent jerk to port broke off both engines from their mountings. The starboard engine splashed into the sea but the port engine dropped on top of the cockpit while the propeller cut through the roof like a scythe, right between me and the wireless operator behind me, raining pieces of aluminium and wiring on our heads. I quickly climbed through the top hatch on to the cockpit roof and saw that the plane had broken into three pieces. It was a miracle that no one was killed or even hurt. Only the wireless operator and I had head wounds, but strangely enough we hadn't even felt anything until the operator pointed at me, shocked, and said: 'Sir, you are bleeding!' Whereupon I replied: 'Just look at yourself!'

We were picked up by a sloop and an American ambulance quickly came to fetch us and take us to hospital. (There were still a large number of Americans in Biak.) To my surprise I saw there was already another man in the ambulance, moaning on a stretcher. He had apparently been driving his jeep along the coast when we made our spectacular landing, and while watching us in shocked surprise, he had tumbled off the cliff into the sea.

I was soon visited in hospital by my 'sympathizing' ex-120 Squadron colleagues, who were still stationed in Biak.

'What are you doing on such a dangerous flying boat, anyway? You should have stayed with us!'

Come to think of it they were right. I had got through the entire flying training and all the operations against the enemy, including two emergency parachute jumps, with nothing more than a few insignificant scratches, and now I had to walk about for the rest of my life with some interesting scars on my forehead, without being able to tell an exciting war story to go with them.

But that was the last straw for me. Once I was back at Rose Bay, after the wounds with at least ten stitches – in addition to a concussion – had successfully healed, I asked the C.O., Commander Wil Aernhout, to instruct me on the 'Cat' so that in future I could handle the controls myself. But it just so happened that the Navy had recently taken over a number of second-hand C47s (Dakotas) and that was more in line with my experience on land-based aircraft.

My instruction on the Dakota was extremely brief. I received a real crash course from an experienced sergeant-pilot: three landings on Mascot Airfield at Sydney in daytime, and three night landings the same evening. One day later I was sent to Perth in West Australia as brand-new captain with my crew and a cargo of spare parts and equipment intended for HMS *Jan van Galen,* one of our destroyers. Our plane had just come out of maintenance, and unfortunately the fuel gauges were not well calibrated. This fault, combined with my inexperience (and that of my mechanic), resulted in us taking insufficient fuel on board, when refuelling during an intermediate landing at Broken Hill, for traversing the notorious Nullabor Plain desert.

We soon realised this when one fuel tank after another emptied without the meters pointing to zero! Finally we were flying on the last tank, and with no idea when that one would be empty, while there was still no sign of Perth Airfield. So I decided to jettison some of our very heavy cargo in order to have more chance of a successful emergency landing in the desert, which was indicated on the map with: 'Warning – many rabbit holes!'. We had been in radio contact with the traffic controller in Perth for quite some time, and he was fully aware of our predicament. All at once I heard him saying: 'I hear your engines, you must be very close!'. Naturally radar was not yet common in those days . And then my co-pilot suddenly saw the sun reflecting on a zinc roof, and there loomed the landing strip on the shimmering horizon. I immediately gave the order to stop jettisoning the cargo, but unfortunately the nervous mechanic had already dropped a number of valuable radar parts overboard, instead of the very heavy manila hawsers which we were also carrying.

We were received with considerably less warmth on board the 'van Galen', once they had discovered what was missing from the long and eagerly awaited cargo.

I obviously had a lot of explaining to do when I got back to Rose Bay, but luckily I could share the blame for the stupidity with the maintenance service, and the whole affair fizzled out. But from that day on, I have always had my fuel tanks filled to the brim, regardless of the weight of the load.

We flew a lot in those days, 200 hours a month was no exception. We went to places in the East Indies Archipelago which I had only heard of at school. The Japanese had put down fighter strips where there had not already been an existing airfield, and you could land just about anywhere with the Dakota, although we did sometimes first have to make a low pass to chase off cows or goats. Furthermore weather conditions were an important factor since good weather forecasts were not yet available in those days, so that we were sometimes confronted with unpleasant surprises.

In addition to the flights between the islands of the archipelago, we also flew regularly to Australia for the evacuation of ex-prisoners of war, who had to rehabilitate in Australia.

I particularly remember one of those flights.

While the passengers were boarding the Dakota, I was standing at the bottom of the steps of the aircraft, as usual, to keep an eye on things, when I suddenly spotted the director of my old High School in Semarang standing among the emaciated crowd. I had been summoned to his office countless times to undergo reprimands, and warnings that he didn't think much would ever become of me if I didn't work harder. I even received special mention when he was handing out the diplomas: 'If there is one who doesn't deserve it … etc.' after he had praised the ones who had excelled.

When I went up to him, he recognised me almost immediately, and I could see him thinking:

'Do I have to go with *him?*'

Unfortunately it was not a pleasant flight, lots of bad weather on the way, and we finally landed in a heavy tropical rain storm with visibility not much more than a hundred metres. But this time he couldn't hold anything against me, and he even seemed grateful that I had put him back safely on the ground.

During one of those flights, my colleague Leen Nifterik (who later became a KLM captain) and his crew were flying their Dakota when they got caught in one of those notorious North Australian storms. When the engines failed, he had to make a belly landing in the vast steppe of Arnhemland. His radio had ceased functioning earlier on, so he had not been able to report the problem. A search operation with our Dakotas was started as soon as they were reported missing, but with no result, until one fine day when a lady sitting in a Qantas passenger airplane on the way to Darwin, called the hostess and said: 'Miss, there's an airplane lying down there!'.

Initial disbelief soon turned into joy when, after the Captain had been informed, he spotted the Dakota and the madly waving crew. When they were picked up a few days later by Australian Army trucks, it appeared that they were all in fairly good condition thanks to the 'emergency rations' they had used : a couple of crates of oranges, a crate of beer – and a pedigree dog bought by a colleague in Australia…

I also had a strange, though less precarious, experience in that same notorious region. At the beginning of 1947 we were flying with a Dakota somewhere between Cloncurry and Port Darwin in terrible weather. We were using the automatic pilot (AP), but the co-pilot and myself both continued to assist manually so as to unburden the AP from the heavy strain and prevent possible damage. Every now and again we would look sideways out of the cockpit windows at the wing tips, which were clearly flapping up and down. The story went that as long as the wings of a Dakota kept flapping, there was nothing to fear. It was time to start worrying if they *didn't* move any more (due to metal fatigue). Suddenly a blinding light filled the cockpit and for a few seconds we couldn't see a thing. Gradually we recovered our sight and, stunned, we were still looking at each other when the wireless operator, who sat a bit to the side behind us, came rushing up, deathly pale, and stammered that he had seen a white luminous ball, the size of a small football, come straight through the cockpit window in between the two pilots and roll slowly back through the gangway until it disappeared into thin air. We all smelt a strange sulphur-like odour, but did not see any damage.

With co-pilot Jaap Kalker and mechanic de Bruijn in front of our Dakota on the grass airfield at Den Pasar, Bali.

When I got back, I naturally tried everywhere to find an explanation for the phenomenon, until I learnt much later that it must have been 'ball lightning' – a very rare occurrence during electric storms.

At the end of 1946 the Rose Bay Detachment was disbanded, and we returned to the East Indies where we were to carry out transport flights and special missions. The most noteworthy flight was perhaps our journey through the 'Big East', as the outer regions of the East Indies were then called. Our passengers were a group of airfield engineers and air traffic controllers, who wanted to make an inspection tour of all the airfields to asses their usefulness. It was an extremely interesting trip. One event I remember well. We had arrived in Hollandia, the capital of Netherlands New-Guinea, where a day of rest was scheduled. Therefore I was glad to participate in a welcoming party that had been organized for us, which naturally entailed drinking, in my case beer. All at once the newly appointed Governor came up to me and asked if I would be willing to fly him and his civil servants, in addition to my group, the following morning to see the isolated Baliem Valley in the mountains from the air.

The incredibly lush and fertile Baliem valley, which had been farmed by Papuan tribes for nine thousand years but only discovered by the Dutch from the air in 1938, had recently been in the world news because of the crash of an American C 47 (DC-3) there. A spectacular rescue of the survivors had been organised by the Americans, who gave the Baliem valley the name 'Shangri-la' after the imaginary remote valley in the Himalayas from the novel Lost Horizon by James Hilton.

I was far from sober, but I hated to refuse the Governor, which I really should have done, of course. So still under the weather we were sitting in the cockpit a few hours later – the co-pilot, Jaap Kalker was in no better shape than I was – and we took off. The flight proceeded normally for a while until suddenly one engine started missing. A quick check revealed that both engines were connected to the wrong tank, which was almost empty, so that any moment we could go into a 'glider flight'. Switching over to the right fuel tank was done in a flash, and just in time. By then we were both completely sober.

A pleasant occasion was on the day I arrived in Batavia, where we were to be stationed for a while – at last we could eat good Chinese food again – and it so happened that Eugène Poublon, an ex-colleague from 120 Squadron, was getting married that same day, as I heard from another ex-colleague on the airfield. So I went along as an uninvited but nevertheless welcome guest to take part in the wedding festivities.

Paul Verspoor was also there and in an unguarded moment I invited him to go along the next day in a flight to our Navy Base in Surabaya. Paul readily agreed and arrived on time at the airfield, where to my dismay I had just been informed that I would be having the Flag Officer Naval Air, Rear Admiral H. Schaper, RMWO (equivalent of VC) on board as a passenger! Regulations had meanwhile been tightened to such an extent that you couldn't just take a lieutenant of the KNIL along on board as a non-registered passenger. However Paul, inventive as ever, quickly removed the pads with stars and the pilot wings from his shirt, concealed his officer's cap, and pretended to be an extra mechanic, much to the amusement of the real mechanic. It became really interesting when the Admiral affably started talking to the crew members one by one, who, as was customary, were lined up smartly to attention next to the steps of the aeroplane. When it was Paul's turn, the Admiral asked him how long he had served with the MLD, and if he enjoyed the work, etc. and he didn't seem to notice that this rankless mechanic was dressed in a very smart khaki uniform. Paul managed to get away with it, and could not then foresee that Schaper would one day (after his transfer from the navy) be his boss as Commander-in-Chief of the Netherlands Royal Air Force, nor, for that matter, that Paul himself would end up as major general in that same Air Force.

Notwithstanding the interesting and busy activities, my homecoming to the Netherlands Indies was not what I had imagined it would be. Although I had already been informed by the Red Cross that my parents and brother Peter had all three survived the war, it had not yet been possible to meet them.

My father, who had worked for three years on the infamous Burma railway when he was a Japanese prisoner of war, was the first one I met after the war. Upon his return to Java, he was appointed as Head of Transport for East Java, and posted in Surabya, where I was able to meet him briefly on a surprise visit when I was passing through. He was in a meeting, but I asked his secretary to fetch him 'for urgent reasons'. He came out looking slightly disturbed, and then for the first time in my life we embraced! It was not so common between men in those days.

He had endured the hardships of the camps remarkably well, as opposed to the thousands of Dutch, Australians and British who had perished. All that he would ever reveal about that terrible time is how, aided by his experiences in tropical forests and his Spartan way of camping (which I knew only too well), he always managed to find something nutritious to eat. One way was by catching lizards with self-made snares on the banks of a river, and then using them together with bamboo shoots to make a nourishing soup. The Japanese guards were fairly lax because there was nowhere to escape to anyway in that immense jungle. Furthermore he often swapped his sugar ration for rice and salt; the British and the Australians could not do without sugar, whereas that was the least essential part of the tropical diet. Only his eyesight had suffered through lack of certain vitamins.

My mother and Peter had the misfortune to be in Malang in East Java, where they had been interned during the war, and where the Indonesian rebels were now active. These 'Pemoedas', as they were called, were notorious for their savage cruelty, but fortunately my mother and Peter would eventually be liberated unharmed, and were then transported to Holland before I had a chance to meet them. My mother was in bad shape because she had damaged a vertebra when working as a voluntary ambulance driver just before the capitulation to the Japanese.

I found that life in my beloved Indies had completely changed. So much had been destroyed, and there was also a lot of poverty. The hostility of at least part of the population also made me realize that there was little left of the old, familiar Indies. It gradually became clear to me that this country, where I was born, and where I had had such a wonderful childhood, was in fact not my country any more.

And then the first so-called Police Operation (in effect a military operation) began, against a kind of guerilla war by the Indonesian freedom fighters, as they called themselves, and which in fact they actually were. But naturally at the time we didn't see it that way, and neither did a large proportion of the Indonesian population, for that matter, for they only longed for the peace and relative prosperity of old.

Queen Juliana presenting the 'Vliegerkruis' (Dutch equivalent of the DFC).
Admiral N.A. Rost van Tonningen looks on.

For us this entailed mainly reconnaissance flights over East Java for the advancing Marines, and transport for the various units. One time it looked like the real thing. It was in a Catalina to which I was assigned as co-pilot to Lieutenant Commander 'Bas' Sjerp, an experienced Catalina pilot. We received a number of hits in the starboard engine nacelle. The dry, hard ticking of small calibre bullets sounded familiar, but couldn't compare with the 28 mm blows that I had taken before. I therefore felt quite blasé once it became apparent that no serious damage had been done.

The same Sjerp finally found time to give me proper instruction on the Catalina, for which up to then there had been no opportunity. He was an excellent pilot and also a good instructor, and after a number of demanding lessons, including the spectacular 'stall landing' in a strong swell, I was solo.

I shall not easily forget those stall landings. To make it as real as possible, Sjerp had directed me to an area off the south coast of Java, where you could always count on a strong ocean swell of several meters. It was a matter of putting the plane down – at absolute minimum speed, just before stalling, and if direction and strength of the wind allowed – in a 'valley', parallel to – and between the waves. But it became really interesting if there was too much wind, and moreover, across the waves. 'Hanging on the propellers', just above the waves, you had to let the flying boat plop into the sea between two wave crests by suddenly cutting the throttle. The result was that the next wave came right over the cockpit, so that you literally felt that you were submerged. Rough stuff.

I did get a real scare, however, on another occasion. We were again flying in a Dakota, doing reconnaissance for the Marines, who had just landed on the coast near Pasir Poetih in the Eastern corner of Java. We were flying at very low altitude above a paddy field when all of a sudden I heard a loud bang, and simultaneously I was covered with bits of broken glass and blood. For one fleeting moment I thought that my time had come until I felt the wind on my face, and saw white feathers mixed in the blood. We had hit a so-called 'blekok', a large heron, which had come straight through the cockpit window on my side.

Actually I was glad when I was 'repatriated' to the Netherlands at the beginning of 1948, together with other ex-war pilots, to help reconstruct the Netherlands Naval Air Service.

Still, saying farewell to the Indies was not easy and it was with a melancholy feeling that I thought back on the day in November 1945 when I first set foot again on 'my' country's soil after the war, at Makassar, in Celebes. I was with Wim Landman, who, regardless of his faults, was nevertheless born and bred in the Indies, like myself, and when we were driving from the harbour into town in a jeep with a military escort, we suddenly saw a 'warong', a small eating stall, at the side of the road. We looked at each other simultaneously, and Wim ticked the driver on the shoulder, and said: 'Stop here!'.

And to the surprise and amusement of our escort, we dashed into the warong, sat down on the sawn-off palm tree trunk, which traditionally serves as seating, and both ordered a couple of large pieces of 'Tempeh Goreng' (a kind of soy bean-cake) .

7.   The Helicopter Foundation 1948-51

I was stationed at the Naval Air Base Valkenburg (MVKV) at Katwijk, near The Hague. There was not much flying to start with, because first a selection had to be made among the reserve officers, which in fact we all were, of the ones the Royal Navy wanted to keep on as career officers for reconstructing the post-war Naval Air Service. This was done by means of a demanding course in The Hague, where we were put through all kinds of tests. The ones who were found suitable, were offered a contract for professional service, and I was one of them.

I had little motivation to start studying medicine at this stage since it would take at least another six years, and in fact I really liked being in the Navy, so I signed up and was given the rank of Lieutenant.

At the beginning of 1949 I was posted to the General Services Group, a mixture of various types of aircraft, including the well-known B 25 Mitchell bomber, with which my colleagues had earned fame during the war in England with 320 Squadron.

I had an interesting experience with this aircraft during one of the first international exercises before NATO was established. The exercise was called VERITY, and we were stationed at St. Eval on the coast of Cornwall. On the flight there from the MVKV I got radio contact with the control tower of St.Eval when I was some distance away. After I had reported, I was told that a fog bank from the Irish Sea was in the process of spreading over the air base, and that I could either turn back or make a GCA landing. I had never heard of GCA. This was a then new system developed in the United States, whereby you were 'talked' into landing from the ground with the help of radar, hence the name Ground Controlled Approach. The GCA Controllers were people who had been very carefully selected. When I had informed my Controller of my ignorance, he enquired in a calm, almost fatherly manner, how many hours I had, and which types of aircraft I had flown. This apparently reassured him and I was accepted. His optimism was obviously not shared by my co-pilot, a sergeant; we didn't yet know each other very well and he didn't trust me. He almost begged me to go back safely, but I didn't feel like giving up straight away. We finally made a successful landing in fairly thick fog, and my co-pilot recovered.

There wasn't really much going on at the MVKV in that initial period, and I was beginning to get bored so I decided to read law at Leiden University with an old friend from the navigator school when I first joined the Naval Air Service in 1941. There was always an opportunity to study on the air base in daytime, and we went to nearby Leiden in the evening where we had a private tutor, an undergraduate student, who would test us and help us along. We made fairly good progress and were ready for the first examination in July 1949.

But by then a memorable event had taken place. On the 27th of May, 1949 a helicopter landed for the first time at the Naval Air Base Valkenburg – a Sikorsky S 51. None of us had ever seen such an apparatus, which was not surprising since this was the first and only helicopter in the Netherlands. I was immediately fascinated, and I made sure I was one of the lucky ones to have a ride in it. When I then heard that the pilot of the helicopter, Lieutenant Senger, would soon be resigning as temporary director of the Helicopter Foundation, in connection with his departure from the Royal Navy, I didn't hesitate for a minute and promptly filed a request to be nominated in his place. My request was granted, but it did mean that I had to stop my law studies because now I didn't have the time anymore.

The Helicopter Foundation was established in 1947 by a number of government organisations such as the Ministries of Agriculture, Defense, and Works and Roads, and also the Postal Service, the National Aviation Laboratory (NLL), the Netherlands Institute for the Development of Aircraft (NIV), and companies such as Fokker, the KLM and Avio Diepen. The latter firm had taken the initiative when it appeared that the American aircraft manufacturer, Igor Sikorsky, had produced the first really usable helicopter, the S 51, and they dispatched their test pilot, Hein Bulten, to the United States to become the first Dutch helicopter pilot to be trained at the Sikorsky factory.

The foundation was set up at Ypenburg Airfield, close to The Hague. The then Flag Officer Naval Air, Rear Admiral Schaper (whom I knew only too well!) made a smart move by making Naval Air personnel available, consisting of a pilot (Eduard Senger), a very experienced flight mechanic, sergeant-major Harmelinck, and two other flight mechanics, van den Berg and Toet. Harmelinck had been replaced by Piet Visser just before I arrived. Visser had already established his reputation the very first day he got acquainted with the helicopter. Accompanied by Harmelinck who had to show him the ropes, they were standing at a given moment on top of the helicopter while Harmelinck laboriously explained the functions of the various parts of the very complicated rotor head with its nine hinges and three dampers. While he was listening, Piet started rubbing with his forefinger on one of the three arms of the rotor head, to which the rotor blades are attached.

'What are you doing, Piet ?'

'It's got a crack in it'

'Come off it man, that's impossible, it's titanium.'

'No, look!'

'Well I'll be damned … you're right!!!'

Within a few days a Sikorsky team was flown over with a new rotor head – this was *not possible*, and according to them, it had never happened before.

At the Helicopter Foundation with flight mechanic sergeant Bogert (right) and the mechanics Toet and van den Berg.

The task of the foundation was to investigate whether a helicopter could be of use to the participating institutions. In addition, the engineers of the NLL and NIV wanted to find out all there was to know about the helicopter and stuffed it with all kinds of measuring instruments, and sometimes let us carry out tests, which were enough to make your hair stand on end. Although it must be said that they came on board themselves during the tests, at least the younger ones like Lucassen, Kuipers and Meyer Drees.

I started at the foundation in September 1949, and my first concern was the handling of a helicopter, which was no easy task. Hein Bulten was my instructor, and I have never had a better one. In order to master the very different coordination of the flight controls, I had first to practice sitting on a chair with two broomsticks: the one in the left hand represented the 'collective stick', the other in the right hand, the 'cyclic stick'. After about six lessons, I was flying solo, but I had never before been through such a hard time. The PH-HAA, as the helicopter was then registered, had extremely heavy controls, which was most exhausting, certainly for a beginner. Most instruction flights didn't last longer than twenty to thirty minutes.

A very interesting time was now beginning, with completely different work from what I was used to. Many meetings with representatives from the participating institutions, who naturally all had their own special requirements. For instance I transported post, sprayed field crops, carried out autorotation tests with the aeronautical engineers, and gave countless demonstrations at all sorts of events, such as exhibitions and air shows.

For one of those demonstrations I used to lower our mechanic, corporal van den Berg, during the flight into a lorry driving beneath us. This stunt always received a lot of acclaim, and when one day we were visited by test pilot Alan Read from Westland, a British helicopter factory, who was trying to sell their helicopter, he wanted to show the same stunt with his helicopter to prospective buyers. His own mechanic didn't feel a bit like it, and van den Berg told me straight away that he would only cut these capers with me. Alan was faced with a dilemma, but I didn't want to let him down – he was an ex-Navy pilot – so I volunteered for the stunt. It was nevertheless a strange sensation dangling at the end of a cable under a flying aeroplane and being let down at exactly the right moment onto the back of a moving lorry, and then loosening yourself in a flash so as not to be dragged out again. But I knew that Alan was a good pilot and I had every confidence in him.

One very interesting experiment was night flying. It was universally known that a helicopter, dangling under its rotor, was a so-called 'inherently unstable' apparatus, but the National Aviation Service still wanted to find out if flying on instruments would be possible in bad weather. To this end the ingenious American system of 'two-stage amber' was applied. The cockpit windows were covered with yellow plastic, and I was given spectacles with blue glass: through the contrasting colours I could therefore not look outside, but I could see my instruments, which had meanwhile been supplemented with an artificial horizon. It soon became apparent that flying on instruments was only possible with some foreward speed, whereby a certain direction stability was obtained. But vertical take-off and landing was impossible. Modern helicopters are gyroscopically stabilised, so do not have that problem any more. However with adapted airfield lighting and a searchlight that was mounted under the nose of the helicopter, it was possible to take off at night and land in the light cone. And so the entry was added in my helicopter licence from the National Aviation Service: 'The bearer of this document is qualified, exclusively for experimental purposes, to fly helicopters on instruments (IFR) and at night (20-1-1950)'.

Flight mechanic van den Berg on his way down to the lorry.

I got on well with Frits Diepen, whose firm, Avio Diepen, did the maintenance of the helicopter. Once he invited me for a private talk over lunch in a chic restaurant, 'The House of Lords' in the centre of The Hague. We drove there in his Maserarti 3500 sports car, and I was already most impressed. Then when he ordered plover's eggs as a starter for lunch, which I had never eaten before or seen anyone else eating them for that matter, and he deftly flattened his little egg on the palm of his hand, I thought for a moment, in my uncertainty, that he was having me on, but then I thought it best to go ahead and follow his example …

It turned out that the purpose of the lunch was to sound whether I would eventually be willing to go and work for him. I was flattered, but of course I politely refused all the same.

When the experimental programme of the Foundation was drawn up, it had been agreed that at the end, all the participating institutions could delegate a pilot, who would then be given a short orientation course on the helicopter. The Ministry of Agriculture was especially interested in the possibilities of the helicopter for crop spraying. For the bigger fields winged aircraft were used which were equipped with spraying booms on both sides. The drawback, however, is that the edges of the fields, where high trees often grow, are difficult to reach for an aeroplane because the pilot has to be able to pull up in time. This is quite a dangerous affair in view of the often heavy load of spray liquid tanks and the ensuing risk of stalling. The irony of fate was that this was demonstrated only too clearly when my pupil from the Ministry of Agriculture, Hamming (an ex-KNIL fighter pilot) crashed with a spraying aeroplane in the 'classical' way, shortly after his first instruction on the PH-HAA helicopter.

To my consternation, the Director of the Foundation, the former Director-General of the Postal Services, Van Houwelingen, requested me to inform the wife of Hamming of the fatal accident; because I was a fellow pilot, he felt that I was the most suitable person to do it. I could not refuse, although I had hardly known Hamming, and had never met his wife.

As a precaution against eventualities, I decided in any case to take a doctor along with me, and I looked up a doctor in the telephone directory who had his surgery somewhere in the neighbourhood. I was lucky for I quickly found a young, sporting doctor who made himself available without further delay. I was given a car with a driver for the purpose by Avio Diepen (my own mode of transport in those days was a motorbike), picked up the doctor, and together we went to Mrs. Hamming. After my carefully chosen words, my role had ended, and the doctor had to take over.

It was an interesting experience for me to see how the various pilots reacted differently to the very different flying characteristics of a helicopter. For instance, one of the pilots with the least experience, a glider pilot, had relatively less difficulty than other more experienced pilots. One of these, a big Air Force captain with enormous hands, even stopped altogether:

'This brute is not for self-respecting pilots!'

He wasn't all that wrong, perhaps, as illustrated on an ill-fated day when I was instructing Lieutenant Jaap Schwartz, who was actually my best pupil, which is perhaps why I let him do things that were still beyond his capabilities. As a result the PH-HAA fell on its side after a hard landing, and the rotor blades broke off.

The timing of the accident was not all that bad because the helicopter was due anyway for major maintenance and several modifications had to be carried out. One was the replacement of the linen-covered wooden rotor blades by metal blades. This would be a big improvement: when standing still; the old blades were apt to absorb a lot of moisture, resulting in severe imbalance and vibration during take-off, until the moisture was flung out by centrifugal force. Also, this unfortunate incident probably saved many lives later on. When the repair took place, in addition to the rotor, the very heavy control system with wires and pulleys, was replaced by an hydraulic system, so that the controls became much lighter. This would come in very useful for hoisting people two years later: it would have been very tricky without that modification.

Obviously this was the right moment to close down the Foundation. All the participants had had the opportunity of estimating the value of a helicopter for their purposes. It had become clear that the helicopter of that time, with its short flying duration and relatively low lifting capacity, had considerable limitations in many areas. For instance it had been proven that a fixed-wing aeroplane was much more economical for spraying field crops, much to the disappointment of the participants from the Ministry of Agriculture.

The accident with the PH-HAA which probably saved many lives two years later.

Summing up, it could be said that only where vertical take-off and landing, and hovering were a necessity, could a helicopter be of use. This did offer perspectives therefore for the Royal Navy. I wrote a final report to the Flag Officer Naval Air and pointed out that the helicopter would be absolutely ideal as rescue airplane on board our aircraft carrier, H.M.S. Karel Doorman (ex British HMS Venerable and named after Rear Admiral Doorman who was killed in the battle of the Java Sea in 1942). He agreed, and a year later on the twentieth of December 1951 I was able to fly our first navy helicopter over from Ypenburg to the Naval Air Base Valkenburg, where she was given the registration H-1.

8.   Aircraft Carriers 1951-53

As already mentioned, while the helicopter was being repaired, the Foundation was dissolved, since the aim had been reached. It was now time to do something about my own future. I asked for an interview with the Flag Officer Naval Air, still Rear Admiral Schaper, and requested a posting with my old love, fighter planes. 860 Squadron, which had earned its spurs in the war with Swordfishes, nicknamed 'String Bags', on board aircraft carriers, was just newly equipped with the Hawker Seafury, at the time the fastest propeller fighter in the world with its speed of more than 700 km per hour. Actually, Schaper considered me a bit too old at twenty-seven (!). At any rate as far as seniority was concerned, because, he said, there were plenty of younger pilots most keen to join. But I had just done well by tipping him off about the helicopter being up for sale after the repair, and he granted my request.

First I had a few other jobs to do, one of which is worth mentioning. Avio Diepen, one of my former 'clients', had a contract with the Navy for major maintenance on some of the Naval Air planes, such as the Mitchell bomber and an amphibious sea plane, the Sea Otter, which was used for rescue operations. Their test pilot, Hein Bulten, did not consider himself qualified to fly heavy aeroplanes, and certainly not sea planes, and suggested to me that I could apply for the job of test flying after major maintenance. Which is what I did, although I was not sure how the Naval Air High Command would react to this; so I didn't ask them.

Flying the Mitchell was no problem, of course, but the Sea Otter was another matter. Not only had I never sat in one of them before, but, apart from the few lessons on the Catalina flying boat four or five years earlier, I had very little experience as a pilot where 'water' was concerned. The water landings took place on part of Westeinder Lake that had been marked for the purpose, and I soon discovered that the plane was very docile and easy to land. Everything went well until one day when I had to fetch a Sea Otter from Yeovilton on the south west coast of England. Unfortunately it was not good weather there, but worse still, I was unexpectedly given a passenger to take back with me, the Commanding Officer of Naval Air, Captain Rombeek. Naturally he knew me well, and was surprised to find me on a flying boat. But he was a sport (or else he was in a hurry to get home), and cheerfully climbed on board. I was somewhat less cheerful, however, because bad weather with snow showers and ice above the English Channel had been forecast, and I was soon confronted with it. In fact the weather deteriorated so much that I decided to turn back and make a GCA landing on the nearest airfield, which was Manston.

I shall not easily forget that landing in what had in the meantime become twenty centimeters of snow on the runway; skis would have been more fitting. After landing I was advised to stay where I was, because taxiing in that mess was too risky. Captain Rombeek, as cheerful (or relieved?) as ever, insisted on getting out to pee. He had to pay for it dearly for as soon as he stepped on the ground, he slipped on the snow, with a concussion as a result. Luckily an ambulance managed to reach us, and the Captain disappeared to the sick bay, while I watched him go, dismayed and not knowing how all this was going to turn out for me. But it ended all right. Only, the Naval Air authorities thought that there were sufficient other pilots available for test flying, with thousands of hours of experience on sea planes.

It was now time to report to 860 Squadron, which had just been reinstalled, and already stationed in England at the Naval Air Station St. Merryn in Cornwall, to prepare for boarding the British carrier HMS Indomitable since our own carrier, the Karel Doorman, was in maintenance.

My colleague, Hans Goossens – nicknamed 'Goose' of course – and myself had had some familiarising on the Seafury at Valkenburg Naval Air Base. It was a delightful sensation to sit in the narrow cockpit of a fighter again after so many years. What was most noticeable during that first flight was the relatively low noise level as compared with the P40 of old. This was because the enormous engine was equipped with slide valves. Moreover with its 2480 hp it had more than twice the power of the Allison engine of the P40. In fact all that horse power caused an awe-inspiring torque, which you had to handle very carefully at low speeds, such as in take-off and landing, when you had insufficient pressure on the rudder to counter the torque effect.

I once witnessed a very spectacular landing by a colleague at Valkenburg. He made a bad wheel landing, bounced off again, and then tried to recover with a burst of throttle – which he should never have done. The result was that the engine torque promptly turned the plane on to its back, with a 'back landing' as a result! I raced on to the runway with some other colleagues, and saw, to my horror, an arm just sticking out of the upside-down cockpit wreck, the hand moving spasmodically. The pilot survived the crash thanks to the armour plate behind the cockpit seat which sticks up above the head, although he had to walk about for months in a plaster corset (decorated with lots of signatures of well wishers).

But for the rest, the Fury flew like a dream: light on its controls but not too nervous. Aerobatics were a joy. She didn't have any nasty surprises, but would punish too rough a hand with a violent snap-roll in a stall turn. Especially in dog fights it was wonderful to handle when thrown about just below the shuddering stall warning.

Take-off and landing always took place with the cockpit hood open, which in the winter did not exactly add to your comfort, but was customary for single-engine fighters in those days in case of engine failure when you would have to make a belly-landing and quickly abandon the cockpit.

On a beautiful summer day – in the meantime it was August 1951 – I took off, together with my colleague and fellow latecomer 'Goose' in our brand new Furies for St. Merryn. My plane had registration number '13', a number that most colleagues didn't like. It was the practice that each pilot had his 'own' plane assigned to him (except when it was in maintenance, of course), and I defied fate and chose the '13'. Curiously, all the mishaps that I would encounter with the Seafury in the course of time were never with the '13'.

I should mention here that our Navy had been closely cooperating with the British Royal Navy for quite some time, and one of the arrangements was with the Fleet Air Arm, enabling our carrier squadrons to be boarded on British aircraft carriers when our (only) carrier, the Karel Doorman was in maintenance.

On arrival at St. Merryn we reported to our commanding officer, Lieutenant Commander 'Bert' Bruinsma. The first officer was Karel Labree, and the next in rank and seniority was myself, so I became the Senior Pilot', or senior 'P' as the British called it. However, this Senior 'P' still had a lot to learn since, as opposed to the others, I had never been on deck. So I was hardly given time to unpack my suitcase, and began immediately with the 'dry deck' landings, called DDL's. Before you were accepted on board, according to regulations, you had to have at least 120 DDL'S registered in your logbook, and I had exactly ten days time. However, I knew that Bert was not above committing a bit of forgery if there were no other way out, and that would prove to be only too necessary.

On another lovely summer day, the 31st of August, 1951, our Queen's birthday, fate struck again. Up to then everything had been normal routine: I took off in the morning as number three in the usual fighter formation of four under the leadership of Bert. Now and again you had to get away from those DDL's, which exacted maximum concentration.

I was on my back at the top of a loop doing 'follow the leader' in line astern, when I heard a muffled bang: an oil pipe of the engine had broken, and the windscreen was soon covered with black oil, while thick, black, greasy smoke was filling the cockpit. The enormous five-blade propeller was suddenly standing still in front of me – a strange sight. I rolled the Fury out of the loop, and Bert, who had seen the long smoke trail behind my plane, calmly called over the radio: 'Ruud, bail out!'. That was all the encouragement I needed for I was already preparing myself for my third emergency parachute jump!

And here you had one of those remarkable lucky coincidences, which not only make life more pleasant, but can also sometimes extend it. The Seafury was known to be very dangerous to leave by parachute, following the usual method for single-engined fighters of turning the plane on its back so as to fall free. It had happened a few times that the pilot was then thrown against the tail fin, with fatal consequences, so that instead it was advised to 'ditch' – land in the water – if the necessity arose. Not a very pleasant activity either since the Fury with its large radial engine in the nose, was also a bad 'ditcher'. As soon as the aircraft, ploughing through the water, slows down, the nose goes down, causing the engine to scoop up water, and the resulting drag turns the aeroplane over on its back. It was then important to stay calm and loosen all the belts while still in the rapidly sinking and darkening cockpit, removing the oxygen tube last of all because that allowed you to breathe a bit longer. Then you climbed out, gave a tug on the CO^2 bottle to inflate the lifejacket, and up you went!

But there was another way. Very recently a British pilot had got out in really quite a normal manner by jettisoning the cockpit hood via the emergency system, which also opened the little panel on the port side, so you could simply step out on to the wing and be immediately blown away, free of the dangerous tail.

'Just like getting off a moving bus, old boy, nothing to it!'.

This valuable information had been distributed in the usual manner through the 'Notice to Airmen', and I had literally read the leaflet that very morning at the briefing, and automatically made a mental note of it, because ditching did not appeal to me at all.

It was indeed easy: trim full nose-up, jettison cockpit hood, loosen oxygen tube and radio connections, then the belts, climb on the seat bending down, turn round so as to face the tail – and out!

'Twenty-one, twenty-two, twenty-three', pull the parachute ring, and that was it.

So there I was once more hanging under a parachute and I soon realised that again I would not end up on the ground, because we had been flying over the Irish Sea. Luckily close to the coast so at least I didn't have far to swim. But first I saw to my amazement that my Seafury, which I had carefully steered in the direction of the sea, dived down from the high altitude we had been flying at, and turned inland (caused by the increasing speed and its trim), to crash and explode on the only house in the vicinity.

It was reassuring to see my three colleagues of the formation flying around me in a wide circle until I splashed into the sea. Then with Bert leading they flew right over me at high speed and minimal height, waggling their wings to congratulate me and wish me luck. Bert had meanwhile given the customary 'MAYDAY, MAYDAY' emergency call over the radio with the position for the Air Sea Rescue Service.

Meanwhile I was floating in the sea, which luckily in August had a reasonable temperature, and I rid myself of parachute, helmet and oxygen mask, actions which we had regularly practised in a swimming pool, the so-called 'wet dinghy drill'. In particular I had been able to bring into practice what we had been taught to do in case of a parachute landing in water.

The wrecked Sea Fury and the gash it tore in Mrs. May's cottage.

Freak Plane Crash Traps Housewife

MAN DEFIES FIRE TO SAVE HER

By Daily Mail Reporter

AMID blazing petrol and exploding ammunition, Mr. Robert Henry, a 75-year-old retired hotel proprietor, yesterday tore at the rubble of a Cornish cottage smashed down by a pilotless plane, to rescue a woman buried in the rubble.

With his bare hands he uncovered the ruins of her kitchen, and dragged out 47-year-old Mrs. Eliza Constance May, of the hamlet of Lower Trefreock, Port Isaac, badly burned about the face and neck.

"Save my dog," she said, "he's worth more than I am." But as Mr. Henry ran back he saw the dog, a pedigree Samoyad, valued at £100, already burned to death.

The accident is one of the biggest freaks of the air. The pilot, Lieut. Idzerda, of the Royal Dutch Naval Squadron, at St. Merryn, exercising with the British fleet, developed engine trouble in mid-air.

TURNED ROUND

He set the aircraft—a Sea Fury—to fly to sea, then baled out. As he was falling, the plane, by some trick of an air current, turned on its track, and dived into the back of Mrs. May's cottage.

Lieut. Idzerda landed in the sea. Then he swam nearly half a mile, and climbed 150ft. of cliff to the waiting coastguards.

"I must go and see what has happened," he said, and ran nearly three-quarters of a mile to the hamlet to see if he could be of any help.

People in Trefreock took cover as exploding ammunition whizzed down the street. Others were evacuated from their houses.

Mrs. May was taken to Wadebridge Hospital, where she is seriously ill with burns and suspected fractures.

Last night Mr. Samuel May, her husband, and his nephew George were digging in the ruins of the cottage for his life savings, which had been hidden in the bedroom.

Newspaper photo plus article from the Daily Mail.

There is a risk that after landing in water, the nylon canopy will fold on top of you like a 'death shroud,' impeding your breathing while you are struggling to free yourself from the parachute lines, often with fatal results. The technique to avoid this is the following: nearing the surface of the water, already loosen the parachute harness by a blow on the central lock on the chest – but take care to hold on to the harness straps since it is easy to misjudge the distance! Only when your toes touch the water, loosen the straps in a flash, so that the freed canopy will be blown away by the wind before touching the water.

I was about a quarter of a mile away from the coast, and decided not to use my dinghy, the small rubber boat which serves as a cushion folded on the parachute pack on the cockpit seat, but rather to swim to the coast. This inflatable dinghy, which I therefore had to release, is attached with a canvas strap and a twist lock to the life jacket (which I did keep on, of course).

In view of the strong breakers and steep cliffs of the Cornwall coast, it didn't seem such a good decision after all, the more so because just as I had clambered up the 150ft high cliff with some difficulty, the rescue launch arrived below to pick me up. But going back down the cliff was naturally not on, and I waved to them gratefully, thinking: 'A pity you didn't come a bit sooner!'

So I went on my way, following a path, sopping wet, but quite pleased with myself, and it was beautiful weather. Soon I met two smartly dressed young ladies. I expected I would give them a fright, the way I looked: tattered flying overall, torn gloves and bloody fingers from the sharp rocks, and moreover soaked. But they just gave me a polite nod, said 'Good morning, sir' in chorus, stepped calmly past me, and continued, undisturbed, on their way as if it were the most normal thing in the world. Somewhat dazed, I stood looking after them, while a puddle of water from the Irish Sea was collecting around my feet …

After a while I arrived at the coast guard cottage and tried to find out if anyone had been injured by the crashing plane, but no news was yet available. Soon an ambulance came to fetch me and back on the station, I didn't have much explaining to do. Bert said:

'I could also have advised you to ditch, but you like jumping so much, don't you?'

Indeed, with this third emergency jump I had unintentionally established a record, at least a Dutch one, which to my knowledge has never been broken.

The only thing I regret is that I never had a chance to keep the steel ring, the so-called D ring, which is attached to the chest harness to open the parachute with, as a souvenir. After my first jump somebody pointed it out to me: you should keep that thing with you when you jump, even if it's only to prove how calm and collected you were (to even think of it!). During my second jump with the Japanese enemy around, I had more urgent matters on my mind, and when I landed in the sea after my last jump, I couldn't take it with me because I had to swim.

But there was no time to lose now that I had lost one valuable day, and the next morning I was doing another seven DDL's. I never made the required hundred and twenty, I only got as far as a hundred, but Bert didn't bother about a slight counting error in my log book, and signed for my proficiency without blinking an eyelid.

This lack of practice would soon tell. It started on September the 8th when the complete squadron arrived above the 'Indom' (HMS Indomitable), waiting for us in the English Channel. When I looked down out of my cockpit on to that 'postage stamp' far below me, I wondered for a short moment what on earth I was getting myself into. My self-confidence was given a further knock when first all the others were let on board before I was allowed to try. This was standard procedure in case the newcomer would crash and obstruct the flying deck before the others had a chance to land. At last it was my turn, and as in a trance I carried out everything I had been taught.

First at an altitude of 500 ft past starboard side of the carrier with flaps at 10°, wheels and deck hook down, which are then checked from the flight bridge. As soon as the ship re-appears under the rear edge of the port wing, left turn past the bow of the ship while descending to 300 ft, open cockpit hood, detach parachute harness, oxygen tube and radio connections (in case you landed in the sea and would thus be in a hurry to get out), flaps to 30°, turn through to opposite heading, reduce speed to 100 kts, and go down to 100 ft. As soon as the ship's stern is at port, turn into finals while descending and reducing speed to 90 kts, and then follow the signals of the batsman. I arrived on the flight deck of HMS Indomitable with a hard smack, the deck hook grasped a wire, which brought me to a full stop, and I was immediately pushed back into position to take off again and make the prescribed seven deck landings so as to 'learn it once and for all!' Psychologically a good thing, of course.

And indeed, when after the last landing I could finally fold the wings and be directed to the fore deck by the deck crew, and climb out of the cockpit utterly exhausted, I had the feeling that I would be able to master it. What confused me momentarily was that Bert had asked me to report to the flight bridge – a kind of balcony on the port side of the island – straight after the final landing so he could introduce me to the Commander Air. But I had never set foot on an aircraft carrier before, and promptly got lost. An amused sailor showed me the way and ultimately I arrived on the flight bridge.

In the cockpit of the Seafury. Note the small emergency exit panel on the edge of the cockpit.

In the meantime, my Seafury, my faithful F 13, which never even received so much as a scratch, was brought via the front lift (one of the two large lifts on the flight deck) to the enormous hangar below deck, where its own permanent mechanic immediately took over. As a rule, pilot, mechanic and aeroplane stayed together as long and as much as possible – until the plane had to go into periodic maintenance – which intensified the team spirit. The pilot -

mechanic relationship was also important; after all the safety of the pilot was largely dependent on the care of the mechanic who had to prepare the aeroplane for flying every day. Further, the mechanic assisted the pilot with fastening the parachute straps, and the lap and shoulder belts, and finally handed him his helmet with oxygen mask, and checked that everything was properly attached. In this way a good and lasting contact often developed between pilot and mechanic.

I shared a cabin with a British Royal Marine Officer, a rather introvert man, who had a batman at his disposal who daily polished his uniform buttons and his shoes; in return for a small remuneration he also did little jobs for me.

'My' Nr. 13 full throttle just before take-off on the catapult

Landing on deck was not easy. I was handicapped not only by lack of practice, but even more so by the fact that being an experienced pilot, I found it difficult to follow more or less blindly the directions of the batsman. The batsman, a pilot who had been specially trained for the purpose, was indispensable for landing safely on the relatively small and narrow flight deck, while moreover the ship was often rolling and pitching, and the pilot himself could not see the deck properly because of the large engine in front of him. The batsman stood on a special small platform on the port edge of the flight deck at the stern, and indicated by means of signals with his bats, somewhat like large ping pong bats, whether you were too high, too low, too fast or too slow, and whether you were lined up properly. If everything went well, you got the 'cut' (close the throttle), and in the last two to three seconds you quickly looked in front of you to finish off the landing. You came down with a hard smack and the intention was to catch one of the ten steel, hydraulically braked, arresting wires, which were stretched across the flight deck, with the landing hook – which you had let out beforehand together with the landing gear – positioned at the back of the tail of the aeroplane. This brought you to a standstill after some twenty to thirty metres from 80 knots to 0.

A normal take-off.
In the foreground, the second barrier is lying down.

A less fortunate take-off by a colleague.

If you missed the wires, you ended up in the barriers, a kind of steel tennis nets, of which there were two installed, one behind the other across the deck, to prevent you from crashing into the other aeroplanes parked on the fore deck. If you were not in the right position according to the batsman, you got a wave-off, and that meant that you had immediately to give full throttle and go round again for another try. My problem especially was the scary low speed of no more than 90 kts at the end of the circuit, just above the sea. I liked to keep an eye on the speedometer for an extra knot or so (1.8 km per hour), instead of leaving it entirely to the batsman. Consequently I often came on deck slightly too fast, which time and again resulted in a reprimand from our own squadron batsman, Guus Hagdorn, at the debriefing. Guus was new to the job. He had recently had his training for Deck Landing Officer in the U.S. and kept strictly to the rules. Some experienced batsmen took individual peculiarities into account – usually too much speed – and gave a so-called 'early cut' so that you could glide on a bit before touchdown, which was actually against the rules.

Landing on the 'straight' deck in those days exacted utmost concentration, and was not easy. According to statistics, you could count on an average of one crash in the barrier every 160 landings with the Seafury, which certainly wasn't a bad 'deck lander'. However, on my 25th landing I already had my first 'barrier', but then I was suddenly cured of my excessive tenseness, and after that I finally began really to enjoy this top-performance flying. Indeed, in those days if you were a carrier pilot, you could say you belonged to the elite of military flying.

A classical barrier crash.

It became much easier later on when the so-called 'angled deck' was introduced, which had an angle of 8 to 10° to the longitudinal axis of the ship, so that you could simply go around again if necessary since there were no obstacles in front of you. Moreover, instead of the batsman, the angled flight deck is equipped with a hollow mirror on the port side, in front of which a light source is positioned which thus reflects in the mirror. Horizontal green lights are mounted on both sides of the mirror. On the approach the pilot then has to adjust his gliding angle in such a way that he sees the reflected ball of light lined up with the green lights in the middle of the mirror.

The story goes that the idea for an angled deck suddenly came to an officer of the Royal Navy when he and his wife were dressing to go out for dinner. He stood behind her to knot his tie in the mirror of the dressing table while she was applying her make-up. The relative movements of the two of them in the mirror gave him a sudden brainwave: he took her lipstick, made a dot on the mirror with it, moved his head from side to side – and the landing mirror for the angled deck was invented!

A British colleague in distress on HMS Indomitable.

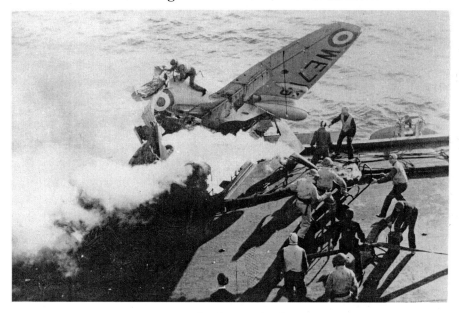

… but he survived.

That period with the 'Indom' generally entailed exercises with other units, alternated by an occasional weekend ashore, usually in Gibraltar where the Royal Navy had a large base.

Some remarkable events took place there. The Royal Navy is (or was?) on the whole rather formal. For instance it was always evening dress for dinner. Before and after dinner you were in the bar of the Officers' Mess with your colleagues, where there was plenty to drink. But if you knew you had to fly again the next day, you limited yourself to one or two glasses of gin and lime, the favourite navy drink at the time. Everything changed, however, when we were in port and the formal British sometimes went absolutely mad. All kinds of wild games were played in the Mess such as 'crash in the barrier': two heavy leather arm chairs were placed against each other, one turned upside down, and you had to somersault over them. Risky fun.

But the favourite game was: 'Are you there, Moriarty?' (from Sherlock Holmes of course), and the best way to describe that spectacle is my own experience. During a competition in the Mess I once had to oppose the Captain of the 'Indom', who was specially invited for the party. Normally the Commanding Officer of a ship just doesn't go to the Mess, but stays aloof in his own State Room, the same as in our Royal Navy. And so that evening I found myself in evening dress lying on my stomach, blindfolded, on the floor, and opposite me on his stomach the Captain, similarly attired, with all his ribbons. Our left hands were tied together with a table napkin and in our right hands we held a club in the shape of a rolled-up newspaper filled with flour. The idea was then to call out in turn: 'Are you there, Moriarty?' and then quickly turn your head away because your opponent, guessing the direction your voice came from, would try to hit you on the head with his 'flour club'!

I do not remember who won, only that we split our sides laughing and almost suffocated from the flour, which had turned our navy blue uniforms white.

I did bear this Captain a grudge though, for the following reason. When planes are landing on board, a carrier always steams at high speed against the wind so as to reduce the landing speed on deck, which naturally makes a difference to the braking by the wires. But evil tongues alleged that the Captain wanted to make a good impression on the Admiralty Board – and so be awarded the OBE

(Order of the British Empire) – by keeping the fuel consumption of his ship as low as possible by secretly steaming a couple of knots slower than we were entitled to. The result was extremely hard landings, especially mine, as I was inclined to cheat with a couple of knots, anyway.

Ultimately, our Captain (with his OBE) ended up as First Sea Lord.

However, on the whole I have very pleasant memories of that first acquaintance with both carrier operations and the British Royal Navy. It was the British humour especially that appealed to me. One example of this was when we encountered HMS Illustrious, another British carrier, off Portugal in the Atlantic Ocean. It was a beautiful day and moreover a dead calm which is quite unusual for those parts. There was no flying because in that case we would have had to steam at maximum speed, and for some reason that was not on. All of a sudden 'All hands on deck' was broadcast on the ship's tannoy (public address system), which seemed a strange command, but of course we complied. There was a tremendous commotion when more than a thousand men hastened on deck by way of the numerous ladders and stairs. Once on the flight deck we saw the ship's brass band already present and greeting us with lively marches. When everyone was lined up, the Captain came to the microphone and informed us of what we had to do. He said that in a few minutes we would be meeting our sister ship HMS Illustrious, and that we should greet our colleagues in an appropriate fashion. When the band beat a roll on the drums, all hands had to run on the double to port, then after the next roll on the drums back to starboard, and continue like this for several goes. So we did as we were told and to my amazement that enormous ship of some 36.000 tons began rolling in a most stately manner and it must have been a very strange sight on that glassy smooth sea. And that was naturally the intention for just at that moment Illustrious passed us on opposite heading!

Another strange custom was that when you were in a port with other ships, and you naturally visited each other, you tried to acquire a 'souvenir' from your colleagues, in fact steal one. Obviously the victims of the theft tried to retrieve the object, usually a squadron emblem or a flag or a mascot etc., at the very next opportunity, and preferably with something extra. We knew that there was a gold-painted fish, carved from wood and measuring more than a metre, on the flight bridge of Illustrious. This fish was held out on a stick in its belly every time a pilot flew past after having received a last minute wave-off because something was not right; for instance the ship was not properly in the wind yet or did not have enough speed. The meaning was: 'Not your fault but the 'Fishheads'. That's what the colleagues of the 'sailing' navy were called by the 'flying' navy.

Obviously everyone realized that this 'Goldfish' was a most coveted object to be stolen, so it was very well guarded and never left alone on the bridge. Therefore an extra challenge for the Dutch!

Once when we were berthed on the *Indomitable* in Gibraltar at the same time as *Illustrious*, a plan was worked out with the utmost precision. Two of our officers, 'Bill' van den Brandeler and myself, went to the bridge to talk to the officer on duty there. One of our sailors was standing close to the door leading to the flight bridge, a bit behind him another sailor, behind him another, and so on. While I distracted the attention of the British officer on the bridge by talking to him, Bill managed to quickly snatch the fish away and pass it on to our man at the door, who just as quickly handed it to the next man. My conversation partner saw it just too late, and sounded the alarm, but the fish had already disappeared, on its way to a hidden place on the Indom. Even we didn't know where it was kept because when we asked our shipmates they just laughed and said: 'Leave that to us, Sir'.

They were right because the colleagues on Illustrious did everything they could to find the beast, even our cabins were searched when we were not on board, but there was no way they could begin looking for it in the immense quarters where our crew were berthed. Only when we were back with the squadron at our home base Valkenburg did a delegation of the men formally present the fish to the commanding officer, Bert Bruinsma. Later on it was again put to use on our own carrier, Karel Doorman, and heavily guarded! Now the Goldfish has been given a place in the Netherlands Naval Air museum on the Naval Air Base, de Kooy.

A small incident took place in the Mess. The food on board was poorly prepared; although the ingredients were of good quality, it was usually overcooked. Our men especially complained because they missed the typical Dutch rich and spicy navy food.

In the meantime I had been promoted to First Officer because Karel LaBree had been transferred to take command of his own squadron. One day I was warned in the Mess by a steward that one of our men wished to speak to the C.O. Bert was away so I went in his place to see what the matter was. A group of four men were standing there waiting, led by 'Tarzan', our muscular corporal-armourer, a real tough type from the province of Zeeland. He was holding his cap with both hands and thrust it in front of me, saying:

'Sir, this garbage is not fit for human consumption!'

An indeed very unappetizing-looking potato, cooked to mush, and in the skin to boot, was lying in his cap. You really couldn't do that to someone from Zeeland – where reputedly the best potatoes in the world come from. I managed to pacify them, and Bert later arranged a special allowance for our men so they could buy extra food in the ship's canteen, such as biscuits and chocolate.

An equally original complaint was made in the officers Mess, this time anonymously.

'Devil on horseback' had again been served with our drinks in the mess. This typical English snack consists of a boiled prune wrapped in a piece of fried bacon and is very tasty if well prepared and crispy, but apparently beyond the skill of the ship's cooks. There was the customary book of complaints in the Mess, and we had often wondered if anyone ever bothered to look in it. In any case at least one time because, as the story goes, the Commander of the 'Indom', who was president of the Mess, opened up the book at a suspiciously bulky place, and, to his disgust and anger, he discovered a whole 'devil on horseback' stuck to one of the pages, and written underneath: Unfit to eat for man or beast!'

It was during this period, Autumn 1951, that we received word that the Dutch Royal Navy had decided that all ships and institutions would henceforth carry an emblem, i.e. an official coat of arms, following the custom of the British Royal Navy. This naturally also applied to our Squadron 860, and it was decided that I would design the coat of arms and my colleague Guus Hagdorn, the only one who had studied Latin at school, would compose a suitable motto. Since one of our main tasks was providing a protective fighter screen for the fleet, a 'fighter umbrella' as the British called it, my first idea was an armour plated umbrella, but of course it had somehow to rest on the prescribed waves of the sea, and a very imaginative genius suggested a floating cork from a Bols gin bottle. The submitted design was promptly returned with the remark 'ridiculous!'. I then drew the coat of arms as it exists today, portraying a winged and armoured fist, which represents a defence against lightning flashes from the enemy above. It was then beautifully painted on cardboard by corporal-sickbay attendant Jeekel, and subsequently dispatched. The High Council of Heraldry finally approved this design and Guus's motto: Arcens Affligo' ('I strike while defending').

In addition, Hans Goossens made a cover for the squadron line book with calfskin bought in Gibraltar, and which he completed with a very attractive representation of our new squadron emblem; working with leather was his hobby. This line book is now also in the Naval Air Museum.

The emblem of 860 Squadron.

The flying programme on board HMS Indomitable consisted mainly of interceptions of 'enemy' aircraft, coming from ashore or from other aircraft carriers, in our role of 'combat air patrol', alternated with attacks with our four 20 mm guns or with rockets on a target towed by another aeroplane, or on ground targets, in the role of tactical fighter-bombers.

A visit to Loch Eriboll, the most northern loch in Scotland, turned out to be a very special occasion. We had been doing gunnery exercises on cliffs near Cape Wrath, and now had a day of leisure ahead, at anchor in the loch. That region is practically uninhabited, and I was greatly impressed by the wild beauty of the area, which we could observe from a distance. A few of us were given permission to go ashore, and were dropped there by launch. When the launch had left, a quiet descended upon us like nothing I had ever experienced before. Naturally the sensation was caused by the contrast with the usual noise on board the aircraft carrier. Although you were no longer aware of it, you actually lived in a constantly noisy environment and now the only thing we heard, apart from the ringing in our ears, was the rustling of the wind and sheep bells far away.

At the end of 1951 we returned to Valkenburg. In the meantime the helicopter, now registered as H-1 with the Naval Air Service, had been repaired and was ready to be test flown. The first thing I noticed was how light the controls had become; an enormous improvement.

I was now able to complete the training of Jaap Schwartz, who was destined to succeed me as helicopter pilot when the time came. HMS Karel Doorman was also out of maintenance, and would now for the first time have a rescue helicopter on board; also the first in Europe to have one since even the British didn't have one yet. The so-called 'plane guard' function was normally carried out by an escorting frigate or destroyer, which was positioned right behind or next to the aircraft carrier, ready to haul any unfortunate air crew out of the water. A helicopter was obviously a big improvement: it was not only infinitely cheaper, but was also able to get there much quicker.

In January 1952, 860 Squadron boarded HMS Karel Doorman for the trip to the Netherlands Antilles and Morocco. For me personally it was an especially interesting time, because half the day I flew my Seafury nr.13 and the other half the helicopter. Luckily there were no accidents for which we had to go into action, so Jaap and I could confine ourselves to demonstrations and taking eager passengers along, because everybody wanted to sit in that novel apparatus.

No flying was allowed during the crossing, which is customary in peace time on account of the lack of alternative possibilities in case the flight deck should be out of order after a crash. The problem was then how to keep your pilots usefully occupied. Usually all kinds of lectures and lessons were given, but even that got boring after a while. Naturally this problem did not apply to the ground crew who had enough jobs to do on the aeroplanes in the hangar.

Jezebel in her role as 'plane guard', just before the signal: 'start engines'.

Jezebel taking off for her 'plane guard' position on port side.

It so happened that we had a well-known cardiologist on board, Doctor Hazenberg from Amsterdam. He was overworked (nowadays it would be called 'stressed') but didn't feel like going on holiday, when a colleague reminded him that he was a reserve officer in the Royal Navy, so why not let himself be called up for active duty. The Navy immediately reacted positively, and so our cardiologist was posted as Surgeon Lieutenant-Commander, Royal Navy Reserve on board HMS Karel Doorman, a ship full of healthy young men.

That was my chance. 'Doc' was a very witty and voluble fellow, and I managed to persuade him to give a number of talks on medical subjects for our pilots. He did so with great enthusiasm and humour, so much so that we sometimes wondered how many of his stories were really true. However this could not really satisfy his zest for work either, so he continued looking around for something to do. Until he discoverd a steward with enormous floppy ears.

It is not known how he managed to persuade the young man (it was rumoured that he first got him drunk), but all at once the steward was serving at the dining table with a thick bandage around his head. And not long afterwards he was proudly walking about with a pair of trim, flat ears. Doc's reputation was made. He then started eyeing a young officer as his next patient, but this one was a descendant from an old aristocratic family, who apparently all had floppy ears, so the baron felt obliged to decline the offer in honour of the family's characteristic.

But soon there was a 'real' patient: a sailor with an acute appendicitis. The Commander of the ship, Commander Van Oostrom Soede, RMWO (highly decorated ex-submarine captain in the Second World War) and myself were invited to see the Master at work. In view of my youthful plans of old, I was very interested, and Doc exhibited a true work of art. He made an opening no bigger than a large buttonhole, deftly wriggled out the swollen appendix, cut it off, and closed up the wound with a few stitches that he called the 'tobacco-pouch' stitch. All this in the course of a few minutes! Alas, the Commander had to miss part of the show because he felt faint and had to sit down for a while to recover …

During our stay in Curaçao, where nobody had ever seen a helicopter before, the H1 drew an enormous amount of interest.

Jaap and I had to give many a demonstration, and high-ranking authorities, including the Governor-General, lined up for a ride in it.

During that visit the H 1 was given the name 'Jezebel', after a very popular song hit at the time, about a wicked woman – rather appropriate!

On the return journey the 'Doorman' went past all the islands of the Antilles, and we often had to deliver mail with 'Jezebel'. Once we took the padre and the dentist to Saba. This landing on Saba was not simple. Saba is the smallest island of the Netherlands Antilles, and is actually an extinguished volcano, rising steeply out of the sea, so it was not easy to put Jezebel down on a slope. What happened next is described in a very lively manner by Gerard Casius in his article 'Jezebel on Saba' in the July number 2002 of 'The Spinner', a publication of the Netherlands Military Aviation Museum. Part of the article is quoted in the following:

> *Not until 1946 did the people of Saba get to see an aeroplane from close by. It was a Vought OS2U Kingfisher float plane belonging to the Compagnie Aérienne Antillaise (CAA), an unlicensed company, operating from French St. Maarten. It landed in Fortbay, the only bit of more or less calm water on the coast of Saba, and it was naturally a great sensation. Since the government did not have a high opinion of the technical reliability of the aircraft of the CAA – and rightly so – the requested concession for an air line was not granted, and Saba's hope for an air link remained unfulfilled. The only aeroplanes they saw were civil and military aircraft flying over the island.*
>
> *However, in 1952 a miracle occurred, at least in the eyes of the people of Saba.*
>
> *The aircraft carrier HMS Karel Doorman was exercising in the Caribbean area – it had also transported the Fairey Fireflies of Squadron 1 to Curaçao – and was passing in the neighbourhood of Saba. By chance the wife of the Governor of Saba had just given birth to a child, and their wish was to have the baby christened by a minister of the Reformed Church, which was not possible on the island that was mainly Anglican and Baptist. A telegram was sent to the 'Doorman' asking whether the Navy Chaplain could go ashore to perform the christening. Now for the first time the 'Doorman' had a helicopter on board, the famous Sikorsky S-51 'Jezebel'. It was therefore a challenge to fly the chaplain to Saba with Jezebel, and so it was decided. It was fairly late in the afternoon of the 14th of February when Jezebel took off from the*

'Doorman', with Lieutenant Ruud Idzerda, the first helicopter pilot of the Netherlands Naval Air Service, at the controls, and headed with the Chaplain on board for 'The Bottom', the main village of Saba.

The name 'The Bottom' is a degradation of the word 'botte' (from Zeeland) meaning 'basin', and that is a good description of the lie of the village. It is surrounded on all sides by fairly high mountain slopes, and this turned out to be an unsurmountable obstacle for the S-51. It was possible to land, but for a safe take-off from this elevated and hot, tropical location, the helicopter had to be able to make some forward speed, and there was not sufficient space for that there. Meanwhile practically the whole of the population of Saba (one thousand) had gathered in The Bottom to witness the wonder of the helicopter landing on their island. Idzerda hovered above 'the basin' and made several attempts to land, 'egged on by the crowd as if it were a football match', as the Antillian historian, Dr. Johan Hartog, wrote. But the pilot decided not to land there after all. A message to this effect was thrown down on a roll of paper, and Idzerda looked for a more suitable location. He found one on St. John's Hill, by road 800 meters away from The Bottom. A location where the Jezebel could, as it were, just 'fall off' the hillside when taking off.

The people of Saba were naturally terribly disappointed that the Jezebel did not land. But then word soon came that the heli had landed on St. John's. 'A bomb could not have had more effect' according to Dr. Hartog, 'because the whole crowd went tearing up to St. John's along roads, steps, and any way they could find up the mountain side; scattered every so often by a hooting jeep forcing its way through, and crammed to the mudguards with passengers.'

Now in those days there wasn't a proper road in Saba. The way up to St. John's went steeply uphill with hairpin bends and consisted of large steps. That didn't stop anyone from dashing up the mountain. A neighbouring resident of St. John's presented the helicopter crew with a hurriedly gathered bunch of flowers, and someone else came running up with a large Dutch flag, tied in haste to a long branch. The climax of the reception was a series of twenty-one salute shots fired by someone with a hunting rifle. The Navy Chaplain and the pilot then proceeded to The Bottom where the Governor's baby was christened. After this short ceremony they returned to St. John's, and the helicopter took off from Saba without any trouble. As it left the ground, the multitude spontaneously began to sing the national anthem.

The whole of Saba turned out for Jezebel.

It was interesting to identify clearly the two original communities of the island: sandy-haired people with freckles, descendants of British colonists, and black descendants from slaves.

The landing on the island of St. Maarten with Jaap Schwartz was another memorable occasion, also because we had to collect some lobsters that had been ordered. Our ships paymaster, a renowned gourmet, knew that beautiful lobsters were to be had there, and organised a subscription list in the 'Long Room' (as the mess is curiously called in the Netherlands Royal Navy) for those who were interested, and who had to pay in advance, for a festive lobster dinner. I entered my name too, of course.

The visit to St. Maarten late in the afternoon got a bit out of hand because in their enthusiasm they had organised a festive reception for this first helicopter visit to the island, complete with speeches and brass band. I was getting slightly nervous because I knew that the Doorman was meanwhile steadily steaming away from us at 18 knots, on the way for the crossing to Morocco.

At last we were able to break away. The lobsters in two large baskets were loaded on board the helicopter next to Schwartz and we speeded after the Doorman while night was falling. Luckily some smart individual on board had meanwhile directed a searchlight straight up at the clouds above the ship, which was a very welcome beacon for us. We landed without any problem on the illuminated deck, and I had just switched off the engine when I heard Schwartz swearing and ranting that 'those damned beasts are loose and pulling at my shoe strings!' A mechanic came running up to help and was promptly bitten in his fingers. Then an officer came up to me and said that I had to report immediately to the Commander Air, Witholt.

This Commander was known as an amiable and somewhat phlegmatic person, but now he was really angry. He accused me of coming back too late on purpose so that I could be the first to make a night-landing on the Doorman! Indeed, during its last maintenance the Doorman had just been fitted out for night-flying operations, and these had yet to take place. I tried to convince him that it hadn't even occurred to me, also because landing in the dark with a helicopter was really nothing very special. I then handed him a formal letter that the Governor of St. Maarten had given us for the Commanding Officer, and we had had to wait for that, surely? I think he was only half convinced.

But the lobster feast made up for a lot. We had agreed to wear evening dress for the occasion, and we sat at a separate table where the lobsters were tackled, accompanied by champagne. The colleagues who had not put themselves down on the list did look rather envious …

The visit to Morocco was very worthwhile, although it didn't start off so well. I had to take the commander of the flotilla, Commodore Bientjes, and Commander Witholt to a military airfield near Casablanca. When we arrived at the airfield, we saw a troop of soldiers lined up close to the landing place. I was thinking, well, a guard of honour, how courteous of the French. A number of képis were blown away as we landed, which somewhat disturbed the decorum, whereupon a furious French officer came rushing up, and snapped at me:

'Pas ici! Nous attendons notre général … allez-vous en!'

And so I realised that I was at the wrong airfield …

While we were anchored on the roadstead off Agadir, one of the highlights was the invitation that our Commander of the Flotilla, who had embarked with us for an exercise, had received for a visit to an old fort in the desert, called Tiznit. I was one of the lucky ones who were allowed to go along. That fort could have come straight out of the film 'Beau Regard', from the book with the same title. The fort was encircled by a towering stone wall, and we were received at the enormous wooden, bronze-studded gate, by a guard of honour of Spahis, striking horsemen in flowing robes and armed with long lances. In those days Morocco was still a French colony, and these Spahis were an Algerian unit of their Foreign Legion.

Inside we were welcomed in style by the Commanding Officer and his staff. After being taken around the fort, it was time for champagne, at eleven o'clock in the morning! But it tasted very good in that scorchingly hot, dry, desert atmosphere. We were then joined by a very exotic looking group. Huge men in brown 'burnous', a long coat with a hood attached, and with a kind of black cord wound around their bald heads (traditionally for pulling up a bucket of water from a well in the desert), fairly light brown skin, and some of them had blue eyes. It appeared that these were 'Goums', warriors from the Berber peoples, who are not Arabs, and apparently the original inhabitants of that part of Africa; quite mysterious because they were originally a white race. The Goums had the reputation of being fearless warriors, a fame that was further strengthened when ultimately they were able to overpower the Germans at the notorious battle of Monte Casino in Italy during the Second World War, after many unsuccessful attempt by other units.

These Goums were indeed covered with medals, and it was curious to see them standing there clutching a glass of orange juice in their coarse fists: they were Muslims.

Our visit to Casablanca was also memorable for two very different reasons. The first was meeting an American film crew who were filming there, and had been invited to a reception on board the Doorman. The leading man was Van Heflin, a well-known film star at the time, who told us that he was of Dutch descent. He was a very nice person, as opposed to his wife, a red-haired 'femme fatale', who was doing her best to seduce one of our young officers. I could have forgiven her for that, until at a dinner, for which Van Heflin had invited me and a few other colleagues ashore after the reception, I saw her stubbing out her half-smoked cigarette on her not even half-eaten filet mignon on her plate.

The other event was very special, like a fairy tale. We were invited to a reception at the palace in the capital, Rabat, given by the French Governor of Morocco, together with King Hassan.

When we arrived at the gateway, two black giants were standing at the gates in colourful dress with baggy breeches and turban, and with drawn scimitars. The gardens, where the reception was held, were decorated with Chinese lanterns hanging in orange trees, and the people present were all equally colourful, especially the French officers of Spahi regiments and the Foreign Legion.

After this, the Doorman steamed to the Mediterranean, first to visit Oran, the French naval base in Algeria. During the weekend I had just finished my watch as duty officer, and found myself practically alone at the Sunday lunch table, together with the two navy chaplains (Protestant and Catholic). Although I was certainly not a 'customer' of either of them, I naturally knew them and got on well with them. So when they asked me if I felt like joining them to visit an ancient convent of the 'Sœurs Blanches' some distance from Oran in the desert, I readily agreed. We were accompanied and driven by a French priest, who with typical Gallic driving style – full throttle and using his hands as much for talking as for driving – raced through the desert in his old Peugeot. We arrived at a large complex surrounded by a wall which looked a bit like Fort Tiznit in Morocco. Only here we were not greeted by Spahis, but, after knocking, first carefully sized up through a small opening in the enormous door, before being let in by a surly-looking nun in a white habit. After we had been parked in a waiting room, two much friendlier, giggling Dutch nuns came in and greeted us with the unmistakable accent of the Catholic southern provinces of the Netherlands.

After refreshments had been served, we were shown around. I was particularly struck by the large inner garden, including an orange orchard with oranges bigger than I had ever seen before. Underneath the trees, the ground was covered with oranges and I made a comment on the waste. Then we were shown a laboratory where especially biological research in many different fields was carried out.

I noticed a number of boxes in a kind of terrarium, and when I asked what was in them, the accompanying nun said: 'Put your finger inside, then you will know!'. I didn't think that was such a good idea, so then she carefully opened the box, and the biggest scorpion I had ever seen was crawling inside! 'Very naughty!', I said, wagging my finger at her. But she made up for it when we were given two baskets full of those enormous oranges to take with us when we left. My earlier remark had apparently gone home, and I would have liked to keep most of them for myself, but my two religious travelling companions thought that the sickbay was a more appropiate destination for that delicious fruit.

After the Doorman took to sea again, eight fighters from our squadron flew off to visit the French naval air base at Oran for the day. I noticed during lunch that our French hosts (pilots!) were calmly drinking wine (although they did add some water), which would have been a mortal sin for us.

We were to return to the Doorman, which was waiting for us off the coast, later in the afternoon. When taxiing for take-off, it is customary to request permission from the control tower in English, the international language in the aviation world. Not so for the French. Naturally we were aware of their sensitivities, and it had been impressed upon us to request permission in French. In English you ask: 'Request permission to enter the runway for take-off.' In French it is: 'Demande permission pour pénétrer la piste et décoller.'

And so the leader of the second flight of four, who took off after me, Willem de Kluizenaar, nicknamed 'De Kluis', a real wag, called over the radio: 'Demande permission pour pénétrer le décolleté!'

The French air controllers could obviously appreciate his humour because they burst out laughing.

Later on 'De Kluis' would be in the news in a less pleasant way. When landing on board the British carrier HMS Illustrious, on which we had embarked in September, he made a hard landing, one wheel gave way, the port wing broke off rupturing the fuel tank, and everything burst into flames. De Kluis was able to save himself by jumping right through the blaze on to the deck, which unfortunately resulted in a broken ankle – but also a most spectacular photo.

Kluizenaar jumping for his life.

In the meantime at Valkenburg, in between trips abroad, I had formed a formation stunt team, with a view to possible participation in the National Stunt Competition the following year. I had carefully selected Hans Goossens, Taco Mulder and Frans Harte on the basis of their flying skill and enthusiasm. Whenever we had a chance, we practised all kinds of stunts in a 'diamond' formation: loops, slow rolls, rolls off the top and 'chandelles'. The engine cowlings on the Furies at our disposal were painted orange, with the numbers '860' in black.

One day, when we were back in home waters, we had the Defence Committee of the Lower House of Parliament on board for an official visit. As part of all kinds of demonstrations during this visit, my stunt team, which had meanwhile been christened '860-Aerobats', was also requested to give a show. Everything went according to plan until we came in to land. I came down alright but the damper of the deck hook sprang an oil leak, so that the hook started to bounce, and only just caught the last wire. The result was that the Fury (but of course not my '13' which was in maintenance) dived into the first barrier, and remained there standing on its handsome orange nose. No harm was done except for a broken propeller, and I put my cap on and calmly climbed out of the cockpit. The deck crew quickly put the Fury upright again and pushed it away to make room for my team mates who had to land after me. But the impression that this must be an extremely dangerous business had been made. At any rate …a few months later, pilots on aircraft carriers were granted the same extra flying allowance that jet pilots in the Air Force had been receiving recently, and I have always tried to maintain that we could thank my 'demonstration' for it …

Stunt team 'the 860 Aerobats'. From left to right: Rudi Idzerda, Hans Goossens, Taco Mulder and Frans Harte.

The 860 Aerobats in echelon port.

Stunt pilot 'Goose' says 'sorry!'.

During a conversation with one of the members of the Defence Committee afterwards in the Long Room, he told me that he had found it a fascinating show, and made a remark that struck me: he said that the teamwork between all the people involved, the various units of the deck crew with their differently coloured caps, the batsman with his bright iridescent orange jacket, the catapult crew with their black caps, the pilots in their aeroplanes, all seemed to be part of a superbly trained ballet, and the roaring of the engines and the hissing of the cables and the clattering of the barriers folding down onto the deck, made the accompanying music.

He was absolutely right. All at once I saw the context of that intense interplay on board in a new light.

The ballet performance begins in the morning with a bugle sounding throughout the ship (the flight roll call), playing the first notes of the tune: 'Er kwam een vogel aangevlogen' (A bird came flying …an old Dutch folk song), and everyone starts preparing for the work ahead. The aeroplanes are brought from the hangar on the lift to the flight deck, where they are pushed by the shunting crew, wearing their blue caps, to positions indicated by the Flight Deck Office in his yellow vest. The air crews hasten to the briefing room where first the weather forecast is given, then the various missions, and the squadron commanders wind up with last instructions. The adrenaline starts streaming through the arteries as they make their way to the aeroplanes.

We now follow the performance of the two solo artists of the ballet: the pilot and the batsman.

Once on deck, the pilot sees Jezebel standing ready at the front of the ship, surrounded by black-capped deck hands, ready to remove the blocks for the take-off. A reassuring sight, that slender orange Jezebel, who will shortly take up position on port side just above the sea, prepared for whatever may happen.

The pilot arrives at his Seafury and climbs onto the port wing. The mechanic is sitting astride the fuselage between the engine and the cockpit windscreen, ready to help with strapping in. A mutual smile, a nod and a 'good morning'. The pilot lowers himself into the cockpit, where the mechanic has already put his parachute down on the seat, puts the harness on, attaches the dinghy – which also serves as a cushion – with a belt to his life jacket, and then fastens the wide lap-belt, to which he attaches the shoulder straps handed to him by the mechanic. Then the mechanic gives him first the inner cloth helmet with oxygen mask, integrated head phone, microphone and radio cable, and finally the hard outer helmet with visor. Thumbs up, and the mechanic slides nimbly down the smooth fuselage to position himself in front of the aeroplane to check the starting of 'his' engine. The enormous five-blade propeller begins to rotate hesitatingly, a few puffs of smoke and coughs, and then a mighty, sonorous roar of 2480 horse power. With that music in his ears, the mechanic, satisfied, disappears to the catwalk, a narrow passage at the edges of the flight deck where everyone has to stay below flight deck level during take-off and landing.

The pilot now waits for the green light from the flight bridge, and take-off directions from the Flight Deck Officer, while he and his Fury are gently heaving with the motion of the slowly pitching ship that stretches in front of him.

When all the aeroplanes have left, relative calm falls on the flight deck: the 'intermission between the acts'.

Then the 'pas de deux' of the pilot and batsman follows. The 'solo dance' of the pilot intensifies at the moment he turns in towards the ship. He concentrates on that little figure in bright orange on the extreme port edge of the flight deck, who is welcoming him with outstretched arms and

*orange bats in his hands. At that moment the batsman becomes the 'star'
through his unique responsibility for a safe landing. He indicates by
means of arm signals what his partner, the pilot, has to do.*

Bats up.

'Oh, I'm too high, reduce throttle and lower the nose slightly.'

Right bat hitting the right leg.

*'OK, I know, again I'm too fast. A little less throttle, not too much –
come off it!'*

Bats up momentarily.

'Still a bit too high, take a quick 'high dip' with the control stick.'

Bats straight in front of him repeatedly clapped against each other.

'What's that, too slow? Quick, a bit more throttle!'

Bats down.

'And now too low – yeah, no wonder, a bit more throttle.'

Bats horizontal, a slight bending of the upper body to the right.

'Ah, I'm alright, you just want to line me up a bit more with the deck.'

Right bat slapped rapidly against the left shoulder.

'Ha, the cut! The next three seconds I am on my own.'

*Slam the throttle shut – look ahead – there is the deck straight ahead
and underneath the engine cowling, and there looms the 'island' on
starboard side where the Commander Air and the rest are watching
critically – lower the nose – at the last moment quickly and carefully ease
it down and settle to a three point attitude – a hard smack – a tense
fraction of a second – then a sudden strong tug: we've got a cable!'*

*Then suddenly the corps de ballet pops up from all sides behind the
scenes with their differently coloured caps; the blue caps loosen the deck
hook from the wire – a sign to move forward – taxi to the fore deck – give
some throttle – now a yellow cap comes dancing up and directs the pilot
with rapid gestures to the exact place, while the pilot meanwhile folds the
wings of his Fury.*

'Done it again, my friend, you brought me safely back.'

*The music – the humming of the engines – fades, the adrenaline goes
down, and the pilot imagines distant applause …*

9. The Great Flood of 1953

My first task in the new year was test-flying Jezebel who had just come out of maintenance, and had at the same time undergone certain modifications. Not a moment too soon, because in the night of Saturday, January the 31st and Sunday February the 1st 1953 our country suffered the worst flood disaster in centuries, caused by a fatal combination of spring tide and westerly storm. Eighteen hundred and thirty-six men, women and children, and tens of thousands of animals were drowned.

I was called early on the 1st of February from Valkenburg with the message that the dykes had burst in Zeeland and South Holland, and that it seemed useful to go and see if Jezebel, still the one and only helicopter in the Netherlands, could be of help.

Alas, because of the violent storm, we could not set off straight away since Jezebel could not take the strong gusts of wind. I did try by starting the engine in a hangar, but as soon as the rotor blades came outside the protection of the hangar, they began to flap wildly, with the risk of hitting the tail boom, so I had to abandon the attempt immediately to avoid damage.

Bursting of the dykes in Zeeland, February 1953.

We spent the whole day Sunday waiting on the air base, but we could see in the Met office that the weather was not improving. Confused reports of what was happening in the south west of Holland came slowly trickling in, and they were not encouraging.

But on Monday, February the 2nd, we set off first thing in the morning for Zeeland. We did not have much information, only that something was seriously wrong. I had taken Taco Mulder, from my stunt team, along as my helper – at his own request – although he had never been in a helicopter before. I gave him the necessary instructions on the way. Jaap Schwartz went with flight mechanic sergeant Bogert, who had meanwhile replaced Visser, and Corporal Van den Berg, as Jaap's helpers, by car to the nearby Air Force base Woensdrecht, which we were to use as our base. The plan was that Jaap and I with our helpers would relieve each other every time the helicopter had to be refuelled, which was about every three hours. When Taco and I arrived at Hoek van Holland, we couldn't believe our eyes: we could see virtually nothing but water, and here and there a few trees and roof-tops, on some of which we soon saw people sitting. We learned later on that this was Oude-Tonge, but at that moment we had no way of orientating ourselves.

Zeeland flooded, seen from inside Jezebel.

Dropping the rescued at Zierikzee.

Jezebel was equipped with a winch that unfortunately could not lift more than 100 kg at a time. Moreover the cable got stuck after the third rescue, so that we had to go to Woensdrecht for a quick repair. At the end of the cable was a large hook to which the loop of a life jacket was attached, which the person to be rescued had to put on. It soon became clear that this was not satisfactory because some didn't know what to do with the life jacket. We even pulled up a young woman who was just hanging on to it – very risky.

The procedure was as follows:

As soon as we saw someone in distress, I hovered above him or her, following directions from my helper, Taco, who was sitting behind me, because I myself could not look right under the helicopter. This was a matter of good teamwork, such as 'a bit to the left – back a bit – now a bit to the right' etc., but we soon got into the routine. Unfortunately there was only room for two extra passengers, and in view of the urgency – some were literally clinging to rooftops and trees – we first took them to the nearest dry place, often Zieirikzee, so as to gain time.

In any case, it must have been a very frightening experience for most of them. No one had ever seen a helicopter before; it made a terrible noise, and caused a violent downdraft when it was hanging above them. It was a drawback that the helicopter of that time had little reserve power, so that some of the people we rescued, often dressed in as many clothes as possible against the severe cold, and sometimes drenched as well, heavily taxed the lifting power. The irony of the situation was that the very strong wind, that was still prevailing, was a positive factor because hanging motionless requires the most power, and holding the machine into that wind gave extra lift.

I can imagine that the ones we had to leave behind were worried that we would not be able to find them again after we had left with the lucky ones to be dropped in Zierikzee or elsewhere. On the whole, though, we managed, with the help of compass and watch, even if it was very difficult to orientate yourself visually since there were hardly any points of recognition left on that endless expanse of water. We flew from roof to roof, all the while looking if we could see anybody; often people were waving with sheets. I remember that we sometimes saw people in a very critical situation, in agony, while we already had two on board. We only hoped that we could come back in time to save them, but sometimes by then they had already disappeared.

A desperate situation.

The first day I was able to pick up thirty-two people. Some of them were in very bad shape after spending two days in the cold and in mortal fear.

We spent the night in Woensdrecht where the problem with the life jacket was discussed. Bogert found a solution, and during the night he went to the parachute-packing department and made a canvas sling from a discarded parachute harness. I wrote the words 'under the armpits' in big black letters inside the sling. The idea was that the person to be hoisted should put his (or her) head and arms through this sling, slipping it under the armpits. (We heard later on that this 'invention' already existed in the United States.)

Some of the rescues are still vivid in my memory. Among the first to be rescued were a couple of whom the wife was in advanced pregnancy, which was an extra worry. Later on I learned that the baby was indeed born shortly after the rescue, and this would have a sequel nearly forty years on, but I shall come back to that later. After first dropping his wife off, we returned to fetch the husband and his little girl whom he was clutching to him.

Then there was the man who wanted to take his dog with him. Taco called out on the radio: Sir, it's a big bastard!'. To which I replied: 'No way, just suppose it panics.'

Taco gesticulated to the man to try and convince him to leave his pet behind, unsuccessfully, however, because while the man was being pulled up, Taco suddenly saw the dog's snout peeping out of the man's overcoat, so we took them on board anyway. Luckily the animal kept quiet, for the last thing we needed in that cramped space on board was a panicky dog.

Another time, the man we were hoisting seemed extremely heavy, as I could tell from the boost gauge on the dashboard, which indicated how much power was needed to prevent the helicopter from losing height under the weight. When he came aboard the reason was clear: he had a couple of money bags stuffed with large silver coins tied around his waist, and also all his pockets were filled with them. After we had dropped him off, we discovered that in the confusion he had left some coins behind in the helicopter. Later on we handed them over to a policeman, and I can only hope that he got his savings back.

Then there was the man who didn't know what to do with the sling and just held on to it, but he couldn't keep it up, so fell off, landing on his back in the water. We could not get to him because trees were in the way; besides there were many more there waiting to be rescued from their precarious position, so I never knew if he made it. (Fifty years later when I was invited to the memorial ceremony of the Great Flood, I heard from someone who knew the man that he had indeed survived.)

In retrospect one can't help being amazed that under those extreme conditions, most of them did manage to put the sling on properly – although there was one who put the sling on back to front, so that he was pulled up in a very uncomfortable position with the hook behind his back.

One time we saw an old woman standing all alone in water up to her waist, apparently on a dyke with rows of trees flanking what must have been a path. She was clearly in great distress, and didn't react to the dangling sling or to Taco's directions.

Taco shouted: 'Sir, she's drowning, I'm going to fetch her!', and before I could say anything, he had jumped out of the hovering helicopter. This alarmed me considerably because without his directions, I was literally blind to what was going on below the helicopter, and ran the risk of losing both of them. The only solution was to go down, but those trees were in the way. Luckily they were saplings, and moreover, during the last modification of Jezebel, the linen-covered, wooden rotor blades had been replaced by metal ones. So I hoped for the best, and it was a strange sight to see those trees gradually getting shorter on both sides …

Taco managed to push the little old woman into the back, quickly climbed in after her, put his head phone and microphone back on, and reported cheerfully: 'OK, we're ready!'

I could hardly be annoyed with him, and I later put him up for an official Certificate for Exceptional Conduct, which he was promptly awarded by the Flag Officer Naval Air.

Well, the first two days were the worst. The people we rescued were exhausted, after being without sleep and food, and exposed to the bitter cold for two to three days. Jaap and I managed to rescue more than a hundred with our one and only helicopter. The famous 'Bogert' sling, in which all these people have been hanging, was in my possession for many years until I presented it to the Naval Air Museum.

The farmhouse of the Los family after the water had gone down. The survivors were hoisted from under the sagging attic roof. The white sheet, with which our attention was drawn, is still visible.

If we had had more helicopters, several hundred could have been rescued. Alas, many drowned because there were not enough boats there in time either, and moreover boats could not reach everywhere a helicopter could. Several helicopters of the British Royal Navy from England, and of the Americans from Germany, arrived on the third day, but that was too late for the most critical cases, although they did an excellent job evacuating people.

I must mention one exception though, a jolly Belgian pilot from SABENA, called Charles Trémarie, in a small two-seater Hiller helicopter, if I remember correctly, and he *was* there early. However he was by himself and didn't have a hoist. That didn't put him off; whenever possible he just put one skid, (a kind of ski instead of wheels) on the roof of a house, and let the passenger step in!

We stayed in action until the tenth of February, evacuating people, some of whom were injured, in cooperation with the British Royal Navy, who were equipped with a British version of the Sikorsky S 51, the Westland Dragonfly, and a number of American small Bell helicopters belonging to the U.S. Army in Germany. All operations, including those of other units of the Netherlands Royal Navy, were coordinated by Commodore J.F. van Dulm, RMWO (equivalent of VC), another ex-submariner of World War II.

On the seventeenth of February all the helicopter crews, who had taken part in the rescue operations, were invited to Soestdijk Palace. In the morning there was a briefing at Valkenburg when we were informed where we had to land and so on. I was somewhat irritated by the Queen's aide-de-camp, who was also present, a rather arrogant anglophile, a Lieutenant Colonel of the Air Force, who was only interested in the British crews, and hardly paid any attention to us, his fellow countrymen. He had everything all arranged: he would fly with the British Squadron Commander, and they would be in the sole helicopter – because that was all there was room for – to land in the palace grounds. The rest of the helicopters could land in a field a bit further on. I then said that the only Dutch helicopter would most definitely land in the palace grounds of OUR Queen, and that was that. We walked out of the briefing room under furious protest of the ADC, and I whispered to Trémarie: 'Suivez-moi!'. Together with Schwartz and Mulder, I got into our waiting Jezebel, which had already been warmed up by our ground crew. We took off straight away and set course for Soestdijk, followed by Trémarie in his little Hiller.

It was quite foggy that day, but that didn't bother me much because obviously I knew my way above little Holland. We therefore arrived at the palace long before the others, circled round once to look for a good spot, and then put Jezebel down right next to the terrace at the back, where meanwhile Prince Bernhard and the excited little princesses were waiting for us.

The Queen received us most warmly, and we had already been standing there for some time, holding our glass of orange juice, when the others arrived, led by an angry ADC, who nevertheless didn't dare say any more. Bogert, who had arrived by car, and who had also shaken hands with the Queen, whispered in my ear: 'It will be some time before I wash this hand!'

A very interested member of the Queen's court was the Chief of the Royal Military Household, the highest military function at the court, Vice-Admiral N.A. Rost van Tonningen. The admiral held his head a bit stiffly to one side as a result of a bullet in the neck that he had once received when shot during the war by a resistance fighter, who had mistaken him for the 'traitor' Rost van Tonningen, a relative.

On a reckless impulse, I asked the admiral where he lived, and if there was a field near his house. Luckily he didn't live right up in the north of Holland, but in Haarlem, so not far from Valkenburg, and he said there was a field opposite his house.

'Shall we take you home then, Sir?'

Reception at Soestdijk Palace for the helicopter crews after the flood disaster.
Extreme right Jaap Schwartz and sergeant Bogert.

The admiral immediately agreed, and so it happened that after the reception was finished, we were on our way to Haarlem with our enthusiastic passenger, in the fog which had meanwhile grown thicker. Once we even flew under high tension wires so as not to lose contact with the ground, because instrument flying with a helicopter was not yet advisable in those days, notwithstanding my licence to do so as certified by the National Aviation Service! But by following the railway line from Utrecht to Amsterdam, we found Haarlem without any problem, and with the help of his directions, finally the admiral's house. After circling over the house to warn his wife, we put him down in the field, and took off again straight away, with a farewell wave with an admiral's cap.

This would not be the last we heard of it, as was to be expected. The next day I was visited by the military police who inquired what we had been doing there. You were only allowed to land with an aircraft on an airfield, right? I told him loftily that we had just taken the Chief of the Royal Military Household home, and moreover, I had not touched the ground with the wheels, but hovered just above it. The MP was baffled by that argument, and I heard no more about it. In those days you could still get away with it…

10. HMS Karel Doorman 1953-54

The day after our visit to Soestdijk Palace, I took over the command of 860 Squadron from Bert Bruinsma, my first command, and in June 1953 I was promoted to Lieutenant Commander.

It was now high time to do some more practising with the 860 Aerobats for the National Formation and Stunt competition, to be held at Soesterberg airfield on the 18th of July. Apart from the more usual manoeuvres, we had one speciality: a landing in closed diamond formation. This was especially tricky for the rear aeroplane, number four (Frans Harte), and it had never been shown before. Nevertheless, the first prize went to our competitors from the Air Force, a team of Meteor jets, and we had to reconcile ourselves to the second prize.

I had overlooked the fact that in the so-called compulsory part of the demonstration, you had to land in the normal manner right behind each other, when special attention is paid to the individual distances between the aeroplanes.

Fly past in starboard echelon prior to the landing by the 860 Aerobats during Air Show at Soesterberg Airfield.

Alas, that was something we had not practised properly. When it was over, the president of the jury, the well known veteran pilot, General Versteegh (retired) told me that after the first, free part, we were well ahead of the others … mea culpa.

… and their unique formation landing.

That summer a rather amusing event happened. The Air Force was visited by a brand-new jet trainer, the SIPA Mini Jet, a French machine that they were hoping to sell. With an eye to future developments, the Navy was also interested and delegated me to be present at the demonstration on Gilze-Rijen airfield, near Breda. After the French test pilot had given his presentation – in French, of course – the demonstration was about to begin, and he asked who wanted to go along first. My navy uniform probably stood out among all the Air Force uniforms; in any case, I was the first to go. In the cockpit I was given an explanation in rapid French where all the levers and switches were, and we took off. He soon let me take over the controls, and I found it very easy to fly, although it was strange not to have the familiar propeller in front of me. After flying about a bit, and trying a few stunts, we went back and he even let me do the landing, which went well. We taxied back to the waiting spectators and he got out and said something like: 'Allez, vous êtes solo!'

Such nonchalance (or was it élan) can only be expected from the French.

Although I had understood very little of his instructions, I was reluctant to back out, with all those Air Force colleagues looking on, who knew very well that I had never flown a jet before.

At the beginning of the runway I had to put the flaps down. I had a choice between two handles, but I really didn't know which one it was. So of course, I chose the wrong one, and to my dismay, the nose wheel suddenly retracted: so that was the handle for the landing gear! The little jet was now standing on its nose, but luckily the two main wheels stayed in place after I had put the handle swiftly back again. I next undid my straps, clambered out of the cockpit and hung on the tail, and indeed, the machine came down neatly on its three wheels again. Meanwhile a Peugeot of the French attaché, with the test pilot on board, came racing up with screeching tyres. He jumped out of the car, inspected the nose of his aeroplane, grinned at me encouragingly and stuck his thumb up: 'Allez!'

The flight went without further incident, and after landing, I taxied to the waiting crowd. In the meantime the test pilot had probably been boasting about how easy and reliable his aeroplane was – even a navy clot could handle it. To cap it all, he suggested to the next one whose turn it was, Captain Droste (the father of a future Commander in Chief of the Royal Air Force) that he got in with me. He refused, and I didn't blame him, although I did tease him about it afterwards.

The rest of 1953 was concentrated on the usual flying exercises, and on training a number of young pilots on the Seafury for the next posting on board the Doorman, which was planned for January in the new year. I also took leave of my beloved Jezebel by instructing my old schoolmate, Jan Adriaanse, who had been appointed to form the first helicopter squadron of the Naval Air Service, equipped with the newer and larger Sikorsky S 55, which had meanwhile been purchased.

Before my final farewell, I had one last mission to carry out with Jezebel. On the 17th of December 1953, a Meteor jet belonging to the Royal Air Force crashed into the Ijsselmeer off Medemblik, and the Naval Air Base Valkenburg, with still the one and only helicopter in the country, was asked for assistance. That day North Holland was shrouded in thick fog, but I was in possession of the first instrument-flying licence for helicopters, issued in 1950 (be it 'exclusively for experimental purposes') so I decided to give it a try, together with my faithful helper, corporal Van den Berg. Alas visibility deteriorated to such an extent – less than 50 metres – that I was forced to land at the side of the main road near Heemskerk, and wait for an improvement. It wasn't until the next morning that I decided to risk it and return to Valkenburg, since meanwhile it had been confirmed that the Meteor pilot had been killed. This turned out to be one of the most nerve-wracking flights that I had ever made with Jezebel. I had decided to fly south by following the coastline, where visibility was supposed to be better, but first I had to cross over the dunes to get to the beach. I progressed at walking pace, but so low that once I had to avoid a cow in a field, and several times fishermen on the beach. I could clearly see the surprised look on their faces! The fog remained too thick to whip back over the dunes to reach Valkenburg Air Base, and Ypenburg Airfield was also not possible, so I finally decided to land on a football field near the Laan van Poot at The Hague. I could then telephone Valkenburg from my mother's house, which was nearby, and wait for the fog to lift. I was eventually able to return to base in the afternoon, but not before a crowd had gathered round Jezebel, and a diligent policeman had made an official report – just to make sure, he said.

Jezebel on football field behind the dunes in The Hague.

After the customary 'dry deck landings' (DDLs) at Valkenburg, and 'deck landing practice' (DLPs) on the Doorman off the coast, 860 Squadron boarded in January 1954.

The four comrades of the photo on page 35 – twelve years later.

As Squadron Commander, I was quite an authority on board, at least that's how I felt! I now had my own personal steward, and a cabin with a porthole all to myself. This was new for me, and I recall the changing view when we were anchored somewhere, and the ship swayed with the wind. It also meant that I was once invited to dinner by the Captain of the ship, Captain Koudijs, with whom I got on well. On that occasion he said to me in the course of the conversation: 'I say, Idzerda, you are a smooth talker, wouldn't you like to do something in politics?' He himself was advisor on Defence matters to the Liberal Party, the VVD, and later became a VVD member of Parliament. But thank you – no.

In the Long Room with Commander Van Oostrom Soede (RMWO),
Commander of HMS Karel Doorman.

The Flotilla, which now included HMS Doorman, steamed to Morocco to exercise with the French Navy. When we were anchored off Agadir, an invitation arrived for the Flotilla Commander, the Captain of the Doorman, and, among others, both Squadron Commanders (my colleague had a Firefly squadron) for a typical Moroccan dinner with folk dancing. The food was interesting – a kind of pigeon pie, which you ate with your fingers, after our host, a sheikh, while muttering 'insh-allah', had broken the crust of the pastry with his forefinger, and fished out a piece of meat to offer to his most important guest, the Flotilla Commander.

In accordance with custom, we were lying on the floor on cushions around a large table, and leaning on one elbow; not exactly a comfortable position in our tight uniforms. The dancing show afterwards, which was given outside, was very worthwhile. Meanwhile it had become dark, and we sat around a big camp fire. The dancers were so-called 'femmes bleues': their faces and hands were daubed in blue. It was said that this came from the blue dye of their clothing rubbing off. We heard that when the original supplier to their Toeareg tribe tried to deliver a better clothing material that did not stain, it was indignantly refused. The 'dancing' was done on their knees, apparently because this form of dancing was traditionally performed in tents, in which it is impossible to stand.

Naturally there was also flying going on in that period. One incident is still clearly etched in my mind.

The Atlantic Ocean in those parts is notorious for its frequent, very strong swell, a circumstance which sometimes scared the daylights out of us carrier pilots. Because of that strong swell, HMS Karel Doorman could pitch considerably, notwithstanding her 14.000 tons. For this reason, she was nick-named HMS 'Karel Deining' (in Dutch 'deining' means swell). On board you sometimes felt a violent jolt, following which the whole ship would momentarily shake. This occurred when the ship, after sliding down a high wave, pitched into the next one, before the bow had had time to 'take' it, so that the screws briefly emerged from the water.

For us pilots, a pitching ship implied that you had to be lucky and arrive exactly on time above the deck for the landing, i.e. when the ship was momentarily pausing just between two waves, either on top, or in the 'valley' between two successive waves.

My lucky '13', with droptank.

A perfect landing: that will be the fourth wire! On the right the batsman behind the wind screen after his 'cut' signal.

And so it happened that on an otherwise beautiful day, I came back from an exercise with my 'division' of four Seafuries, and reported for landing. I landed first, and was lucky to be able to land without any problem. I then hastened to the flight bridge to watch my colleagues land. After several wave-offs, with the ship pitching violently, they eventually came on board all right, be it sometimes with a bigger smack than usual.

All except Chris Krijger. After his first wave-off, I wasn't worried, knowing him to be a calm and capable pilot, who did not easily get upset. But then came the second wave-off, and after that the third and the fourth, and I began to feel uneasy. Landing on an aircraft carrier, with a 'straight deck' in those days, was, even under favourable conditions, a strenuous operation, and required the utmost concentration. I knew that after every wave-off, you had to 'recharge' yourself to bring up the required concentration, and I also knew that after four or five times, you would be close to exhaustion. I therefore turned to the Commander Air, Commander Witholt, and said: 'Back to the beach, Sir!' which is pilot's slang for: 'Send him to the nearest airfield ashore'. But that didn't fit in with the sailing programme, because it meant that we would somehow have to get him back on deck again at a later date, which would thus entail considerable delay.

The Commander hesitated, and let Chris go round again. I was getting increasingly worried, and impressed upon the Commander that Chris must be getting short of fuel by now and it was now or never 'back to the beach'. But he still hesitated, and then it was too late, and Chris couldn't possibly make it any more to an airfield, and so *had* to come on board.

Meanwhile the batsman, Jaap Luns, was also exhausted, so our own squadron batsman, Willem van den Heuvel, who had landed just before Chris after several wave-offs, said: 'Let me try'.

After the eleventh (!) wave off, Chris finally succeeded ; I was furious and rushed to the deck to receive him. I had always known Chris as a quiet, self-controlled gentleman, but now he was beside himself. When he got out of the cockpit, his face all red, he took off his helmet and kicked it over the deck! Naturally he took it out on me: 'Sir, this is scandalous – you should never have allowed it – irresponsible!' He was right, of course, and I was almost as angry as he was, but after he recovered, and over a beer in the Long Room that evening, he even found it necessary to apologise 'for letting myself go like that'.

After the visit to Morocco, we crossed over to Gibraltar. During flying exercises, Hans van der Kop, First Officer of our squadron, had a serious and spectacular accident.

*A crash in the parking deck after missing all the wires
and jumping both barriers.*

… but the '13' was spared!

Under certain circumstances, for instance if there is not much wind, or if there is no opportunity for the ship to change to a course with headwind for a normal take-off, the catapult is used. This is a kind of hydraulically drawn sled, sunk in a slot on the port side at the fore end of the flight deck. The pilot taxies the aeroplane towards the catapult, where he is carefully directed to the right position by the catapult crew. Then the aeroplane is anchored at the end of the tail to the deck with a steel rod and a so-called 'break ring', while the catapult sled is coupled to the fuselage by means of the steel 'bridle', which is attached to a hook underneath the fuselage.

The pilot, following directions from the catapult officer, making a rotating movement with a small green flag, gives full throttle, takes his left hand off the throttle (to avoid accidentally closing the throttle again through the force of the shock), gives the thumbs–up sign, and finally pushes his head back against the head cushion on the armour plate behind the pilot's seat, and waits for the 'kick in the pants'.

As soon as the tractive power of the catapult has sufficiently increased, within a fraction of a second the break ring suddenly snaps, and a split second later the aeroplane is shot away over the bow of the ship, from standing still to approximately 100 knots.

However, in Hans's aeroplane, the ring broke before the catapult had reached sufficient tension, so that the Seafury just pottered along at a snail's pace on its own power, and splashed into the sea over the side of the deck, after which the Doorman sailed right over the sinking aeroplane.

As usual I was standing watching the performances of my colleagues; I saw it all happen, and I automatically checked the second hand of my watch. Then I raced to the afterdeck to see if he would come up, and again looked at my watch. After two minutes had gone by, I began to fear the worst, until half a minute later suddenly a very red face emerged in the wake of HMS Karel Doorman.

Hans had literally saved his life by following the correct procedures, which we had practised over and over again in the swimming pool of Wassenaar, close to Valkenburg, the so-called 'dinghy drill'. One part of the drill was that if you ever ended up in the sea in front of the ship, which then went over you, you should never be in a hurry to leave the cockpit because you would come out underneath the ship and the screws. So hold your breath and wait until the shadow above you has gone! For that matter, Hans was somewhat 'aided' by his foot getting caught in the cockpit.

In no time he was picked up by the helicopter.

What happened to me some time later, had a more fortunate ending. The Doorman was berthed in the harbour of Gibraltar, and we were to exercise for the first time with the so-called 'RATOG' (Rocket Assisted Take Off Gear). The aim of this method is to make it possible to take off from a ship, that is lying still, with the aid of the thrust of two small rockets, attached underneath the aeroplane on either side.

As CO of the squadron, I would naturally set the example, and be the first to take off with it. I literally shot off the deck with an enormous acceleration (a bit steep because I did not have the control stick exactly in the middle, as was prescribed) until one of the rockets suddenly and prematurely failed. As a result, the aeroplane got an enormous torque, and began rotating around its axis, only a few metres above the sea.

Instinctively I did everything to get the aeroplane straight again (according to some witnesses, I even finished the roll, but I couldn't remember that), and in those few seconds I really thought that I had had it. But the faithful Fury was obedient, and I got away with a fright.

Back on board, I was called to the flight bridge by the Commander Air, Commander Witholt.

My knees were still shaking when I got there, which I tried to hide, and he looked at me silently, shaking his head. Then he said: 'I'm glad it was you.' A strange compliment.

After returning to our home base, Valkenburg, a horrible coincidence occurred.

From time to time we received posters from the Flight Safety Department, which were then distributed around the squadron quarters to be hung up on the wall. One of these was rather shocking, and not easily forgotten. It showed a desolate landscape in sombre colours, with three hills. There was a cross on each hill, and underneath the poster was a simple message: 'Failing Leadership'. To an insider the message was clear: through an error of the leader of a foursome (fighters usually fly in a formation of four), the three pilots following him had crashed.

A few days later, a formation of four of our Seafuries on their way back to the home base, got caught in bad weather somewhere over Wales. The leader, an experienced fighter pilot, attempting to get under the cloud cover, came out too low over the hilly landscape, and just missed the top of a hill by a hair's breadth. But the three pilots, who were flying with him in formation, and thus had all their attention fixed on the leader, were just too late, and crashed simultaneously. It will be evident why I didn't have the relevant poster hung up in the squadron building – the message was clear enough.

In April 1954, we again boarded for the next trip to the United States and Canada, after the customary dummy deck landings at Valkenburg, although we knew that, as always, no flying would be allowed during the crossing. Luckily this time the famous brass band of the Marines was on board, and they gave many a concert in the hangar.

This would also be my last trip, and therefore, for me, the end of carrier operations and life on board the Doorman.

The visit to Montreal gave rise to much commotion and publicity. In the first place because apparently never before had a ship the size of the Doorman sailed so far up the St. Lawrence river (Captain Koudijs liked the spectacular), and in the second place because this visit naturally had a nostalgic effect on the numerous Dutch immigrants. The complete crew list was published in all newspapers, and on the customary 'open day', the ship was literally flooded. People stood queuing up on the quayside, waiting for their turn. Lots of meetings with relatives and friends took place; I was even looked up by a classmate from my primary school in Bandung.

During that visit, I was invited with some other colleagues for dinner at the home of Mr. Kuyper, of the well known Dutch gin distillery of the same name. In the course of the conversation, I recounted – as an appropriate anecdote – how one evening, a couple of years before, on a British Navy base, while standing at the bar with a number of British colleagues, the conversation turned to whisky. One of the colleagues was Scottish. We were all in civilian clothes, so he was in full regalia with kilt and sporran. He claimed as a true Scot that, blindfolded, he could identify every brand of whisky by taste, and would take on any bets for free drinks. Now the other well known Dutch distillery in those days, Bols, had put its own whisky on the market with the name Angus MacKay, and I happened to have a bottle in my room, which I had brought with me 'duty free' from Holland. I took on the bet, fetched the bottle and wrapped it in a towel. A number of the popular whiskies, such as Johnny Walker, Black & White etc. were poured into glasses out of sight of the Scot, and my 'Angus' was among them. He unfailingly guessed all the other whisky brands – but stopped at my 'Angus'. After a few sips, he said: 'All right, I give up, but it must be from somewhere near Inverness.'

Chuckling, I showed him the Bols bottle – from Holland. He shook his head and paid for my drinks.

After listening to my story with amusement, my host said: 'Mr. Idzerda, you did not win that bet: Bols fetches the whisky by container from Scotland – probably from around Inverness – and fills its own bottles with it.'

Unfortunately, I have never been able to repay the bet.

HMS Karel Doorman with all hands lined up to form the letters
D(oor)M(a)N.

On the journey home, about halfway across the Atlantic Ocean, we encountered, on a cross heading, the MS *De Groote Beer*, the famous passenger ship of the Maatschappij Nederland (a large Dutch shipping company), full of Dutch emigrants on their way to Canada.

In those days, it was especially farmers and their families who were looking for a better life in that immense country.

The Marine brass band was brought on deck as soon as the *De Groote Beer* came in sight. When the two ships passed each other, which the Doorman did as closely as possible, of course, the band played all sorts of popular Dutch tunes, and ended with the national anthem. The passengers were thronging at the railings so as not to miss anything, and through binoculars you could see that many of them were crying.

11.   Staff Work and Jets 1954-61

After that unforgettable last voyage, and probably the most satisfying period of my flying career, a completely new phase was coming up in my Navy career: staff work.

The Naval Staff College had just been re-established, and was commencing with its first post-war course, 'Higher Military Formation', and I was one of the lucky ones. The course, under the direction of Captain Van Oostrom Soede, RMWO, recently promoted and well known to me from the Doorman, lasted seventeen weeks and I thoroughly enjoyed it. When it was finished I was posted as chief of staff to the Commanding Officer of the Naval Air Service, whose headquarters were right next to the Naval Air Base Valkenburg. Two incidents from that period are worth mentioning.

Queen Juliana was going to inspect the restoration operations in Zeeland, and had expressed the wish to do so by helicopter. And naturally Her Majesty wished to be picked up at home (perhaps the Chief of the Royal Military Household had given her the idea). The honour fell on my colleague and old school friend, Jan Adriaanse, who promptly approached me for some tips, in view of my local familiarity!

Landing in the palace grounds with the much bigger helicopter, the S 55, with which the Naval Air Service was now flying, looked too risky to me. For that matter, I would have probably not dared to do it with Jezebel either, in view of the lack of space in case of engine failure. I felt that you could not take any risks with the Monarch on board. So I advised Jan to take the field across the road, and inform the Palace accordingly. Apparently the relative information had not been properly transmitted, because Jan had hardly landed and put his cap on straight to receive his high-ranking passenger, when a Palace limousine came driving up with a very agitated ADC on board: why hadn't he landed in the palace grounds? But Jan was not to be moved, and shortly afterwards, a very displeased Queen arrived, who reproached him that the Princesses were so disappointed, since his colleague at the time had landed in the grounds. Had his colleague then taken unacceptable risks?

Poor Jan; in his worst nightmare he could never have imagined that he would one day be told off by his Queen. I had always known Jan as very calm and amiable, but now he was furious with me, and understandably so. At my insistence, the C.O. wrote an explanatory letter, drafted by me, to Her Majesty, which was hopefully to Her satisfaction. At any rate, it calmed Jan down.

The second incident was very tragic. The Seafuries were equipped with a mechanism under the wings for dropping 250 pound bombs on ground targets. It had happened more than once that a bomb got stuck in this attachment mechanism, after which, for safety reasons, the procedure was to discard the bomb, with the attachment mechanism and all, over the sea by means of the emergency jettisoning system. It was strictly forbidden to land with an already activated and thus dangerous bomb. This problem was discussed by the technicians of the Armament Department, and it was much regretted by the Armaments Officer of Valkenburg that they never had the opportunity of discovering the reason for the defect of the mechanism, which, incidentally, cost the same as a new small car at the time.

It never became clear precisely what happened, only that an experienced pilot (notably the same one involved in the accident above Wales) again had a so-called 'hang-up' during a dive-bombing exercise. We shall never know if he let himself be talked into it, but the fact is that he landed anyway with his explosive load, and during the roll-out the bomb came loose and exploded on the runway with disastrous effect. I happened to be driving my car near by, and was one of the first to get there. The pilot was killed instantly, and burned before my eyes in his cockpit.

In November 1954, a new and interesting development took place. The former Helicopter Foundation had been dissolved, but a few young engineers, G.F. Verhage, W. Kuipers and J. Meyer Drees, still maintained a lively interest in helicopters. Verhage, an electro mechanical (!) engineer, had even invented a simplified rotor head construction, without hinges, and had had it patented, which led to the decision to develop a small, simple helicopter themselves. For that purpose, the 'Society for the Development and Construction of an Experimental Helicopter' was established (SOBEH).

The result was the 'Kolibri', and I was asked to be the test pilot. Unfortunately the development progressed very slowly, partly because of the choice of 'ramjets' for propulsion – a choice to which I had certain reservations, due to the fact that these engines were still in a very early stage of development. Eventually I crashed the machine on landing after engine failure when it turned over, so that after the repair and the first successful test flights, I had to hand over my task in 1956 to someone else. I did end up with a new Volkswagen, however. I had been offered a salary when I was taken on as test pilot, which I was not allowed to accept because of Navy regulations, so instead I was given 'suitable' transport, which I was allowed to keep when I left.

The experimental SOBEH 'Kolibri' airborne for the first time:
a distance of 20 metres at an altitude of 15 cm.

Meanwhile the Air Force had already gone over to jet fighters, and the Navy was also beginning to show interest (of course, they already had one very experienced jet pilot …). So in April 1955, I was sent to the Air Force Base at Volkel, together with my colleague and old friend, Luc Oldhoff, to be instructed on jets. We began on a trainer, the T 33 'Shooting Star', and subsequently flew the F 84 'Thunder Jet', a real fighter. It was naturally an interesting experience, especially the unexpected silence in the cockpit, where I was used to the roaring piston engine right in front of me on the nose of the Seafury. The noise that a jet engine produces, on the other hand, is caused by the mixture of hot combustion gases and air, which is thrust out of the jet pipe at the rear, and is therefore hardly perceptible in the cockpit. But I still found that my old Seafury, with its powerful acceleration from the enormous five-blade propeller, and its manoeuvrability, demanded much more flying skill, and was thus more satisfying, although of course it could not match the speed of a jet.

In the course of that year the Navy rounded off its plans for going over to jet fighters. Initially my role would only be an advisory one: at thirty-two I was slightly 'too old' for the jet fighter business. Luckily I managed once again to convince the Flag Officer Naval Air (but this time it was the successor, Rear Admiral J.M. van Olm) that with my experience I was exactly the right person to set up the first jet fighter squadron of the Naval Air Service. He gave in to my arguments, but at the same time he determined that this would be my very last posting with a fighter squadron, and that I would definitely not go on board the Doorman. Indeed, it was time to think about the rest of my career, and I realised that I could not go on flying for ever.

At the beginning of January 1957, I arrived at Lossiemouth, a Fleet Air Arm base up in the north of Scotland, together with my future squadron colleagues. We were to be instructed on the Hawker Seahawk jet fighter, which the Netherlands Naval Air Service would also soon be acquiring. We were detached to Training Squadron 738, equipped with Hawker Seahawks and two-seater Avro Vampires. The Commanding Officer was Lieutenant Commander Bellamy, a rather rough, red-haired, bearish man. His bushy beard was also red, and after a flying trip it came out of his oxygen mask all crumpled up and curling over his mouth up to his nose. I couldn't imagine how he could breathe properly and in any case he was often difficult to understand over the radio when he mumbled through the clogged microphone in his mask.

The winter weather in those northern regions is often surprisingly good, with lots of sunshine, but bitterly cold. We were accommodated in unheated, wooden buildings, with only a small fireplace in each cabin. The steward would come first thing in the morning to make a fire with logs and coal, after he had first, with a cheerful 'Good morrrrning, Sirrrr!', put a mug of very sweet milk with a drop of tea in it next to my bed.

It was a busy time in 'Lossie', but the weekends were free, of course, and we made use of them to visit the beautiful surroundings. One of these outings was to the famous Drambuie distillery, of which it is alleged that to this day only one of the descendants of the original founders has knowledge of the secret recipe that is kept in a safe. When a fresh supply has to be prepared, that descendant – when we were there it was an old lady – retires, takes the recipe out of the safe, personally mixes the herbs and deposits them in the cask. A lovely story, and I think it happens to be true.

One day I was invited to dinner by the First Officer of Training Squadron 738, Lieutenant Commander Robertson, at his home. I was offered a lift by my instructor, Tony Winterbotham, who was also invited. Tony was the stereotype of the slightly affected 'English gentleman', complete with white handkerchief sticking out of his sleeve.

After a long ride in his fast Lotus 7 through the attractive countryside, we arrived in the dark at an enormous gate, followed by a long driveway. We stopped at an equally imposing stairway, which led to a high front door, through which you could easily ride a horse. Our host received us in a dimly lit, gigantic hall, in which I saw armour shining here and there. I had difficulty controlling my curiosity, and we were then led to a modern, well-lit and luxurious apartment, where the other guests greeted us, all in evening dress, of course. During the conversation I could no longer curb my curiosity, and asked someone where we were. 'Oh, didn't you know? John Robertson is married to the daughter of the Earl of Moray, and this is his castle, Darnaway Castle. The Earl himself spends most of his time on his cattle farm in South Africa'. Now I knew.

The drinks were followed by dinner in another huge room, to which we were led through endless passages. The magnificent table was surrounded by six towering candleholders with large candles, providing the only light there was. The main course was salmon – what else? – freshly caught in the Moray Firth, which lies a bit to the north of Lossiemouth.

When we were shown around after dinner through the imposing Hall of Knights (possibly especially for the benefit of the very interested Dutchman), we stopped at an immense painting of a horribly realistic representation of a corpse, bleeding from various stab wounds. It was apparently an early ancestor who had had a bad day. It became even more interesting when the painting was opened, like double doors, into two panels, on which to my surprise an enormous genealogical tree of the Moray lineage appeared. To cap it all, I suddenly discovered the name 'Milborn', a branch that had left for the Netherlands in the eighteenth century; a certain Hans Milborn had been my best friend at primary school in Bandoeng, and I had at the time heard that he was of Scottish descent. Small world.

Meanwhile I had found out that one of my British colleagues was as much of a gourmet as I was; he had become acquainted with Chinese food when he was stationed in Hong Kong.

Moreover he too, was a gifted cook, and so we decided that together we would treat our colleagues to some of our cooking. Very early one Saturday morning, he took me to the fishing harbour at Lossiemouth, where the shrimp boats had just come in. We immediately bought a couple of baskets of lovely fresh shrimps – they were still jumping – and in the evening we cooked an improvised Chinese banquet, which was a great success with our colleagues.

One very special evening a festive dinner was arranged for a traditional Scottish occasion, but I don't remember which. We were seated according to rank, as is customary, at a huge, horseshoe-shaped table, and in evening dress, of course. The table was presided over by the Commander, and I, as most senior guest, was sitting on his right. A crystal decanter with whisky and two small, silver goblets were standing on the table in front of the Commander.

After dessert, the double doors of the dining room suddenly opened, and a Highland bagpipe player in magnificent Scottish dress, came striding in. While playing, he marched back and forth in front of our table, and the melancholy melodies resounded throughout the large hall.

He stopped in front of the Commander and saluted, standing stiffly to attention. The Commander stood up, poured whisky into the two goblets, and handed one to the bagpipes player, whereupon they both downed their tot with one swallow.

Then the usual speeches followed. Naturally I had my turn too, but of course I was prepared. Then the youngest officer present was invited to speak, as is also customary. The young man stood up and said:

'Confucius said: The longer the spoke, the greater the tire. Thank you'.

Applause!

A fixed daily routine was the so-called 'meteo sortie' early in the morning, for the purpose of reconnoitring the area around the base for possible approaching bad weather. This flight was done in a Seahawk, usually by one particular pilot, Lt. Chris Burke, a gifted aerobatics pilot who had often exhibited his prowess at air shows and the like. He was at the time practising for a special programme for the annual international Farnborough Air Show, where aeroplanes from many different countries are shown. What was so special about his performance was that he carried out the usual aerobatics, such as loops and rolls, at absolute minimum speed, as opposed to the normal high speeds, and also at absolute minimum height. He first came over the runway at low speed only a few metres above the ground, and lowered his wheels and flaps as if for a landing. Then, to the horror of all of us watching, who had never seen anything like it before, he suddenly pulled the Seahawk straight up with full throttle, next in a loop, on his back – he was so low we could see him sitting from the ground – closed the throttle and continued the loop by again quickly retracting wheels and flaps, and at the last moment gave full throttle before the aeroplane could stall. He then skimmed over the runway with a thunderous noise, again at a height of only a few metres.

His explanation for this dangerous exhibition was that usually everybody flew his aeroplane at the highest possible speed to make an impression, so he now wanted to show something different!

I remember once saying to him: 'Chris, you don't give yourself a margin of error, that can't always go alright.' He laughed, and explained that he carefully prepared every flight with the utmost precision, by studying the air temperature and barometric pressure and taking into account their influence on the thrust of the Rolls Royce 'Nene' engine, and adapting his speed and height accordingly.

I was not convinced. I had to think of the saying: 'There are old pilots and there are bold pilots, but there are no old, bold pilots.'

Alas, I was proven right. Some months later I heard that he had been killed the day before the Farnborough Air Show during the general rehearsal. His last words over the radio were: 'Christ … I'm not going to make it!'

The course ended in March, and we returned to Holland where we were stationed at the Air Force base Woensdrecht to further our experience on jet planes with the Gloster 'Meteor'.

An incident in that period, concerning the massive formation flight on the Queen's birthday, the thirtieth of April, is worth mentioning. All the jet fighters of the Royal Air Force participated, so we navy students also took part. I requested a Meteor Mk.7 two-seater because I had promised to take along my former Sea Fury mechanic, Sergeant Dirk Venema; he had obviously never flown in a fighter, whereas he had always looked after them with such care. The formation was led – as I discovered many years later – by my old friend and former 120 Squadron colleague, Paul Verspoor. He flew with his formation past all the airfields of the Royal Air Force, where the squadrons stationed there had to join the formation, so also Woensdrecht. But there something went wrong: the leader of the Woensdrecht formation, in which we were thus also flying with our Meteors, mistakenly tried to join the formation in a right turn instead of the usual left turn. The result was a nightmare of dozens of fighters closing and crossing above and under each other, and there was nowhere to go. I was even at times able to count the rivets on the fuselage of a Meteor slipping in right above me. Luckily everything turned out all right, and the huge formation was able to present itself nicely on time.

After landing on our home base Woensdrecht, I had almost forgotten the incident, until my passenger Dirk came up to me, deathly pale, and snapped at me: 'Thanks a lot Sir, never again!'

Meanwhile a happy event had taken place, which would change my life completely. Through my good friend, Jan Adriaanse, and his Australian wife, Beryl, I met Joy Antoinette, 'Toni', an English girl. It didn't take long before we decided that we wanted to spend the rest of our lives together, and this was sealed on the seventeenth of September 1957.

Alas Jan was not to be around much longer to witness our happiness for he was killed in a Mariner flying boat accident in New Guinea in December 1959. Beryl later remarried an Australian diplomat, Harry Bullock, and after their retirement they moved to Canberra, where they are still living.

Joy Antoinette, 'Toni'.

On the eighteenth of July 1957, the big moment arrived when I could finally fetch our first very own Seahawk from the Armstrong Whitworth factory in Coventry. The journey there went via London, where I was met by Peter de Groot, who was then assistant Naval Attaché at the Netherlands Embassy, and who put me on the train, the well known 'Flying Scotsman', for the trip up north.

Curiously, I had been asked to take my own parachute with me (apparently that was not included in the purchase) in addition to my flying overall and helmet so that I was unexpectedly heavily loaded. The handing over was done with some ceremony because the Seahawks were actually delivered to us via the American Mutual Defence Aid Program (MDAP).

The 'F50' had obviously been polished until it was shining like a Rolls Royce, and when I made a complimentary remark about it, they pointed to a little old man, who was still holding the polishing cloth in his hand, and told me he was *the* permanent fixture of the factory.

Then the F50 was first presented to the American Defence representative, who subsequently handed it over to the Netherlands authority, the Naval Attaché. Then it was my turn, and I was able to make the taking-over flight. To the embarrassment of the technicians of Armstrong Whitworth, who were manufacturing our Seahawks under licence, during the flight something went wrong with the ailerons control. However, I was able to keep control of the aeroplane, and delivered it in one piece to the 'men with red faces'. The fault was soon redressed, and the next flight proceeded with no further problems. It was even a pleasure after the comparatively sluggish, heavy Meteor to be able to fly again in this 'gentleman's aeroplane': noiseless, super light on the control stick, and in a roomy, comfortable bubble cockpit with a magnificent view all around.

The next day I left for Holland, accompanied for a short while by a factory Meteor, a two-seater Mk.7 with a photographer on board who had to record the event.

The Seahawk, the first jet fighter of the Netherlands Naval Air Service, on its way to the Naval Air Base Valkenburg.

My first destination was the air base Woensdrecht, where I had to present to my future squadron colleagues our new acquisition, which they too would soon be flying. The air traffic controllers had naturally been informed, and when I requested permission for a 'low pass', it was promptly given. And so a bit later I shot past the control tower a few metres above the runway, pulled straight up, and made two vertical rolls – something you couldn't do with the old Seafury!

On the way from there to the real destination, Naval Air Base Valkenburg (MVKV), I was, for a short while, escorted by three hastily scrambled Meteors, manned by my colleagues.

Arrival with the first Seahawk on MVKV.

On arrival over Valkenburg, I made the same request to the air traffic controllers, and it was immediately granted. Unfortunately there was low cloud cover and it was also foggy, so my planned demonstration was out. I knew that the Commanding Officer of the Naval Air Service, Captain A.J. de Bruijn, and the Commanding Officer of MVKV, Captain A.W. Witholt would be heading the reception line, and I didn't want to disappoint them. So with permission from the control tower, I approached from the sea, behind the waiting public, instead of over the runway, as is usual, and thundered past them at minimum height. Later I heard that they had all been completely surprised, so our first jet fighter had made a fitting entrance.

Welcomed by Captain Witholt, Captain de Bruijn, and Commander Air, Commander Woudstra.

On the eighteenth of September 1957 the first jet fighter squadron of the Naval Air Service was installed with the usual ceremony under the old name, 860 Squadron.

Soon after, the squadron was at full strength with twelve fighters, and we could start on the training programme.

Alas, we soon had our first serious accident. During a 'follow the leader', I suddenly missed my 'wing man', and immediately heard one of the other pilots of our formation call out: 'He's gone down in a dive!'

A black smoke trail, which came up from the ground below shortly afterwards, confirmed our fearful suspicions. The young Dekker had dived into the ground for inexplicable reasons. At least inexplicable for us at the time since he had not reported any problem at all. However during the ensuing extensive inquiry, the reason quickly came to light: he had had a 'blackout', and had not come out of it in time. This was unacceptable, of course. All fighter pilots at one time or another get a complete or partial blackout because of the great gravity forces, called 'G-forces', which occur during fighter manoeuvres, notwithstanding the special pressure 'corset' that was worn. But normally speaking, a blackout does not last more than a couple of seconds, and you certainly do not lose consciousness. So there must have been something else wrong, and that finally emerged from his medical file. During his initial flying training doctors had already established that Dekker had a very low 'blackout – threshold', so he should never have been allowed to become a fighter pilot. A tragic mistake by someone in the Aviation Medical Service.

It was my sad duty to inform his wife of the accident that same day. They had recently been married. As is customary a chaplain came along too, but he didn't need to say much. She was a very courageous woman, who much preferred to talk about her husband with a pilot-colleague as opposed to her very religious father-in-law, who, moreover, was anti-military, and vehemently opposed to a funeral with military honours. So I also had to mediate between Mrs Dekker and her parents-in-law, in addition to their clergyman of the Reformed Church, who was also brought into the conflict. A compromise was ultimately reached: the military procession would stop at the gate of the cemetery, and there the Church would take over.

Nevertheless, the military salute, with bugle blower and rifle salvos, was still given at the gate of the cemetery.

I was gratified that after the funeral Dekker's father came up to me, and said that he had found it all very appropriate after all.

The training programme proceeded further successfully, and I thoroughly enjoyed these (my last) flying hours in a fighter, moreover a jet fighter. It was very different from how it used to be in the P40 and the Seafury: a jet fighter performs best at higher altitudes, and so, contrary to former times, when you seldom went above 6000 metres, with the Seahawk we were normally at an altitude of 10.000 to 12.000 metres, way above the clouds, and always in the sun.

Although the aeroplane was equipped with a pressurized cockpit, the air pressure during flight at high altitudes still remained below the normal pressure at sea-level. Consequently the fighter pilots were given a special diet for lunch, free of onions and other gas producing ingredients. Furthermore we had permission to have lunch in our flying outfit because the 'immersion suits', which are obligatory when flying above the sea, in addition to the customary 'anti-G' corsets (intended to counteract blood receding from the brain to the legs at high speeds), were difficult to put on and take off. Obviously this did not fit in with the quite formal lunch gathering (at that time), presided over by the President of the Long Room, the Commander of MVKV, so that we were 'banished' to a separate table in the television room.

One of the interesting exercises was the 'maximum performance' flight, in which you had to climb to as high an altitude as possible. The Seahawk's ceiling was approximately 14.000 metres (about 42.000 feet) where the bright blue sky above you already began to get perceptively darker, while the fighter was literally hanging tail down 'on its last breath'. You then turned the plane over on its back with a 'split S', and dived straight down to arrive at the maximum attainable 'Mach number' (Mach 1 is the speed of sound) of the Seahawk: almost M 0.89 (approximately 900 km per hour, depending on altitude and temperature). Then it pulled itself out of the dive before less pleasant compressibility phenomena could arise, as sometimes happened at the time with subsonic fighters. In general, the Seahawk was a docile aeroplane without any unexpected tricks, even during extreme manoeuvres.

The flying program ended with the usual dry deck landings in preparation for boarding the Doorman, which would take place at the beginning of November 1958, and of which I would not be part...

During my last flight in the Seahawk as Commanding Officer of 860 Squadron, I looked up HMS Karel Doorman, (which had meanwhile been fitted with an 'angled deck') which was exercising off the coast in preparation for the coming trip. I was given permission over the radio to make a 'dry run' over the ship. So I did the whole procedure as of old: first past the ship with wheels and deck hook out for inspection, then turn in, flaps out, go down to just above the sea, turn in more to the stern of the ship and the flight deck ...and to my amazement I was given the green light to land!

The temptation was great, but I did not want to deprive my successor as C.O. of the honour of being the first of his squadron to land on board.

Then a new period ashore commenced with again a posting at the Naval Staff College, but this time for a term of three years, initially as lecturer, and subsequently as Head of Instruction.

The Director was Captain A.E.J. Modderman, a small, rather intense man, and it was not immediately apparent that he had the reputation of excellent seamanship.

He once took me along on an annual visit to the Naval Staff College at Greenwich, England, with which we maintained close bonds. Much of our instruction material was provided by them, and updating was therefore required.

The official visit wound up with a tour of the famous Maritime Museum, where countless paintings by the Van der Velde's are hanging, of both the father and the son. Many seventeenth century sea battles between the Dutch and the British are portrayed there in great detail.

The conservator of the museum showed us around and explained details concerning the positions of the British and Dutch ships, and Modderman was also able to give amazingly accurate analyses of the tactics shown, based on the direction of the wind and the position of the sails.

Also worth mentioning is the visit the naval officers following the course at the Naval Staff College paid to the Royal Marine Corps at Doorn. There we were given a demonstration by a special platoon that was trained to gain possession of an enemy occupied building in a surprise attack. Although we were thus more or less prepared, the shock effect was immense.

All of a sudden, the windows were blown in with (harmless) smoke grenades, automatic guns were rattling, and screeching marines with black faces, and in camouflage suits, stormed in from all sides. We were all paralysed with fright – the 'surprise-second'. A foretaste of terrorist combat!

12. The Lockheed Neptune 1961-64

In August 1961 I was appointed as the future commanding officer of Squadron 321, to be stationed at Biak, Netherlands New Guinea. The squadron was to be equipped with the new Lockheed 'Neptune', a four-engined anti-submarine aeroplane, which for its task in New Guinea – where few (if any) submarines were to be expected, was fitted with four 20 mm cannon in the nose.

We were to fetch the Neptunes ourselves from the Lockheed factory in Burbank, California, and so we travelled with the first two crews to the United States in September. We were accompanied by Commander Cor Kuiken, a good friend (and older brother of my friend Koos, killed in 1942), who was to assist me, since I had not flown large aeroplanes over long distances for years, whereas he was very experienced.

The two crews were accommodated in a motel in Hollywood, complete with a large swimming pool. Our Technical officer was Lieutenant M.H. van der Hoeven, who came from the Indies, and on one free Sunday, on a barbecue in the garden of the motel, he roasted for twelve men the best satehs (an Indonesian delicacy, skewered meat) I had tasted in a long time.

For the rest it was again a very busy time: morning classes on the technique of the Neptune, in the afternoon, flying instruction. The Lockheed people were quite colourful: the ground instructor was Mario, an engineer of Italian descent, whose frequent expression was 'orate fratres' (let us pray, brothers), and our flying instructor was a certain Beasly, the senior test pilot, and the only one who had ever made a loop with a Neptune (40 tons). Luckily he did not repeat that stunt with us. He did demonstrate the unexpected capacity of the heavy Neptune, thanks to its two extra Westinghouse jet engines of 1450 kg thrust each, which in this updated version had been added to the two existing Wright Cyclone piston engines of 3700 hp each. For instance he taught us the 'short take-off': brakes on, full throttle on all four engines, brakes off and at the frightening low speed of 85 knots, pull the control stick back, with the result that the Neptune took off after an unbelievably short run in a most spectacular steep climbing attitude.

The 'short landing' was just as spectacular. It reminded me of the dry deck landings at Valkenburg in preparation for boarding the Doorman. But instead of a Seafury of less than seven tons, you were now actually applying the same technique to a forty-ton Neptune patrol aeroplane! With wheels out and full flaps, reduce speed to 90 knots, more throttle to avoid stalling, 'hanging on the props' with the nose up, go down to 200 ft, tight turn to 'finals', aim for the beginning of the runway and close the throttle above the edge of the runway. After a fairly hard landing immediately full reverse propellers, press nose wheel down on the runway, and full brakes. The result was astonishing: with a bit of wind you were standing still in 500 metres!

The Neptune was further fitted with so-called 'spoilers' on the wings, with which you could suddenly stall either the port wing or the starboard wing, causing the aeroplane to make an unbelievably quick and steep turn. The intention of this had to do with the use of the 'Magnetic Anomaly Detector', which was mounted at the end of the tail, and with which a submerged submarine could be detected when you flew over it. The local disturbance of the earth's magnetic field caused by the boat was then indicated in the cockpit on a magneto meter, after which it was essential to turn around as quickly as possible to further locate the target, and possibly treat it to a homing torpedo. The detection radius was small, therefore it was necessary to turn back very quickly.

This characteristic of the big Neptune also lent itself to spectacular demonstrations, as Beasly showed us … and let us do! (A few years later, in June 1964, I had the opportunity of demonstrating these unexpected capacities during an Air Show at Eelde in the Netherlands, where the whole of the Royal Air Force top brass were present. I especially did my best because at the time I still had many old friends and acquaintances in the Air Force. One of the stunts was a very sharp turn around the control tower with an 80° bank at about 30 metres above the ground. The air traffic controllers, who had given me prior permission, were delighted and praised the show. Not so my mechanic, who told me later that he hadn't dared to open his eyes until just before we landed …

Afterwards I was accosted by the Commander-in-Chief of the Royal Air Force, Lt. General A.B. 'Bertie' Wolff, whom I had known since Jackson: 'Rudi, I thought you'd gone mad! Never before have I seen such a large aeroplane doing such crazy stunts.')

Photo of stunting Neptune taken by a truant fifth form High School boy, Peter Jongbloed, later Jumbo Jet Captain with the KLM.

One day Mario said to Cor and me: 'Aren't you both from the Indies? Then you should go and eat in that Indonesian restaurant in Hollywood'.

Cor and I gave each other a quick look and both of us were thinking the same thing, it couldn't be much. However we were willing to try it. And so one evening we arrived at the address we'd been given, and saw to our amazement a restaurant built in a huge concrete imitation volcano, with the exotic name 'The Isle of Java Inn'. In front of the restaurant two girls were posted, who, swaying their hips in very short sarongs, led us inside. I was just about to say: 'Cor, what are we doing here?' when we both simultaneously sniffed up a familiar, delicious, and authentic aroma. We stared at each other incredulously, thinking this can only be real . And it certainly was. The explanation soon came when the owner/cook came out to meet us after he had been informed that a couple of Dutch connoisseurs were sitting there. He was a genuine cook from the Indies, who had emigrated via Holland to California. He went through our order, made a few suggestions and the feast could begin.

It was indeed superb, and his cooking could easily match that of the best Indonesian restaurants in The Hague and elsewhere.

After a period of four weeks we and our brand new Neptune, the 201, were ready for the crossing, and we had to take leave of our Lockheed friends. When Cor and I clambered into our cockpit through the nose wheel hatch, we saw written on the wall in big, black letters: 'ORATE FRATRES'.

The journey went via Alameda, near San Fransisco, with landings at Barbers Point in Hawaii, and Kwajalein, an atoll in the west Pacific. A secret U.S. experimental missile base was situated on Kwajalein, which naturally we didn't get to visit. The local Commanding Officer invited Cor and myself for dinner at his home. He and his wife lived in a very attractive and comfortable bungalow, decorated with a collection of Polynesian artefacts. What intrigued me most was a kind of network of rotan twigs with here and there cowrie shells and pieces of coral woven into it, which was hanging as a decoration on the dining room wall. When I asked what the significance was, our host explained that this was probably the most valuable piece in his collection. It was apparently an ancient sea map of the kind used by Polynesian seafarers when they were still doing their voyages of discovery and colonisation of islands in the

Pacific Ocean in their large catamarans and trimarans, thousands of years ago. This woven work of art, obviously of more recent times, represented the currents, and the shells and pieces of coral, the islands and reefs. Alas nobody is able to read these maps any more.

The next stop was Hollandia, the capital of Netherlands New Guinea, and finally we landed on Biak, our home base. We were enthusiastically received – at last modern equipment to ward off those increasingly troublesome Indonesians. Soon after us, the remaining nine Neptunes arrived one after another in Biak, so that 321 Squadron could start operating (the following year two more Neptunes were to arrive from the Netherlands).

On the second of October 1961, I took over the command from my predecessor, Lt Commander H. Moekardanoe.

Arrival of a Neptune in Biak, awaited by Chief Flight Engineer Sergeant Major Leo Willems. This Neptune, the 201, is now in the Military Aviation Museum at Soesterberg.

President Soekarno of Indonesia had meanwhile broken off diplomatic relations with the Netherlands; the confrontation policy was intensified, and the first Indonesian infiltrations had already taken place.

The first weeks in Biak were fairly quiet, so we could use the time to get more practice and to familiarise ourselves with our operating area. We did so-called 'kampong reconnaissance' (kampong is Indonesian for village), which meant looking out for sawn-off, white-painted palm tree trunks on the beach near a village. If the trunks were lying parallel, all was peaceful, but if they formed a cross, it meant trouble, possibly enemy activity. Also, we had to guard the western part of the coastal strip against possible Indonesian infiltrations. These were often lengthy flights: ten hours and more were no exception.

The temperature on board was 30°C and above when we were flying, and the (tinned) food was often abominable. But some of the flight engineers who had lived in the Indies, found a solution. One of them, for example, Chief Flight Engineer Sergeant Major Leo Willems, who sometimes flew with me, would cook a phenomenal nasi goreng (Indonesian rice dish) on the little electric cooking plate we had on board.

Kampong patrol.

After one of these patrols, we were returning via the 'neck' of the Vogelkop, the promontory in the north west of New Guinea (it is shaped like a bird's head, thus the name Vogelkop, which means bird's head). Peter Varenhorst, my young navigator, gave me a course to Biak.

I was very much aware of the Snow Mountains with tops up to 5000 metres on our starboard side. I thought that Peter's course was a bit too close for comfort, and corrected the course a few degrees to port. An event which had taken place seventeen years earlier was still only too clear in my memory.

We were flying in that same area from Hollandia to Biak with a Lockheed L 12, piloted by a colleague. We had left rather late, and ended up in the inevitable clouds, which form around and above the mountains every day after ten o'clock. My instinct told me that we should turn more towards the coast to avoid those mountain tops because we were well below 5000 metres. A suggestion from me to this effect was not appreciated – a passenger should not concern himself with the navigation – until all of a sudden the cloud broke, and we saw a massive mountain side, partly covered with snow, looming right in front of us. The pilot managed to avoid disaster with an extremely steep turn. Needless to say that afterwards some harsh criticism was expressed.

Peter's pride as navigator was naturally somewhat hurt when he discovered my course correction, and I later told him about that event to explain why: a matter of principle and precaution.

A tragic coincidence occurred not long afterwards when a Dakota, the X 11, of the Air Force, flying in the clouds in that same area, crashed against a mountain side through a navigational error of the very experienced pilot. Apart from the four crew members, the wife of a navy doctor and their baby, and a captured Indonesian paratrooper were also among the dead. Our Neptunes searched for many hours, but it was only seven years later that a missionary flying in a small aeroplane, just happened to see the wreck. Not until 1991 could the human remains be recovered after an exhausting expedition to the location of the wreck, which was extremely difficult to reach at a height of more than 4000 metres. The expedition was led by the son of one of the perished crew members.

Meanwhile a dramatic event took place. Michael Rockefeller, ethnologist and son of Nelson D. Rockefeller, then Governor of the State of New York, and later Vice-President of the United States, was doing ethnographic research in the Asmat region on the south west coast of Netherlands New Guinea, accompanied by a civil servant of the Netherlands Interior Government, the anthropologist, René Wassing. When they wanted to cross the wide mouth of the

Oetoemboewé River, breakers flooded the catamaran, and the outboard motor failed. After drifting about a kilometre away from the coast, the two Papuans, who were also in the boat, jumped overboard and swam back to the coast, arriving hours later to report the news to a civil servant. However, the latter was not able to reach the post of the Interior Government in Merauke until the following day, when the Search and Rescue Service of the Royal Navy was warned, and requested to search for Rockefeller and Wassing. This was immediately carried out, initially with no success until it was the turn of my crew. My navigator, Peter Varenhorst, got a contact late in the afternoon, one of many because our very sensitive radar could even pick up floating coconuts. Then out of the corner of my eye I suddenly saw something unusual floating: it was the half-sunken catamaran, with only one man in it, which later turned out to be René Wassing. We threw a dinghy down which had drinking water and food on board, and which inflated itself upon landing in the water. Unfortunately Wassing, who had obviously never seen such an object before, did not know how to turn the little rubber boat around, so it remained floating upside down.

Luckily we could direct a government boat towards him, which was steaming not too far away, so that he was soon rescued.

René Wassing, all alone on the upturned dinghy.

Later on we heard what had happened. When after a long time, help had still not arrived, Rockefeller, who was a good swimmer, disregarding the advice of his companion, decided to swim to the coast, supporting himself on two empty petrol jerry cans.

During our reconnaissance patrols at low altitude, I had several times seen enormous crocodiles lying on the beach, so-called salt water crocodiles, the biggest in the world reaching more than six metres. Their name is derived from the fact that they prefer to stay on the beaches, mainly in eastern Indonesia and Australia, and move from one river mouth to another. Their eggs are laid on the banks of rivers. They are extremely dangerous, and many victims among fishermen and bathers are due to these monsters, when sharks often get the blame. For me his fate was evident, although I learned many years later that a missionary had heard that Rockefeller had been able to reach the coast, but had been murdered there by Papuans. He was even shown a skull, reportedly that of Rockefeller, although later the origin was denied.

Later on I received a moving letter from René Wassing, in which he expressed his deep gratitude.

Initially the Navy decided to abandon the search for Rockefeller after four days. However this was not to the liking of Governor Rockefeller, who, with his daughter, Michael's twin sister Mary, and retinue, including the press, had flown over from the United States in a chartered Boeing 707. He was able to persuade the Navy High Command to do some more search flights, but these had no further result. Meanwhile Rockefeller had rented the entire KLM Hotel in Biak, and later, when the Navy had again stopped searching, he flew above the area from Merauke, first in a charted Catalina belonging to an Australian oil company, and later in a Dakota belonging to Aerocarto, also with no result. Actually this 'Rockefeller circus' evoked a certain repugnance in us: a strange combination of a grieving father and an aggressive American and Australian press bent on maximum publicity. In any case for more than a week, Netherlands New Guinea was world news.

At the beginning of December, 1961, the Flag Officer of the Naval Air Service came over from the Netherlands to visit us. This was Rear Admiral Jaap den Hollander, a highly decorated pilot of the famous 320 Squadron in World War Two.

It so happened that we had been requested to inspect two former Japanese fighter strips to ascertain if they would be suitable for the Neptune. I knew that the Jefman strip on the 'beak' of the Vogelkop (meaning bird's head) was especially very short, and this seemed to me like a good opportunity to demonstrate to the Admiral, who was a very good pilot, all that the Neptune was capable of. Thanks to Beasly's instruction at Lockheed only a few months before, this went surprisingly well, and the Admiral was impressed. During the subsequent short take-off he sat next to me in the right hand seat, and out of the corner of my eye I could see him holding on to the arms of his seat!

Another important matter was housing. Initially we were all accommodated in the Navy barracks Sorido, in anticipation of a house being allotted to those whose family was coming over. There was a waiting list of nearly a year, but an Air Force colleague had had a detachable building shed shipped out from the Netherlands, and made habitable for him and his wife. When it was their turn for a real house, I was able to take over their shed, so that Toni could come over straight away.

Our 'jungle cabin' was situated at the edge of a forest, and some distance away from other houses. This location had been chosen because there was already a connection to the water main, probably still from the time when the Americans were there during the war. However, we had to take care of electricity ourselves, by means of a petrol generator outside, behind the house.

Before we went to sleep at night, I had to close off the petrol tap of the generator, and then I had exactly five seconds to race inside and dive into bed, before the light flickered out.

That we lived on the edge of a tropical jungle was sometimes brought home to us – literally!

Once I found a giant spider in the toilet, which had just given birth to a nest of dear little spiders (spiders are viviparous), and I hastened to get rid of the menagerie before Toni would be confronted by them.

On another occasion, a confrontation with the rich tropical fauna could not be avoided.

Unfortunately I was away when Toni, sitting in our 'bungalow' with the glass doors luckily closed on account of the 'wambrau' (mistral-like wind), suddenly saw an enormous monitor, a lizard, which was locally known as 'kaki ampat' (Indonesian for 'four legs'), which with its long, forked tongue flashing in and out, and scratching with its claws against the glass doors, obviously wanted to come in. Later on, when I once had my driver take her home, they both saw Toni's 'dinosaur' pottering about, and Toni impressed upon him that he had to tell me about this, just in case I still questioned her alleged claim of more than a metre and a half. But indeed I once encountered the beast myself when I went to turn off the generator late in the evening. I didn't tell Toni, because when I was away at night for an operational flight, she had to turn off the generator herself. Maybe I should stress here that monitors are harmless – if you leave them alone!

In retrospect I have to admire her surprising ability to adapt, because, as opposed to myself, who had more or less grown up with these kind of situations, for her it must have taken some getting used to.

Luckily it didn't take too long before a proper house became available. Because of the rapidly worsening situation regarding the Indonesians, wives with young children decided against coming out to Biak, so that we quickly moved up the housing list.

That new house, next to our friends Guus and Ootje Hagdorn (it was the third time that Guus and I served in the same squadron), was indeed a relief. It was newly built in the traditional colonial style. It was far from simple to make something of the garden: the surface of the coral island Biak consists of an extremely thin layer of humus, underneath which lies coral, as hard as stone. Therefore, before we could plant our hibiscus and bougainvillea, we first had to hire a Papuan to dig holes in the ground with a pickaxe.

For me a very busy time now lay ahead. Indonesia's attempts to add this last remnant of the former Dutch East Indies to their Republic became more and more forceful, and our squadron was patrolling the coasts and seas around New Guinea literally day and night.

In the meantime political tension had been building up further. The authorities decided to increase preparedness, and at the end of November a large scale combined exercise was held. The air defence was tested, and the repulse of an amphibious attack combined with a paratrooper landing was also exercised.

321 Squadron in front of a Neptune.

Notwithstanding all the diplomatic deliberation in the United Nations, the Indonesian government decided to go into action. That became apparent on the fifteenth of January, 1962, when Varenhorst, now navigator on board the Neptune commanded by Moekardanoe, during a night patrol discovered an invasion of motor torpedo boats (MTBs) in the Etna Bay. Not entirely by chance (our intelligence was excellent) HMS *Evertsen* and HMS *Kortenaer* were lying in that area, and after they were warned, they opened fire. A well-aimed salvo caused one of the boats to sink, after which the remaining boats turned back.

At that moment we relieved our colleagues with our Neptune. We oriented ourselves on the burning wreck of the MTB, and were able to fire a salvo with our own four 20 mm guns at one of the fleeing boats, of which the phosphorescent wake was just visible in the dark. With no apparent success, however, but they did fire back enthusiastically. This was a baptism of fire for our crew, with the exception of co-pilot Guus Hagdorn, who had flown operations with Seafuries in Korea. Tracers were shooting past the cockpit.

For the rest, this action was a model example of cooperation between the Fleet and Naval Air Service.

In this connection we were glad that we were also able to cooperate in another way.

A request had reached me from the communications officer of HMS *Evertsen*, Lieutenant L.C. Baron van der Feltz to drop the mail

– which was brought from Holland on the weekly KLM passenger plane – during patrol flights at the ships. This was done by means of a metal container, which was dropped into the sea, and subsequently picked up by a launch. I later heard that this postal delivery was a real morale booster for the ship's crew, who before were often deprived of post for weeks on end during long patrols off the south coast.

An irony of fate was that navigator Aberson, who was a member of my crew in the above-mentioned action against the MTBs, had an unfortunate scooter accident nine days later, and sustained a skull fracture. Helmets were then not yet obligatory on scooters, and the stone-hard coral was literally fatal. We took Aberson the same day to Hollandia to be operated on, with our aviation doctor, Bob Kooper, attending him, and flew at maximum speed on four engines. Alas it was of no avail, and Aberson did not regain consciousness.

He was buried in Biak with military honours in the same hard coral that had proved fatal for him.

Four months later, following directions from HMS Groningen, Moekardanoe was able to intercept an Indonesian Dakota, which had just dropped paratroopers over our territory. Moekardanoe, an ex-fighter pilot, shot one of the engines into flames, after which the Dakota carried out a successful ditch just off the coast. Afterwards the whole crew was soon picked up and taken away as prisoners of war.

Their pilots watches were confiscated and sent to me as war booty. At an 'All Hands on deck' of the squadron, I presented the four watches to 'Moek' and three other crew members.

On that same day, moreover, the seventeenth of May, initially directed by HMS Limburg, and later through our own radar, we had intercepted an Indonesian B 25 bomber, which was apparently an escort for their unarmed Dakotas. We set off in pursuit without further delay and started our two jet engines. The B 25 dived down steeply in an escape manoeuvre, and then flew so low over the sea that his two propellers left wind tracks behind on the water. But we easily caught up with him, and when we arrived at shooting distance, I opened fire with the four 20 mm guns in the nose; after a few shots, they jammed! That did not stop the tail gunner of our opponents firing back at us with his two 12.7 mm guns, luckily also with no effect, although the tracers were shooting right over our cockpit. Out of frustration, and to give the enemy a scare, I then fired two 5 inch rockets, intended for ground targets, at him, with obviously no result. This was the first time I had ever seen an armourer – who was a member of our crew – burst into tears: he apparently felt responsible for those 'rotten guns'!

Presenting the 'war booty'!

Caught by a Neptune: Indonesian vessel towing outrigger canoes intended for infiltration. They were navigating in international waters, so no action was taken.

A bit later on we intercepted an Indonesian Dakota on its way back, which had apparently already dropped its load of paratroopers. Gnashing our teeth in frustration again, we could do no better than treat him to our last two rockets; at any rate, the fiery spectacle should have given him a good fright.

We received a telegram from the Commander-in-chief of the forces in New Guinea (COSTRING), Rear Admiral L.E.H. Reeser, addressed to the 'Mock Fighter Squadron 321', in which he congratulated those involved in the two actions for their performances.

An interesting detail concerning these events is that both Indonesian aeroplanes had at one time belonged to the Netherlands Military Air force, and had been donated to Indonesia at the time of the handing over of the sovereignty of the Netherlands East Indies. Actually, I was glad that the Indonesian crew was unharmed, because in fact I had nothing against them personally, on the contrary. I was already wondering what we were doing there.

For that matter, it was a strange situation altogether: there had been no declaration of war, and we could only react if territorial waters were violated. This was happening to an increasing extent, and in some cases initially successful landings were carried out, such as on the scantily populated island of Gak. Our marines were put on land there, and a new task arose for the Neptunes: fire support for the marines. This took place at their directions from the ground with 250 pound bombs, 20 mm guns and 5 inch rockets, and pamphlets were also dropped. We never saw any results ourselves because of the dense jungle, but we did learn later from an intelligence report that some operations had definitely been successful. The infiltrators had suffered losses, were completely demoralised, and the pamphlets had given the final push to surrender.

On another occasion, a Neptune, in cooperation with HMS Friesland, at night discovered a number of motor boats and landing craft near the island of Misool, and promptly launched repeated attacks with rockets and the four 20 mm guns, despite intense anti-aircraft fire from the enemy. For this fearlessness, I put the captain of the aeroplane, Lieutenant Roel Soffner, and his pilot, Sergeant Major De Roo, up for a decoration for bravery, and to my pleasure some time later I was able to pin the Bronze Cross (equivalent of DSC) on them at an 'All hands on deck'.

There was another reason why I was pleased about this. Earlier on, one of our pilots had also distinguished himself, and I had recommended him too for recognition. By a strange coincidence, not long before a formal letter of disapproval had come in for that same officer in connection with an incident which had taken place before my arrival, and this was still in my safe. It hardly seemed the right moment for me, at this stage, to present him with this negative document, since it would mean a probable limitation of his further career.

After consultation, COSTRING came with a 'Solomon's decision': the two recommendations – the positive and the negative – were cancelled against each other. Nevertheless this situation bothered me for a long time since I was not able to explain to colleagues – as I was bound by secrecy – why I had not put the man in question up for recognition.

One day I received orders for a top-secret mission for the bombardment by four Neptunes of a strongly defended base on the Indonesian island of Morotai. Now it was true that we had been nicknamed 'mock fighters', but bomber was an entirely different matter, and the Neptune was not at all suitable. It did not even have bomb-aiming apparatus, so that the bombs would have to be dropped by visual guessing, 'Eyball Mark One', at very low altitude. In view of my earlier personal experience with anti-aircraft fire at low altitude, I could foresee serious problems arising, but I had no other choice but to begin intensively exercising with night bombing at extremely low altitude. My plan was to carry out the bombing raid at night so that at least we would not be bothered by the Mustang fighters stationed there. I was intending to take four Neptunes in a wide circle around Morotai out of reach of radar, and to approach from the north. Then, whipping low over the mountain ridge in close formation, we would drop our bombs with delayed action fuses at low height over the military base and runway, and make our getaway to sea before the enemy had properly woken up and been able to come into action with their anti-aircraft batteries.

My colleagues could only guess about the sense of those unusual exercises because I was bound to secrecy until the very last minute. They probably thought, especially that closed formation at night was a crazy idea, 'inspired by the fighter pilot background of the C.O'. They were quite right because I knew only too well that in a loose formation of four, the last ones have the worst chance because by then the enemy gunners would be wide awake.

Luckily the staff of COSTRING realised in time that it would be much too risky a mission, thanks to repeated negative advice from Cor Kuiken, who was staff officer MLD there.

The morale of the squadron, however, was very high, despite the many lengthy patrol flights in daytime in the tropical heat, and the continuous efforts of the ground crew to keep the aeroplanes in optimal condition. I once had my doubts about how the 'spoilt youth of today' would react to the enormous work load in quite primitive conditions, but I was soon cured of my scepticism. I remember one striking example of their dedication when one day a petty officer advised me in all seriousness to consign a fellow petty officer to his quarters so that he and his subordinates could finally get a good night's sleep!

The leadership of the men was in good hands. Chief Petty Officer Gerard van Schooten (Bronze Cross with bar and Flying Cross – one of the most decorated men in the MLD) was Chief Maintenance; Chief Petty Officer Leo Willems (Flying Cross) was Chief Flight Mechanics; Chief Petty Officer Henk Kramer (Flying Cross with bar) was Chief Ground Mechanics and Chief Petty Officer Rudy Meijer, a good-natured giant of a man, generally liked and always in good spirits, was overall Chief Personnel.

Our Intelligence Service was first-rate. One valuable piece of information they provided us with was the radio frequencies the Indonesians used, so that those among us who could speak the language – and that were quite a few – were sometimes able to pick up interesting conversations. For instance we were once again on a night patrol in the neighbourhood of the Vogelkop, when Peter Varenhorst suddenly got a 'bogey' (echo of an enemy aeroplane) on his radar screen. We were able to almost cut him off and get behind him, but he was very fast so I started both jet engines. We were gradually gaining on him, as Peter constantly reported: 'Bogey 12 o'clock 4 miles ... gaining ... now 3 miles ... 2½ miles...'

Suddenly I heard on the Indonesian frequency I had on: '(call sign) ... *Awas! Awas! Ada Tuan Andjing di blakan!*' (Watch out! Watch out! There's a Mister Dog [Islamic term of abuse] behind you!') I had hardly recovered from my surprise when Peter reported: 'Bogey speeding up ... now three miles ... 4 miles...'

It was a Lockheed 'Hercules', which, warned by radar from apparently a ground station, gave full throttle with his four 'propjets', and we knew only too well that he was at least a hundred knots faster than we were. Interesting fact was that this Hercules was recently delivered by the same Lockheed factory in Burbank as our Neptunes, and the Indonesian crews had also been trained by that factory, just like us.

In the meantime, infiltrations with small vessels and paratroopers steadily continued. Luckily our squadron had thus far not suffered any casualties, but notwithstanding the high morale, it was nevertheless a sombre time, because you could foresee that we would eventually lose out, if not militarily, then politically. We therefore all breathed a sigh of relief when, at the instigation of the United Nations, a cease-fire was declared on 18 September 1962.

Soon after, an Indonesian Hercules with a delegation on board on its way to Hollandia for negotiations, landed in Biak on the civilian Airport, Mokmer to refuel. Nobody was allowed to leave the aeroplane during refuelling, and two armed marines were posted at the steps – for we were still in a state of (undeclared) war. Then a high-ranking Indonesian officer of the Tentara Republik Indonesia (TRI) the Indonesian Army, appeared in the door opening, called one of the marines and asked in perfect Dutch if he would fetch the Airport Manager, because he knew him. The Manager, somewhat surprised, went along with the request, but warned the marines that they had to come and fetch him if he were not out again in a few minutes. When he then stepped into the aeroplane, he was practically embraced by the TRI officer – it appeared that he was a colleague and old friend from the time of their training for KNIL officer at the Royal Military Academy in Bandoeng before the war, many years ago. When it was time to go, the Indonesian asked if he could bring something with him from Indonesia next time, because obviously his friend suffered all sorts of hardships on this island. To which the Airport Manager replied that if he could spare it from what little he had in Indonesia, a portion of 'petjil Batawi' (an Indonesian vegetable dish from Djakarta, in colonial times called Batavia) would be very welcome. The Indonesian then smilingly corrected him: 'You mean petjil Djakarta?'

About a week later, an Indonesian Hercules again landed at Mokmer Airport, and one of the crew handed to the marine standing on guard, a 'rantang' (a set of little pans stacked on top of each other) containing petjil Djakarta for the Airport Manager.

There was now time for more pleasant activities.It so happened that the District Commisioner of the Geelvink Bay, to which Biak also belonged, was Pim Kouwenhoven, an old acquaintance of mine. I had met him in Biak in 1945 just after the end of the war, and he had told me then of the adventure he had just experienced when he was posted on the island of Noemfoor as a young civil servant of the Interior Government.

Amazons of the shooting club organised by the Armaments Officer, Lt. Commander Frans Bom. Toni standing second from the right.

One morning one of his Papuan soldiers came rushing in to warn him: 'Tuan, the Japanese are coming!' and to his horror, he indeed saw a couple of landing craft full of Japanese soldiers heading straight for him. After they landed, a Japanese officer approached, halted in front of Pim, drew his samurai sword – that's the end of me, Pim thought – and offered it in surrender with a deep bow.

After the renewed acquaintance, we became friends with Pim and his wife Annelies, and Toni was given a unique opportunity to see more of New Guinea because Pim invited her with a friend, Delia, the English wife of my direct superior, Captain J.C. Petschi, to accompany him on a government boat to various coastal villages, sometimes inhabited by extremely primitive Papuans. If the boat could not get all the way to the village, the guests were brought ashore on canoes, hollowed out tree trunks, in which the Papuan who was rowing would sometimes be singing out loud. The villagers took it for granted that Pim had taken his two wives along. One trip was abruptly ended prematurely when suddenly a Beaver float plane, belonging to the Kroonduif Company, appeared in the distance. Pim realised immediately what was up, and said: They are coming to fetch me!'

After circling around to warn Pim, the Beaver landed in the sea. It was clear that the District Commissioner was needed, and in those days it was the only way to contact him.

Now I could take more time off, I was also able to go along on a trip a couple of times, and once to a very special destination: the village Warsa, where I had been an uninvited guest seventeen years before – almost exactly to the day.

It was a very strange sensation for me: I recognised straight away the small bay with the pure, white narrow beach, where so often I had sat between the coconut palm trees, wondering how I would ever get away from there. The village itself, on the other hand, had completely changed, and was unrecognisable to me.

We were received hospitably, and in the course of the conversation, the civil servant, who was accompanying us, mentioned the incident of seventeen years ago to the village head, who then sent for a few old Papuans. When the village head explained to them in their own language who I was, it was moving to see how their memory all at once came back to these old men, for we must bear in mind that these people have no written language to help them remember. They were probably no older than me, but the average age span of those primitive people was at the time not much more than thirty or forty years. One of them pointed to the sky, and gestured something like a parachute, and there was much cackling and grinning with their almost toothless mouths. We were treated to coconut milk, and given a number of coconuts to take with us when we left.

It soon became clear that we would not be staying much longer in Biak, and the return journey had to be planned. For me it was it was a foregone conclusion. We would make a start flying our Neptunes over to the Netherlands, two at a time, just before the transfer of our last colony in Asia to the UNTEA, a commission of the United Nations, which had mediated between the Netherlands and Indonesia. I took off with the first two Neptunes on the first of October 1962, five minutes before the official transfer ceremony began, and the Dutch flag was lowered over this last part of our former Netherlands East Indies.

Our first landing was on the airfield of Saigon, South Vietnam. Hostilities had not yet broken out there, although the tension was noticeable. As with all further landings, we had to spend the night there, because we were not allowed to fly at night over foreign territory with a military aircraft. We were met at the airfield by a gentleman in tail coat and striped grey trousers, and while I was thinking that this was a bit too much of an honour, he introduced himself as the newly appointed Netherlands chargé d'affaires in Saigon, Sir Beelaerts van Blokland. He told me that he had just got back from an official visit to the President of South Vietnam to present his credentials, as is customary. He further apologised for not being able to receive us at his home because he was still camping in his empty house. He handed me a large envelope filled with piastres, and the addresses of the two hotels which he had booked for us.

He was also present when we left the next morning to bid us farewell, and he asked me if I would give his mother in Wassenaar, Holland a call when I got back, and give her his love. All very pleasant and correct, which is usual when navy units visit abroad.

In the evening we went to eat in a Vietnamese restaurant, all twenty-four of us, Everyone agreed that the ordering could best be left to the C.O. in view of his Asiatic experience. That was not easy because the Vietnamese dishes were naturally completely unknown to me, but I didn't let on, and ordered at random – in French, of course – with the well known navy motto in mind: 'It doesn't matter so much what it tastes like, as long as there's plenty of it'. The men enjoyed the dinner, but when the waitress lifted the lid off a large dish, and a collection of dear little birds, lying on their backs with their claws up appeared, it all went suddenly deathly quiet …

The next stop was Katunayake Air Force Base in Sri Lanka. What I remember most from there is breakfast in the Officers Mess, which looked very British, and where the steward asked me:

'English or local breakfast, Sir?'

'Local, of course!'

With an approving smile, I was subsequently served with a dish of curried vegetables. Very good. (I suddenly realise that it is often the food that I remember best).

The next destination was Karachi, Pakistan, where the KLM Manager handed me a telegram from Captain Petschi from Biak, informing me that I was promoted to the rank of commander. That had to be celebrated, of course, with the two crews in the bar of the KLM Hotel, where we were all staying. With the price of beer in that Islamic country, this cost me several months of the salary increase. But it got much worse: the next day, the very friendly Manager offered to take my uniform jacket to a tailor in town to have the three wide gold bands put on. Now I knew that the colour of so-called 'Indian' gold was very red, but not to worry, the Manager said, they had a solution, only it would cost a bit more because they would have to use smuggled 'English' gold. So it was done, and the result was perfect, although I had to swallow a few times when I saw the bill. At any rate, I could boast that I had the most expensive Commander- gold braid in the whole Netherlands Royal Navy.

This was somewhat compensated by my shoulder epaulettes. During the next flight, the gold braid of the shoulder epaulettes of navigator Peter Varenhorst were, without my knowledge, professionally removed – under loud mock protest – by the Chief Flight Engineer, Sergeant Dirk Venema (the same who some ten years earlier in 860 Squadron had been the mechanic of my, or rather *our* Seafury), so as to add a wide substitute band to my epaulettes.

On her journey back to Holland with KLM, Toni had a unique opportunity to stop over in Tokyo for ten days with a friend who had family living there, with whom they stayed.

The KLM passenger plane afterwards also landed in Karachi, at the same time that I was there with our first two Neptunes for two days rest, so we had arranged that Toni would stop over in Karachi for two days as well. The KLM Manager and his wife had organised a day trip by bus for us all, with a picnic at the famous Turtle Beach, where we could amuse ourselves with riding on camels, watching a snake charmer, and swimming.

After swimming, there was an unusual incident. When everyone was out of the water, one of the Petty Officers and I were both looking out over the sea to make sure that each of the twenty-four men were out, when we saw two heads above the water a long way out. We both immediately jumped into the sea again because it looked as if there were problems: the heads were very close together as if one were trying to help the other. However, when we got closer, we witnessed an unexpected, very special scene: two mating giant turtles...

After Karachi we continued our journey to Valkenburg with two nights in both Basra and Athens. There was nothing we could do in Basra because we were not allowed to leave our hotel at the airfield on account of strained diplomatic relations with Iraq. Luckily we were able to relax in a lovely swimming pool because it was terribly hot.

Athens was a rather different story. We were completely ignored there by the Netherlands Embassy. They had taken care of hotel accommodation, but for the rest we had to look out for ourselves. My request to pay my respects to the Ambassador, as is the custom in the Royal Navy, was brushed off with: 'Your gesture is appreciated, but not necessary'.

Not even transport had been arranged, and that in a city where we could not even read the street signs and notices, and where we were hardly able to to make ourselves understood. Such a contrast with Saigon and Karachi. Naturally I wrote a detailed account of the 'reception' in Athens in my journey report, and I was pleased to learn later on that my complaint had ended up at the Ministry of Foreign Affairs, where it was 'duly noted'.

We did visit the famous Acropolis, of course, and that made the day of rest very worthwhile.

When the entire squadron had arrived at the Naval Air Base Valkenburg, 321 Squadron was formally disbanded, and simultaneously reinstated under the name 320 Squadron, which had won so much fame in World War Two flying B25 bombers. At the same time, work began on the modification of the 'mock' fighters' into anti-submarine aircraft. For instance the nose section with the four canons was removed, and replaced by a nose section with more appropriate apparatus for the new task. The crews also had to be retrained, of course, so altogether it was a very busy time. Furthermore, we all had to get used to the climate again – it would turn out to be the coldest winter of the century.

Back from New Guinea and welcomed by the Commander of the Fleet, Vice Admiral A.N. Baron de Vos van Steenwijk.

An interesting diversion came up when at the end of November 1962, a volcano erupted right off the coast of Iceland, and formed a new island there. This seemed an excellent opportunity to put our navigators through their paces in the 'old-fashioned' way, so without the help of radar. It meant more than twelve hours flying there and back over the sea, with no possibilities for land orientation. The last miles to Iceland, however, were simple because the enormous columns of smoke and steam were visible from afar; at least for the pilots in front, but they kept quiet about it, of course.

It was an imposing sight: the primeval forces of nature were displaying themselves most spectacularly. When we got closer we could distinctly smell the sulphur, and we saw large rocks being ejected, some the size of a Volkswagen, and coming all the way to our altitude – a warning not to get too close – to subsequently splash into the sea with enormous clouds of steam. Splendid material for a colourful newspaper article by journalist Ewout Janse of the The Hague newspaper, 'Haagsche Courant', whom we had on board as passenger.

*Forces of nature. The new volcano near Iceland,
photographed from our Neptune.*

I was only too aware of the fact that this would definitely be my very last operational 'flying' post, and I thoroughly enjoyed this task, which was new to me – anti-submarine warfare – with the wonderful Neptune. When the squadron was completely operational again, we took part in various NATO exercises, for which we were stationed on British RAF bases, among others, Bally Kelly in Ulster, St. Mawgan in Cornwall, Kinloss in Scotland, and Gibraltar.

The anti-submarine task with land-based aircraft is carried out by the British through their 'Coastal Command', a unit of the Royal Air Force, not by the Navy, as in our case.

During one of those Nato exercises, we were operating from the British Naval Base at Gibraltar. In the anti-submarine exercise 'Magilex' in March 1964, two Dutch submarines also participated, and we therefore had to hunt them too. This went quite successfully, so that we perhaps showed our complacency a bit too obviously. In any case, one day I was invited with some of my plane captains by the Captain of one of the Dutch submarines, HMS 'Tijgerhaai' (Tiger shark), for a demonstration on board. This consisted in the two submarines submerging – which was already bad enough for us pilots – and then in turn doing a game of leap-frog, when we could clearly hear the other boat crossing right over our boat every time since we could distinctly hear the rotating screws!

Needless to say that at the end of the trip, we were relieved to step ashore again – with deep respect for our submariner colleagues. For that matter, the mutual appreciation between the Submarine Service and the Naval Air Service is traditional.

One special event in this period was the visit of our Crown Princess, Princess Beatrix, who was doing the rounds of the different military units in order to familiarise herself. She was accompanied by a pilot colleague of mine, George Pauli, the first one from the Naval Air Service to be appointed as Aide-de-camp to the Royal Household, something to be proud of. I and some other colleagues were invited by the Commanding Officer of the Naval Air Service, Captain Sjerp (my former Catalina instructor) to have lunch with Her Royal Highness at his Headquarters. I noticed that she was exceptionally well informed (obviously well briefed by George), and also expressed herself with great charm and liveliness – undoubtedly due to the genes of her father.

Crown Princess Beatrix visits the Naval Air Base Valkenburg.

13. NATO Headquarters Brussels 1968-70

On the first of August I was posted to the Admiralty in the Hague as Head of the Department of Planning. This signified the definite end of my flying career, on which I could look back with great satisfaction: through circumstances I had been able to fly a total of thirty-two different types of aircraft, either in single-seat fighters, or as first pilot.

The Admiralty building was at that time situated in the Koningin Maria Lane, The Hague, at cycling distance from Smidswater, where we lived. My right-hand man was Lt. Commander Kees van Westenbrugge, and he and his wife Lydia later became good friends. Kees had a keen intellect, and he soon brought me up to date with my new work. The most interesting part was our contribution to the Defence Bill, a task which entailed countless meetings with staff officers of the other military forces and various civil servants. I had frequent and good contact with the Secretary of State for the Navy, Vice Admiral (ret.) A. van Es, which perhaps contributed to my next very interesting posting to Brussels as military adviser to our NATO Ambassador at NATO Headquarters at Zaventem.

So we moved to Brussels in May 1968, to a house in the suburb of Kraainem.

This diplomatic post was again an entirely new experience, both professionally and in our private life. It signified an almost daily routine of social obligations, lunches, cocktail parties and dinners, occasionally all three in one day, all very interesting, of course, but after a while quite tiring. Professionally, it entailed a succession of meetings about subjects which were in general as yet new to me.

It already started the first day when I presented myself as was customary in full dress uniform (with sword), to my new boss, Ambassador Boon, who addressed me benignly:

'Commander, although I have been informed that you can only stay two years with us instead of the usual three – apparently even more important tasks will be waiting for you – I bid you welcome, and I suggest that you go straight away to participate in the subject committee meeting this morning about the NATO alarm system, so as to familiarise yourself. I look forward to reading your report on the matter.'

Still slightly bewildered I wandered through endless corridors to one of the countless meeting rooms, where it soon appeared that the meeting was presided over by a French Colonel, who immediately started off with a long and complicated account – in French, of course. Like most naval officers, I had hardly spoken a word of French since my schooldays, so I did not catch more than 20% of the Colonel's argumentation. A looming disaster, I couldn't turn up with that for my Ambassador. I therefore accosted the Colonel after the meeting and asked him if I could drop by for some more information, because – I thought I might as well be frank – 'I was not able to follow your fascinating presentation entirely'.

'Mais bien sur, Commandant. Venez avec moi!'

So we walked to his office where he was very helpful, and I finally managed to put together an acceptable report. This was presented to the Ambassador in the usual memo (through his secretary, of course), and the next day it came back initialled, and with the remark: 'You are already getting into your stride!'

The final straw came at a cocktail party a few days later when I saw 'Mon Colonel' standing in a group, and I joined them, glad to see at least one familiar face, and to my amazement heard him conversing in fluent English …

Meanwhile, on a visit to the Flag Officer Naval Air, my former plane captain, Peter de Groot (who – in view of the scars on my head still owed me something), informed me that my next post would be Commanding Officer of the Naval Air Base Valkenburg, later followed by the function of Commanding Officer of the Naval Air Service. Then he added somewhat cryptically with a smile: 'And after that, the sky's the limit!' This also explained the short two year posting in Brussels.

Another indication came when after a meeting I was walking with the ambassador through the interminable corridors of NATO Headquarters, and he suddenly turned to me and said: 'I heard from Secretary of State van Es, whom I just visited in The Hague, that you have a bright future ahead of you, and I'm very pleased.'

It was customary that the national Commanders-in-Chief paid an annual visit to NATO Headquarters, and so I heard that my top boss, Commander in Chief of the Netherlands Royal Navy, Vice

Admiral J.B.M. Maas would soon be arriving with his wife. After discussing it for a while, Toni and I boldly decided to invite them for lunch at our home. After all, I was the only Naval Officer at the Netherlands NATO Embassy, and so it was 'my Admiral'. Nevertheless, we were pleasantly surprised that the Admiral promptly accepted. I should perhaps mention here that I had met him once before in 1964 when I was Commanding Officer of 320 Squadron and he was Captain of HMS Karel Doorman. I had to be on board HMS Karel Doorman for a debriefing of a fleet exercise in which my Neptunes had participated. The ship was alongside the quay of the harbour of Bergen, Norway. When I arrived on board, I approached the Commander of the ship to find out which cabin he had allotted to me. He seemed rather nervous and preoccupied (later on I learned that he did not get on at all with Captain Maas, and in fact was scared stiff of his Captain), and said that they were actually full up, but that he would see about it later. When I left his office somewhat perplexed, I almost bumped into that feared Captain Maas.

'Why are you looking so down, my friend?'

'I think I shall have to sleep in one of the aeroplanes, Sir.' I said jokingly and explained the problem to him.

'Well, then you just take my Stateroom, because I'm sleeping in my sea cabin on the bridge anyway. Steward, prepare my bunk for the Commander'.

That is how Maas was, and you were either afraid of him, or there was nothing that you would not do for him. Needless to say that from that moment on, I belonged to the second category.

As a souvenir from Bergen, I took two live lobsters home with me; the memory of that lobster feast after the helicopter visit to St. Maarten, was still fresh in my mind. However this time we had to prepare them ourselves, and that led to some hesitation on our part...

Back to Brussels. I had arranged everything with the Admiral's aide-de-camp (ADC) down to the last detail.

Mrs. Maas, who came directly from The Hague, would be brought straight to our house. After his meeting in Mons at the Military Headquarters of SACEUR (Supreme Allied Command Europe), the Admiral would be driven to his hotel in Brussels to get changed, after which I would fetch him.

Head of Planning behind his desk.

Unfortunately, there was an overly diligent staff officer in Mons, who had been informed that the Admiral would be having lunch at our home, but was not acquainted with all the arrangements that had been made. He thought he would make a good impression by giving the Admiral's driver detailed instructions on how to get to our address in the Avenue des Frênes, which he had looked up on the map of Brussels. Thinking that there had been a change of plan, meaning he would not first be able to change out of his uniform, the Admiral willingly let himself be taken along. Alas, the staff officer had made a mistake, and had given another Avenue des Frênes in the middle of town, instead of in the suburb Kraainem. Moreover it was not a very nice neighbourhood either, so I can imagine what the Admiral was thinking. To make matters worse, the driver got a fit of nerves and suddenly needed to pee, but didn't speak French, so the

Admiral, in full uniform with gold braid up to the elbows, had to ring the doorbell of a house, and ask if his driver s'il vous plaît could just come in and do 'pipi' …

Luckily it was a very friendly and helpful woman who opened the door, and she even looked up the correct address in the telephone directory for him.

In the meantime, Toni was sitting at home with Mrs. Maas, also British, all the time waiting for us to arrive, after she had shown her guest around the house and garden, and had had her shell collection from New-Guinea admired, while wondering about her crab soufflé in the oven. Finally the Admiral arrived at our house, obviously much too late, and … alone.

'Isn't my husband with you?', Toni asked in surprise.

Meanwhile I was busy tracking down my missing Admiral, and was still waiting for him in his hotel after an agitated telephone call to his aide-de-camp in The Hague, when the receptionist called me over. Toni on the phone: 'The Admiral has just arrived!'

Apart from the telephone ringing three times during lunch (twice the ADC for the Admiral), and also just during the main course, the familiar beggar ringing the doorbell for his monthly alms, everything went well. The Admiral and his wife were charming guests, and it turned out to be a very pleasant afternoon. I admired the Admiral for not showing any signs of annoyance for what had happened, on the contrary, but I admired Toni even more for her composure.

When Mrs. Maas left, she complimented Toni for coping so well, and for the excellent lunch.

Nevertheless, the whole event was a clear example of over-organisation.

Not long afterwards, a friend and colleague, 'Dicky' Wentholt, formerly Communications Officer on board HMS Karel Doorman, came on official business to NATO, and I took him home for lunch. He was telling us about a fantastic small hotel in Tossa de Mar on the Spanish Mediterranean coast. We were in the process of planning our holiday, and immediately showed interest, but then he hesitated; we had to promise not to tell anyone else about it.

The hotel was indeed very special, magnificently situated in the middle of cork oak woods, populated by an improbable number of nightingales, who also sang in daytime!

The owners were a very tall Icelander, an artist, and his Spanish wife who was a marvellous cook. Her talent turned out to be more in demand than his paintings, and the small hotel with restaurant became a huge success.

One day at lunch the Icelander came up to our table with an anxious look on his face.

'A telegram, Sir. I hope it's good news.'

It was a telegram from Brussels, sent by the thoughtful Kees van Westenbrugge (who at the time had a NATO function at the Military Representative) with the message that I had been promoted to Captain. That had to be celebrated, of course, together with the other guests, and with Spanish 'champagne', which tasted surprisingly good.

When the two 'Brussels years' had gone by, I was transferred to the Naval Air Base Valkenburg to take over the command. But first we were offered a stylish farewell dinner at the home of Ambassador and Mrs. Boon.

On my last day at the office I took leave of all the Embassy personnel. After the kind words of the Ambassador, it was my turn to speak. I naturally mentioned the interesting time, how much I had learned etc., but I also referred to the (for me) unusual working method. My contact with the Ambassador, whose military advisor I was, had almost exclusively been limited to writing memos, several hundred in total, which I then got back initialled, and sometimes accompanied by his remarks.

This clearly caused some amusement, everyone there being well aware that the Ambassador liked to maintain a certain distance. But afterwards, his Excellency came up to me and asked with a concerned look on his face:

'But you did like it here, Captain, didn't you?'

14. The last stage 1970-75

My command of 'Valkenburg' would only be for one year, really too short to be able to oversee everything that went on in such a large organisation with over two thousand men, but luckily I had an experienced staff at my disposal, who in fact could have also done the job without me. Therefore my main tasks were especially representative and ceremonial, such as oath of allegiance ceremonies for newly appointed officers, handing out wings, and receiving high-ranking authorities who were in the habit of using our naval airfield when visiting or leaving The Hague.

One very foggy morning I had the pleasure of keeping our Minister of Foreign Affairs company, the well known Joseph Luns (also the uncle of my First Officer, Jaap Luns), while waiting for better weather so his plane could take off. Or rather he kept *us* company, for he entertained us with his inexhaustible supply of anecdotes and jokes, and I was not surprised when he confided that he had once really wanted to be an actor.

Reception given by Prince Bernhard at the 'Zwaluwenberg'. Kees van Westenbrugge is absorbed in thought.

The Parade Commander reports to the Commanding Officer of the Naval Air Base Valkenburg during the parade at Katwijk for the Queen's birthday.

An interesting event took place on another very foggy morning. The telephone rang, and the Commander Air, my good friend Commander 'Bill' van den Brandeler (partner-thief of the goldfish), reported that a transport aircraft of the U.S. Air Force was circling above the base, and had requested permission to be allowed to land, in spite of the fact that we were closed down. Because they were getting short of fuel, and moreover the captain was reported to be in possession of a so-called 'Master Green Instrument Ticket', which allowed him to attempt a landing with bad visibility at his own risk, I gave permission. I opened the window of my office to listen to what was about to happen, and I soon heard the reassuring noise of 'reverse thrust' and squealing brakes. A bit later the telephone rang again:

'Sir, there is a 'chicken colonel' on board the aircraft.'

The distinctions of a Colonel in the U.S. Air Force are small, silver eagles (chickens) on the shoulders or lapels. I replied:

'I'll send my car, ask him if he would like to come and have lunch with me.

Inspection of the Marine Band prior to the Allegiance ceremony.

Newly appointed officers taking the oath.

Bill again on the phone. 'The colonel is pleased to accept your invitation, but apologises for his flying overall.'

That was no problem, of course, and a bit later a tall man stepped into my office. He immediately looked vaguely familiar; as opposed to names, I rarely forget a face. It was a very pleasant lunch, and we were soon exchanging each other's war experiences. It then appeared that he had been stationed in Hollandia, New Guinea, with an A 26 bomber squadron directly after the Americans had recaptured the town in 1944, while we were still in Merauke with our 120 Squadron. A number of our pilots visited that squadron to exchange information, and some of us, including myself, were given the opportunity of flying with them 'piggy back' at the back of the single-seater attack bomber. It is hard to believe, but my guest, Colonel Collins, was one of those pilots who had taken a Dutchman along. Unfortunately, neither of us could say for certain whether we had indeed flown together then, but it was nevertheless a very remarkable coincidence.

In between the busy activities, there was still time for other things. Together with Jaap Luns, I had resolved to obtain the medal of the Association for Physical Culture, which entailed swimming, long jump, fencing, rope climbing and a 15 km walk in two hours. For quite some time, the personnel of 'Valkenburg' were treated in the late afternoon after work to the spectacle of a Commanding Officer and his First Officer training to exhaustion. It was not easy, even if the requirements were adapted to our age, but we made it.

One day we were invited by the director of the swimming pool in Wassenaar (where our flying crews practised their periodic dinghy drill), to come and inaugurate the recently installed sauna. This was promptly accepted, and from then on it became a permanent routine that early every Monday morning before work started at eight o'clock, the Commanding Officer, the First Officer, the Head of the Technical Department (the Commander Air dropped out after the first time), the Paymaster and the Medical Officer sweated it out together.

That one year at the Naval Air Station Valkenburg flew by, following which I was appointed as Commanding Officer of the Naval Air Service (CMLD) in a building just outside 'Valkenburg'. As a function I found it far less interesting than the previous one, but it was a necessary step leading up to my next post. As operational

Commanding Officer, it did give me more opportunity to fly: I only had to telephone one of the squadrons, and an aeroplane would be waiting for me.

It was also a busy time ceremoniously and socially, and Toni and I had to attend many an official reception, and also receive at home.

With Admiral Sudomo, Commander-in-Chief of the Indonesian Navy. First meeting of former enemies after the conflict in the Etna Bay in 1962.

An interesting event in this period was the visit of the Commander-in-Chief of the Indonesian Navy, Admiral Sudomo and his wife. I was requested as CMLD to offer the Admiral – or 'Laksamana' in Indonesian – a helicopter trip above the Delta works (the reconstruction works after the great flood). Accompanied by our wives, it turned out to be a very enjoyable outing, the more so because both the Admiral and Mrs. Sudomo spoke excellent Dutch. The Admiral had even had part of his training with our Royal Navy in Den Helder, and spoke with fond memories about the trips to The Hague during the weekends, which always ended on Sunday evening with eating delicious pork chops at Hotel Centraal opposite the railway station.

'But Admiral', I said, seemingly disconcerted, 'that was naughty, you as a Muslim eating pork chops?'

'But Captain', he replied, 'I am a Christian!'

His accompanying staff included two captains, who had also followed training courses at the Royal Institute of the Navy in Den Helder. When they met a number of former fellow students, who under the Dutch promotion system were 'only' lieutenant commander or commanders, there was teasing back and forth.

'Look, you have simply chosen the wrong navy!', the Indonesians said.

This is characteristic of the good atmosphere which prevailed during the visit – and then to think that only ten years earlier as enemies we had exchanged fire in our Neptune with the motor torpedo boats of the 'Ankatan Laut', the Indonesian Navy, in the Etna Bay of the coast of New Guinea ... commanded by the then Commodore Sudomo.

With Admiral Sudomo and our wives in an Augusta Bell helicopter for a trip to the Delta works in Zeeland (a system of dykes constructed after the Great Flood in 1953).

My last operational flight was as formation leader of ten Neptunes for a 'Fly Past' over Den Helder on the occasion of the farewell of the Commander-in-Chief, Vice Admiral Maas. In view of various happenings in the past, I felt a certain bond with him, and was glad that as Commanding Officer of the Naval Air Service (CMLD), an operational command, I was in a position to take leave of him personally in this manner, in addition to the customary official farewell dinner in the 'Palace' (the residence of the Commander of the Fleet) in Den Helder, for which Toni and I were also invited.

On the thirtieth of June 1972, I was promoted to the rank of Rear Admiral, and appointed as Flag Officer of the Naval Air Service, and also as Deputy Chief of the Navy Staff for Aviation matters.

The morning of that important day began early and exceptionally well. Without my knowledge, Toni had purchased a flag and a flag pole (she thought she couldn't do less for a 'Flag Officer'), and hidden it in the garage of our neighbours, Macie and Hein Steman.

A hole for the mast was secretly dug in our front garden by Hein and another neighbour, KLM pilot Cees de Hoogh, and neatly covered with grass sods.

I was still half asleep when I was suddenly awakened by the sound of a bugle; I immediately recognised the seven o'clock reveille signal, jumped out of bed, saw through the window a real navy bugler standing in our back garden, and called out to Toni: 'Bring me my cap!' I quickly put on my new cap with the double gold braid, and went out on to the balcony in my pyjamas to receive the honours, much to the amusement of all our neighbours, who were all in on the plot. Hein had thought up the idea of a bugler, and had fetched him personally from the Naval Air Base Valkenburg. Then the gathering moved to the front garden, where the flag was hoisted, again to the accompaniment of the bugler, who blew the signal 'Hoist the flag'.

The transfer of the command that same day from my predecessor, Guus Ehbel, and its attendant ceremony was very impressive, because at the same time the Colours of the Naval Air Service were handed over. After the roll call, the Colours were solemnly handed over to me by my predecessor before the entire company of the base and the invited guests, including Toni, and preceded by the usual speeches. A march past then followed with the military band.

In the late afternoon we gave a reception at home with champagne for friends and neighbours, which my navy steward took care of, prior to the big, official reception later in the evening at the Naval Air Base.

The Colours of the Naval Air Service during the transfer of the command.

The following three years constituted a succession of meetings, where in the light of the worsening economic situation of the country, which obviously also had repercussions for Defence, I sometimes had to defend the organisation and even the very existence of the Naval Air Service.

The weekly meeting of the Admiralty Board, of which I was now a member by virtue of my new function, was presided over by the Commander-in-Chief of the Royal Navy and Chief of the Naval Staff, Vice Admiral Eric Roest. The atmosphere was generally businesslike and pleasant, not least through the dry humour of Eric. The presence of the Flag Officer Personnel, Rear Admiral Harry Heckman, a witty colleague from the Indies, who could masterfully imitate an Indonesian accent, also contributed to this. Once, while looking around the table at his fellow Flag Officers he remarked:

'Adoeh, if I would clap my hands now, we would all climb up the nearest coconut tree!'

Indeed, with the exception of Eric, we all came from the former Netherlands East Indies (Rear Admiral Jan Langenberg had even been in my class at High School in Semarang).

Years later, Kees van Westenbrugge remarked: 'We called you The Asian Mystic Power!'

The Admiralty Board in front of the portrait of Admiral de Ruyter.

At one meeting of the Admiralty Board, the 'long hair' problem had again been on the agenda. As opposed to the Army and the Air Force, this especially formed a problem for the Navy because of the voyages abroad. In the middle of the discussion about the problem everyone suddenly fell silent, and all eyes turned towards the large painted portrait of our greatest national naval hero, Admiral Michiel Adriaenszoon de Ruyter (which always hangs on the wall behind the desk of the Commander-in-Chief), in full regalia of shining armour, and his hair flowing in waves down to his lace collar …

Then there were naturally the ceremonial and social obligations, which were sometimes quite enjoyable. For instance, at one of the usual Monday morning meetings of the Admiralty Board, Eric informed us that an invitation had arrived from the Ethiopian Imperial Navy to send a Netherlands warship to the Naval Base at Massawa on the Red Sea, for a Navy Day on the occasion of the eightieth birthday of His Imperial Majesty Haile Sellassie, the Emperor of Ethiopia. Eric wasn't keen on sending a ship especially for that purpose all around the Cape of Good Hope, since the Suez Canal was still closed. I then saw my chance:

'What about one of Her Majesty's aeroplanes? Fast and cheap!'

The idea immediately met with approval, and naturally I was appointed to represent the Commander-in-Chief. The Honorary Consul of Ethiopia in the Netherlands, Mr. Van Ginkel, and Vice Admiral Frits Kruimink (ret.), Head of the Military Intelligence Service, also went along.

That visit was an unforgettable event. We flew with an 'Atlantic' patrol aircraft of our Naval Air Service via Crete, where we spent the night, to Asmara, because Massawa itself did not have a suitable airfield. From there we were taken by road to Massawa with an armed escort, because already then it was not safe in that part of Ethiopia (the present Eritrea), and we were accommodated on the Naval Base.

On the day itself, a so-called 'Sail Past' was to be held for the Emperor by around thirty Navies who were represented. In such a 'Sail Past', all the participating warships sail in line across the bow of the stationary Admiral's ship, which carries the most important authority, thus in this case the Emperor. Therefore, in the absence of a Netherlands warship, I had arranged with the Captain of our 'Atlantic', Lieutenant Commander Kees Plat, who had served in my

321 Squadron in New Guinea as a navigator, and who had stayed behind in Asmara with his aircraft, that I would telephone him from Massawa with the exact time, so that he would be able to represent us there properly at the right moment.

The 'Sail Past' was taking place the morning after our arrival. The Red Sea was as usual smooth as a mirror, and visibility was slightly hazy. Because I did not have a ship, I was invited on board His Imperial Majesty's warship, HIMS Ethiopia (an ex-Netherlands ocean minesweeper) to take part in the ceremony. There I was standing on deck, arrayed in white uniform with medals and sword, in anticipation of what was to come, and chatting to various magnificently attired officers of the represented Navies.

All at once an officer with a friendly, round, brown face came up to me and said in Dutch with an unmistakable 'adoeh' (Indonesian) accent:

'Admiral, may I present myself?'

It was an Indonesian naval captain.

'Of course, Captain', I said, 'what a surprise to hear Dutch spoken here.'

Then the Korean officer I had been talking to, looked at us in turn with a surprised look on his face, and said: 'Excuse, please, you ex-colony, you ex-colonial master, you speak friendly? Please I make picture, yes?'. So we both posed grinning for the photo, but unfortunately the promised photo never reached me.

But then the long column of ships came in sight, led by the Georges Leygues, a French light cruiser (inevitably nicknamed 'Gorgeous Legs'), which had the most senior officer present, a French admiral, on board. They were coming closer all the time, and still no sign of the Atlantic.

And then, just before the first ship was about to cross the bow of the Emperor's ship, out of the haze our Atlantic suddenly appeared right in front of the bow with a thunderous noise, and literally a few metres above the surface of the sea. You could almost touch the letters 'Koninklijke Marine' (Royal Navy), and I got a lump in my throat from pride.

While I was affably acknowledging the many compliments, a pitch-black Ethiopian naval officer suddenly appeared in front of me, and informed me that His Imperial Majesty wished to speak to me. Oh no, I thought, of course we have upset the protocol, because in fact 'Gorgeous Legs', with its now probably furious French Admiral, should have crossed the bow first!

So feeling rather uneasy, I followed the officer to the bridge where the small Emperor, sunk deep in an enormous cane armchair, with a minute little dog on his knees, gazed at me with his piercing black eyes.

Now the story went that if that rotten little dog began to yap at you, the Emperor would lose interest, and you might as well take to your heels. Fortunately the little yapper kept quiet, and the Emperor said with his extremely soft voice, in French, that he had very much appreciated the Netherlands presentation, and asked a few questions about the Netherlands Naval Air Service. Before my French vocabulary was completely exhausted, and after the Emperor had thanked me, I could thankfully take my leave, and concentrate on the champagne with the other naval officers.

The champagne brings to mind the shocking and shameful contrast that had struck me since our arrival, and especially the evening before at the banquet offered to us by the Emperor at the Imperial Palace. On arrival in Massawa I had already noticed the many emaciated, poor people wandering about town in tatters. When the gala dinner began, the Imperial cortege entered, led by the Emperor in full dress, followed by his family and the royal household, nearly all of them big and fat, and laden with jewels, the women wearing diamond tiaras. The endlessly long tables were magnificently laid with fine china and table silver, and there was a present lying beside each plate: for the ladies a bottle of perfume, and for the men a bottle of after-shave (mine was Dior).

The food had been specially flown over that morning from the Ritz in Paris, and it was indeed fabulous; that is if you could forget those poor wretches out in the streets.

Later I noticed that the Emperor read his speech without reading glasses!

The second evening appealed more to me. We were to dine on board the USS La Salle, an enormous supply ship, but because the US Navy is not allowed to have alcohol on board, we were invited for drinks before dinner on board of the British cruiser HMS Antrim. This ship had Princess Anne on board as a guest, and I also exchanged a few words with her. To my surprise she spoke quite critically about our Ethiopian hosts, but she was absolutely right.

After all, she is the daughter of Prince Philip, who is also known for his sometimes less tactful, if entirely justified, remarks. Also, she appeared to be well briefed by her father (President of World Wildlife Fund UK at the time and later President of WWF International), when she remarked on the profusion of eucalyptus trees in and around Massawa. She mentioned that both Ethiopia and Eritrea had at one time been quite verdant, until most trees had been chopped down by the ever-increasing population for fuel and building material. In an attempt to repair the damage and to prevent further erosion quick-growing Australian eucalyptus trees had been chosen, foreign and of little use to the indigenous fauna.

By Command of

His Imperial Majesty Haile Sellassie I, Emperor of Ethiopia,

The Minister of the Imperial Court

has the Honour to request the attendance of

Rear Admiral R. J. Idzerda

at a Dinner at the Imperial Palace,

on *12-2-1973* at *8 p.m.* *Dress: Black Tie*

Invitation card from His Imperial Majesty.

The British had the Royal Marines band on board, who treated us to a concert while countermarching in dress uniform along the quayside in front of the ship.

This provoked a comment from the Russian Rear Admiral, who was our host for drinks on board the *Skritnii* – a 'Sverdlof-class' heavy cruiser. After the dinner, with ice-water served by the Americans, he exclaimed: 'The Yanks provide the food, the British the floorshow, and we the vodka!'

On the way back I just had time to get a kilogram of coffee beans from a little Italian shop in Asmara, keeping in mind the fact that coffee originated in Eritrea, although the Arabs claim that it was in Jemen. In any case, on the way back a delicious fragrance of freshly roasted coffee beans pervaded the aeroplane.

5th March, 1973

Rear Admiral R. J. Idzerda, R.N.N.
Flag Officer, Royal Netherlands Naval Air Force
c/o Ministerie van Defence
Toresnstraat 172
Den Hague
The Netherlands

Dear Admiral Izerda

I was so pleased that you were able to attend this year's Navy Days, and that a Breuget Atlantic 1150 aircraft should be flown out especially for this unique occasion. I was also pleased to have had the opportunity to discuss briefly with you matters of mutual interest.

May I say how much I appreciated the framed early map of Holland which together with the plaque I have hung in my office in Massawa, will serve as constant reminders of your country's participation in this special occasion.

I do hope you enjoyed your short stay in Massawa and that you had a pleasant flight back to the Netherlands.

Yours sincerely,

Alexander Desta
Rear Admiral

Naval Headquarters, Addis Ababa, Ethiopia

Letter from Rear Admiral Desta, the grandson of Emperor Haile Sellassi.

I could not then foresee that not long afterwards neither the Emperor nor his grandson, Rear Admiral Alexander Desta, the Commander-in-chief of the Ethiopian Navy, would survive the revolution which was soon to break out. On my desk I still have

Desta's personal gift to me, a silver ashtray embossed with the Imperial arms, and set in a slice of ivory from an elephant's tusk.

Another memorable and more business-like journey was in connection with the planned replacement for the Neptunes, and the purchase of new helicopters, two projects which were partly my responsibility. It began with a visit to an 'Orion' squadron of the US Navy. We were especially interested in the Orion as the replacement for the Neptune. Subsequently I was flown to the headquarters of the Commander-in-Chief Eastern Atlantic (CINC Eastlant) in Norfolk, Virginia. I was his guest, and had already met him when his Task Force had visited Rotterdam.

It so happened that Netherlands Task Force 5 was also in Norfolk, under the command of Rear Admiral Paul van der Mehr Mohr, an old friend of mine. My host and his wife were invited for a reception on board the flagship, and took me along with them, as an uninvited guest.

When we went up the gangway, I was walking behind the Admiral and his wife, and I saw the Admiral suddenly stiffen – he actually almost halted. The reason for his shocked reaction was clear: among others standing at the top of the gangway, there was a duty officer with long hair down to his collar …

Paul was pleasantly surprised to see me there (in civilian clothes) in the wake of the Americans, and when I later told him about my host's reaction, he shrugged his shoulders:

'That's up to the Defence Minister, he approved it. Besides, the men with long hair do just as good a job as the rest.'

During a sailing trip at Key West in Florida at the weekend with another American Admiral who was my host there, I went to grab the foresheet at one particular time, and at the same time saw my gold wristwatch, which Toni had given me as a gift for my promotion, splash in a wide circle into the Gulf of Mexico. 'Fifty fathoms' was the dry comment of my host, so I could forget about diving after it.

The journey remained unlucky because after this sailing trip in the burning hot sun, I caught a bad cold through lying on my bed in an icy cold room, where the air conditioning was on maximum, in accordance with good American custom. But my very busy programme had to continue, and I had to keep myself on my feet –

literally – with the help of pills and powders, while my cold gradually developed into pneumonia.

But first there was the visit to the Kaman helicopter factory, after which we were brought to New York Airport in the company plane, a fast 'Learjet'. That flight was a new experience: the pilot was the only crew member, and after take-off, he put on the automatic pilot, loosened his belts, opened a little cupboard in the wall, and asked with an inviting smile:

'What would you like to drink, gentlemen?'

Meanwhile the Learjet shot up like a rocket to 42.000 ft, about the maximum height of my beloved Seahawk of yesteryear, and then with a kind of ballistic curve began the descent for the landing!

Members of the Admiralty Board with their ladies at the farewell dinner for Vice Admiral P.P. van de Vijver, Flag Officer Materials. Toni is the fourth lady from the right.

A very special occasion was the thirtieth anniversary of 'D-Day', the sixth of June 1974.

Although in 1944 I was at the other end of the world, and thus did not take part in the operations in Normandy, I was delegated by the Commander-in-Chief, Eric Roest, to attend the ceremonies to represent the Netherlands Royal Navy.

The endless rows of crosses on the immense burial grounds especially made a lasting impression on me. Such a waste of young lives.

There had apparently been heavy fighting shortly after the landing at a narrow bridge over the Orne River (if I remember correctly). The story goes that at a certain moment there was a lull in the shooting, and the ensuing deathly quiet was suddenly broken by the sound of bagpipes played by a Highlander in his kilt as he crossed the bridge. It was said that this was just the morale boost the British needed, and the bridge was recaptured soon after.

I had just heard this story, and was standing with a group gazing at the bridge and lost in thought, when all at once we heard the melancholy sound of bagpipes – and there came that same Highlander in his kilt and bandy legs marching over the bridge. Several of my companions, veterans of the invasion, were deeply moved, and I also had to swallow a couple of times.

An interesting event was the official visit that Toni and I, accompanied by the Head of the Naval Air Technical Service, Captain 'Rob' Jager, paid to my British opposite number, Vice Admiral J.D. Treacher. We flew to the Royal Naval Air Station Yeovilton in an Atlantic of the Netherlands Naval Air Service, and Toni and I stayed with him and his wife in their mansion, Wales House, which belonged to the Royal Navy. We had a lovely room where we slept in the bed of Queen Victoria and Prince Albert, which came from the royal yacht Victoria and Albert. The bedstead was made of silver, and decorated with their monogram, very beautiful, but not all that comfortable.

On the way to London to catch a plane back to Holland, we stopped at Stonehenge, which was then quiet and deserted, and we walked around freely, in contrast to a visit some twenty years later when the surroundings were full of car parks, souvenir shops, cafés etc., and crawling with tourists. Moreover, an entrance fee was then charged, and part of it was no longer accessible to the public.

In October 1974 I paid a short working visit to our Naval Air Detachment in Curaçao, West Indies. The journey went by Neptune via the Azores and Bermuda, and the captain of the plane, Lieutenant Commander Niessink was courteous enough to let me also do a landing. Luckily, it's just like riding a bicycle, once you've learned how, you never forget. On the journey back I flew with KLM, and I was somewhat taken aback when the hostess came and asked if I were Mr. Idzerda, and in that case would I then kindly come to the cockpit.

There I was surprised to find Menno Fris as Captain, whom I had instructed on the Neptune ten years earlier in 1964, when I was Commanding Officer of 320 Squadron. He had been in a group of civilian airline pilots, who had just finished their training at the National Aviation School, where the KLM obtained most of their young pilots. Through temporary economic circumstances, there were no vacancies for them at KLM, so the Royal Navy took care of them by allowing them to do their national service as pilots in the Naval Air Service.

Menno let me sit in the co-pilot's seat for a while, and I was thus able to express my satisfaction that my ex-pupil had turned out so well.

The Spring of 1975 was entirely focused on my departure from the Royal Navy.

On the fourteenth of May I made my last flight in a Neptune, accompanied by the Commanding Officer of 320 Squadron, Commander Kandau. This was combined with some festivity: my Admiral's flag with two stars was stuck by the mechanic during taxiing through the opened astrodome above the fuselage, and after landing I was presented with a huge farewell cake.

My last flight in a Neptune, with the Rear Admiral's flag hoisted.

At the controls for the last time.

The following day I had my last helicopter flight in a 'Wasp' helicopter from the Naval Air Station De Kooy. I was presented there with a small replica of the ship's bell, made of copper, of which the clapper was provided with a rope with many of the knots that I had had to learn thirty-four years before, like all sailors at that time.

At the farewell dinner at the Naval Air Base Valkenburg, I was given as a memento a magnificent wooden shield with all the emblems of the Naval Air squadrons (eight at the time) and the emblems of the two Naval Air Bases, and in the middle of the shield, in a frame behind glass, a replica of the Colours of the Naval Air Service. This was done in the original silk, imported from Belgium, and the beautiful embroidery, done by the wife of a Petty Officer, had taken sixty hours to complete.

Toni was presented with a model of a .22 calibre target shooting rifle by Captain Frans Bom, as a memento of our stay in Biak, New Guinea, when he as the Armament Officer of the Base gave target shooting instruction to the Navy wives.

The official transfer to my successor, Commodore Willem van den Heuvel, took place with the usual ceremonial on the sixth of June 1975, only this time not in dress uniform as this had meanwhile been done away with for reasons of economy (it was reinstated later on).

The feelings which gradually came over me those last few weeks are difficult to describe. On the one hand I could look back on an exceptionally interesting career, with the satisfaction that I had attained the highest possible position in my branch, on the other hand a feeling of sadness because after thirty-four years I had to take leave of what in fact for me had become one large family, the Royal Navy and the Naval Air Service in particular.

Farewell to the Royal Navy.

15. World Wildlife Fund 1975-84

In my last year in the Navy, I had often discussed with Toni what I would do after I left the Navy. After all I was only fifty-one years old.

I had received two offers, one from Hughes Aeronautics and one from Fokker Aircraft. But actually I felt like doing something entirely different, out of the Defence sphere.

I had always been very interested in nature, and for a long time had been a donor to the Netherlands branch of the International World Wildlife Fund, WWF, (now called World Wide Fund for Nature) and I liked the idea of doing something there.

HRH Prince Bernhard, whom I had met several times, was at the time President of WWF-International, and also of the Netherlands branch of the WWF, and I decided to request an audience with him. An opportunity soon arose when I was invited for the annual reception which the Prince was wont to give in his function of Inspector-General of the Armed Forces at the Zwaluwenberg Mansion for Flag Officers, Generals and Commanding Officers.

The Prince's secretary, Ted Vernède, was an ex-Navy colleague whom I knew personally, and I took him aside and told him what my intentions were.

'Well, he's standing over there, go and make an appointment with him!', he said, and brushed my doubts away. 'He won't mind at all.'

So I made my way through the circle around His Royal Highness and was able to attract his attention.

'Your Royal Highness, could I ask you something?'

Certainly Admiral, what is it?'

And I explained briefly what I had in mind. His reaction was unexpectedly quick and positive: he pulled out his diary, and an appointment was made for a Sunday afternoon at five o'clock at Soestdijk Palace, which is near Utrecht.

On the arranged day I turned up at the gate of the Palace grounds, where the sentry on guard let me in, and at the entrance door to the Palace a footman was waiting for me who led me straight to the Prince's study. I made use of the opportunity to look around at the countless elephants, in all sizes and made from all kinds of material.

Prince Bernhard had a special affinity with elephants, and once this was known, he was often offered one as a gift. Even the holiday home of the Royal Family in Porto Ercole on the Italian Peninsula Argentaria is called 'The Happy Elephant'. But very soon Prince Bernhard came walking in with outstretched hand.

'Admiral, what would you like to drink?'

A cup of tea, please, Sir.'

'Well, at this time of day I usually drink something stronger. Won't you join me?'

'In that case, I will gladly join you, Sir.'

He then got straight to the point.

'This is a real coincidence; we have just received a McKinsey report at WWF concerning a highly necessary reorganisation, and one of the recommendations was to take on a manager who can occupy himself with the coordination between Headquarters in Switzerland and the twenty-six National Organisations, and I think that is something for you: a bit of 'military discipline' won't hurt them.

The pleasant conversation which followed, and the quick response to a matter, was typical of Prince Bernhard. In the coming years I would repeatedly be hearing from different people in various countries how valuable his involvement was; with his natural charm and naturally also his status, he could achieve much where others had failed. Also, his motivation was enormous; he told me once that 90% of his time was devoted to the WWF.

I remember one illustrative example when he was visiting Venezuela and was received by the President, a dictator at the time. Venezuela has vast tropical jungles, which, however, as is so often the case, were being threatened by increasing population pressure and uncontrolled felling of trees for the timber trade. Notwithstanding many attempts by UNESCO and other nature protection groups, no one had as yet succeeded in persuading the Government of Venezuela to set up a Nature Reserve. At his meeting with the President during an official event, and within easy hearing distance of the many high authorities present, Prince Bernhard said in fluent Spanish:

'Senõr President, I have heard that you have just proclaimed a National Park, and I would like to congratulate you on this very wise and noble decision.'

In no time the Dictator gave the necessary instructions, and the National Park was a fact.

It is undoubtedly true, especially in the often difficult times in the beginning when nature conservation was not all that common, that Prince Bernhard was of inestimable value to the WWF, and to nature conservation in general. It is therefore not surprising that when he retired as President of WWF-International, he was honoured with the title of 'Founder President'.

Back to my interview. I had never thought of Switzerland, and that naturally first had to be discussed with Toni, but she was immediately enthusiastic about it. So I accepted the offer, and a week later I had a meeting with the Swiss Director-General of WWF-International, Dr. Fritz Vollmar, when on a journey he was able to make a stopover at Amsterdam Airport. He proposed the function of Director of National Organisations Coordination, and suggested that I attend a meeting shortly to be held in London at the home of one of the Trustees of the Executive Committee, Mrs. Sonja Bata (her Tsjech husband was the Bata shoe manufacturer), which I did.

This was my first acquaintance with a very diverse international gathering, including the Directors of the National Organisations, at that time twenty-six. I also met there an energetic young man, Charles de Haes, who made himself known as 'Special Advisor' to Prince Bernhard (usually referred to as PB in WWF circles). The place where the meeting was held was rather special: a large room containing a private collection of literally hundreds of shoes from all corners of the world, including some very old and primitive specimens. This was a foretaste of the sometimes very exotic company I would be mixing with from then on – a greater contrast with the orderly and uniform (literally) life in the Navy is not conceivable.

And so I began my 'second career' on the first of August 1975 at WWF-International at Morges, Switzerland, as Director of International Coordination, although when I arrived that first day, I found that the door was locked – it was the Swiss National Holiday.

At least I had a chance to admire the outside of the beautiful old villa 'La Gracieuse' where WWF Headquarters were seated. For that matter, the whole town Morges, situated on Lake Geneva with a wonderful view of the Mont Blanc and the Alps, is itself a good example of the picturesque, typical French-Swiss architecture.

Director of International Coordination at the WWF.

My entrance the next day was quite remarkable: I was taken by the secretary-administrator Jean-François Buvelot, who seemed somewhat ill at ease, to the office of the Director-General ('DG'), where to my surprise I saw sitting behind the desk next to Dr. Vollmar, the 'Special Assistant' to Prince Bernhard, Charles de Haes. I was told that as a result of the above-mentioned McKinsey report, from now on two DGs would lead the organisation: Vollmar for the scientific and educative side, De Haes for the business side, and I had the honour of being the first to be confronted with the new situation. Indeed, a bit later on, the staff was called together to be informed. I couldn't help thinking that it was an odd construction, 'two captains on the bridge', that could never work for long. And that turned out to be the case, because after a length of time, which was characterised at times by great tension, only Charles de Haes remained, and I again had only one boss.

I should now say something about the organisation of the WWF. On the eleventh of September 1961 the Fund was established at Morges, Switzerland, as a result of a number of initiatives by people who were alarmed by the fact that in many parts of the world, and especially in Africa, things were going very wrong with nature in general, and with wild animals in particular. It was clear from the very beginning that improving the situation could only be achieved with money, lots of money, so that the task of the Fund would have to be mainly fund raising, and naturally information, because you can not raise funds without a message.

The scientific base, on which the organisation had to be supported, was formed by the already existing 'International Union for the Conservation of Nature and Natural Resources', the IUCN, which was established in 1948. This Union is one of those rare combinations in which both governments and non-government organisations (NGOs) work together as partners, resulting in an alliance, in which more than eight hundred members in a hundred and twenty countries participate with a network of more than a thousand specialists, spread all over the world, who keep the 'finger on the pulse'.

The beginning of the WWF was very modest: within six months of the establishment, a Secretary-General, the Swiss Dr. Vollmar, was appointed, and he was given one secretary (Danielle, whom he later married – to make sure she stayed on, as she once jokingly told us!) .

Not until 1967 was it possible to increase the staff gradually with an assistant, the Swiss Jean-François Buvelot, and in 1970 with two more members, the British journalist Peter Jackson for information and the German Dr. Hartmut Jungius, a biologist. Fritz Vollmar told me that there were times when he could hardly pay the salaries of the staff. As will appear later, an ingenious solution was found for that problem.

Peter Jackson was a former correspondent for Reuter, and had once made a big scoop when he was posted to India. During a visit to India, USSR Secretary Khrushchev had 'dropped a bomb' at a garden party given in his honour. He informed the surprised gathering that the Soviet Union had just exploded a hydrogen bomb for the first time.

The press, who were present, dashed off to get this sensational news off to their editors as quickly as possible. One of them was able to grab a bicycle, the fastest mode of transport for getting through the heavy traffic of New Delhi, so Peter knew he had lost out.

He resignedly took a taxi and on the way to the telegraph office he calmly typed out his story on his little portable, which he always carried with him. When he arrived at the telegraph office, there was already quite a commotion; the irritated functionary couldn't read the hastily written scrawl of the bicycle correspondent, and handed it back to him, after which Peter calmly slipped his neatly typed message in front of him. It was immediately accepted, and Peter had the scoop.

Much of the initial success of the WWF was due to the enthusiastic direction of Vollmar, but as so often happens with new organisations, it was exactly that success which threatened to outgrow him. The result was the decision to appoint a second DG, as described before.

The international governing body consisted of a Board of Trustees, formed of influential persons from many different countries, naturally all honorary, of which Prince Bernhard was President. Out of the Board of Trustees an Executive Committee (EXCO) was formed of persons who were willing to spend much time and attention on the WWF, and who met twice a year with the Board of Directors to discuss policy. One of these meetings was combined with the yearly Board meeting, when the representatives of the National Organisations held their meeting at the same time.

The members of the International Board of Trustees were mostly interesting people, such as Sir Peter Scott, who was the first Chairman of EXCO, Dr. Luc Hoffman (Hoffman La Roche), who was the Vice-President of the WWF, Dr. Anton Rupert (Rothman Group), Sonja Bata (Bata shoe manufacturers), Mrs. Mars (Mars Bars), David Ogilvy (Ogilvy and Mathers, Public Relations), Stewart McLain (McKinsey), John Loudon (Shell), Suzi Agnelli (Fiat), Fleur Cowles (painter and author), Thor Heyerdahl (anthropologist and writer, i.a. Kontiki) and Sir David Attenborough (film-maker).

Luc Hoffman, an ornithologist, was a rather reserved, extremely modest man, who had found his life's work in the French Camargue wetlands, a protected nature area, Tour du Valat, which he had established, and which had a study centre where water fowl such as flamingos, swans and geese were studied.

Susi Agnelli was a tall, handsome lady with the features of a Roman aristocrat. I once fetched her from Geneva Airport. It was the time that sensational kidnappings were taking place in Italy, such as that of the well known politician Aldo Moro. She was the sister of Giovanni Agnelli, President Director and owner of the Fiat concern, and at that time the richest man in Italy. I asked her if she felt safe travelling alone as she did. She answered, taking a spray gun of tear gas out of her handbag, 'They would get an eyeful!'

Fleur Cowles had been United States Ambassador to Argentina during the rule of the Perons. The musical 'Evita' was based on a book that she had written about Evita Peron. She told me that this fact was not acknowledged until after a formal protest, and then the acknowledgement was included in the programme of the musical. She didn't think much of the musical except for the song 'Don't cry for me, Argentina'.

Her favourite themes for her paintings were flowers and the cat family. I once asked her who her favourite painter was, and she replied: 'Albrecht Dürer'. Naturally she knew his magnificent copper engravings which I had so admired in my youth, from the book Brehms Thierleben.

I first met the Norwegian, Thor Heyerdahl, in Italy where he lived. He told me that he thought Italy was the most beautiful country in the world, an opinion that was not entirely shared by his Norwegian wife, since she still spent a lot of time in Norway.

The Board of Directors is charged with the daily management, and is composed of remunerated professionals, who at least initially were lent to WWF on a temporary basis. The permanent staff ultimately numbered about thirty of ten different nationalities, although English was the language generally used.

It is interesting to clarify the involvement of Sir Peter Scott, also because it illustrates the dedication of many other prominent persons. Sir Peter was the son of Robert Scott, the famous adventurer who perished in 1912 together with his four companions, after having reached the South Pole and the disappointing discovery that the Norwegian Amundsen had got there more than a month ahead of them. On the way back, Robert Scott had written a farewell note to his wife which was later found on him, and in which he wrote: 'Teach the boy to love nature …'

Robert Scott became a national hero in Great Britain, and at the same time an example for his son Peter, who would strive his whole life to carry his name with honour. He was certainly very successful in this: he was a well known painter (mostly of ducks and geese), and author. He also won the British championship for glider flying, and an Olympic bronze medal for sailing.

Sir Peter, an ornithologist, had been an ardent hunter, a combination with nature conservation which is certainly not uncommon. One day he shot a wild goose, but unfortunately only wounded one wing. The goose went down on a sand bank in the middle of the mouth of a river out of Peter's shooting range, and with the tide coming in, he had to watch helplessly as the bird slowly perished. He was so moved by the sight that he decided there and then to hang his rifles up for good – as he said himself – and became deeply involved in the protection of nature.

Among other projects he set up the 'Wildfowl Trust' for water birds at Slimbridge, Gloustershire, and it was known that he could recognise every individual wild swan by its beak. He was therefore the obvious person, and one of the first, to set up and devote himself to the WWF.

He put his mark on the WWF for good by designing the Panda, the emblem of the WWF, for which he used the famous Chi Chi from the London zoo as a model.

My arrival coincided with more radical changes in the Board of Directors of WWF-International. It had been decided to draw on a number of Directors from the business world who were seconded to WWF by – and at the expense of – their firms, who were willing to contribute to the WWF in this way, with the aim of bringing more professionalism and business experience to the organisation.

And so the staff was ultimately enlarged with a Director of Finance, a Director of Public Relations, and a bit later a Director of Fundraising, all real professionals, who in the beginning did not fit in very well with the rather amateurish, albeit enthusiastic WWF atmosphere of the time.

The Director General, Charles de Haes, a Belgian who grew up in South Africa, came from the Rothman Group where as a junior director he was charged with the sale of cigarettes. He was himself a non-smoker, but he cleverly managed to hide this by always having a packet of cigarettes showing in his breast pocket.

The Director of Public Relations was Max Bisset (the brother of film actress Jacqueline Bisset) and was seconded by the large international advertising firm Ogilvy and Mather. He was quite a character, who confided in me when he arrived that he couldn't tell the difference between a rhinoceros and a giraffe, but of course that was not what he was taken on for. He soon settled in, and after a short period of familiarisation, demonstrated his worth for ever at the weekly Directors meeting when he suddenly remarked that he could not discover a fixed pattern, a clear policy in our organisation – in short a *Strategy* was lacking.

This met with immediate agreement and the task of drafting an official 'Conservation Strategy' was assigned to our scientific sister organisation, the International Union for the Conservation of Nature and natural resources (IUCN). After a few months a first draft was presented, which was naturally also discussed at our Directors meeting, after we had all had the opportunity to study the document and form an opinion on it.

Over the past years I had gradually become more and more convinced by all that I had seen and read, for example in the reports of the Club of Rome, that the threat to nature resided in a basic problem, the population explosion, especially in the so-called Third World, where, moreover, the most pristine nature could still be found. There was no mention of this in the new strategy given the title 'How to Save the World', although there were six other priorities tabled. So I asked, why the omission?

The Director-General of IUCN, who was also present with some of his staff to elaborate on the concept, quickly exchanged glances before saying:

'You are absolutely right, and of course we have thought about it, but it has been decided from high-up that this subject is too sensitive for various religions and population groups .'

Incredible!

Not long afterwards I once asked Peter Scott if he could still be optimistic about the future of nature conservation. He thought for a moment, and then said: 'I have to be. I can't afford *not* to be.

We were often visited at Headquarters by people who devoted their energies in one way or another to nature conservation. One of these was the film-maker Hugo Baron van Lawick, who was then married to Jane Goodall, the well known chimpanzee specialist, and I was greatly impressed by him. But I was most fascinated by the stories of Diane Fossey, the 'Gorilla Woman', whose story was later told in the film 'Gorillas in the Mist'. It was very moving to hear her tell how, when she was studying a gorilla family, after months of patient attempts to get closer, she was suddenly approached by the leader, an enormous 'silver back' (adult male gorillas have a silver grey back). After some imposing chest-beating and deep growling, he went and squatted next to her. Diane went numb with fear, huddled up, avoided eye contact as she had been taught, and started picking leaves which she put in her mouth to show that she was only eating and so meant no harm. All of a sudden, an immense hairy black hand came into view, and gently picked up her notebook from her lap. The gorilla just smelled it, put it back on her lap, and quietly moved away. Diane told us that she then burst into tears – understandably, for she had been accepted! Alas it ended badly both for 'Digit', as she called the gorilla leader (he had one finger missing), and for Diane. They were both murderd by poachers.

My new job entailed a lot of travelling since I naturally had to visit the National Organisations (NOs) of the WWF at their home base to learn their methods – and their weaknesses. Most of the NOs functioned moderately well to poorly. Practically everywhere personnel merely consisted of underpaid, enthusiastic amateurs and volunteers, who were more interested in nature conservation itself than in collecting funds so to be able to realise that goal, which was the real aim of the WWF.

To bring about an improvement required much patience and especially tact since these NOs were in fact independent organisations, and only linked to WWF-International by the name, the Panda emblem, and a fairly open contract.

Obviously I could not occupy myself with all of the twenty-six NOs. Furthermore, some of them had no need of my intervention since they were already operating quite well or reasonably so. The best two were the Netherlands and Switzerland, followed by the United States and the United Kingdom.

To start with I concentrated especially on Belgium, where I was able to find a new Director, an ex-Proctor and Gamble man, who later succeeded in bringing WWF Belgium to the (relative) top.

The procedure which led to this successful result was an interesting experience, and I made use of it later on when working with other NOs. The first step was always to find an influential person locally who was well disposed to the WWF, and then get down to work through him or her to find a suitable director.

In Belgium this was Henri Count de Launoit, who was President of the Banque Lambert in Brussels. He was a most likeable person and I got on well with him. I had a sumptuous office at my disposal on the top floor of the skyscraper where he himself had his seat, with a magnificent view over Brussels, in addition to the assistance of his secretary when necessary. In that office I subsequently interviewed the candidates who had reacted to advertisements, or who had been sent by WWF connections. The very first person, who came in on the very first day, was one of the three best candidates I chose, from which the Board of WWF Belgium had to make their choice, and he became the new Director: Yves Boulpaep, a good-natured, humorous Belgian, who became a good friend. Moreover, more importantly, he achieved good results, which was naturally also good for my reputation.

With Prince Bernhard and Yves Boulpaep, Director WWF Belgium.

In the meantime WWF Headquarters had been relocated in a much larger, modern building in Gland, a short distance from Geneva. The new building was financed by an anonymous donor.

One of my first visits was to WWF Austria, accompanied by the Director-General, Dr. Vollmar and the Director of Conservation, Dr. Hartmut Jungius, and one of the first things I noticed there was that the subjects in discussion bore little relation to conservation. The people we talked to were mainly important businessmen and politicians, who had one thing in common, their passion for hunting, although as I have remarked earlier on, a passion for hunting can easily be combined with a passion for nature conservation. However, in Austria the collecting of funds to conserve that nature hardly came up for discussion.

One day a large meeting combined with lunch had been organised in a nature reserve in the south east of Austria. I remember the large numbers of storks nesting in the trees there; there were hardly any left in Holland at that time. Before lunch speeches had to be made of course, and our host introduced us, as is usual in extremely formal Austria, with full titles, which were also constantly used in the course of the conversation:

'Und nun, meine Damen und Herren, möchte Ich Ihnen gerne vorstellen Herr Doktor Vollmar, General Direktor, Herr Doktor Jungius, Direktor für Naturschutz unde Herr …' then he stopped for a minute because he couldn't think of a fitting title for me, until Fritz Vollmar whispered to him: 'Konteradmiral!' … 'Herr Konteradmiral Idzerda Direktor Koordination.'

It had been a long time since they had had one of those in their midst, and my reputation was saved.

WWF Austria became one of my 'clients', and I became good friends with the Director, Winfried Walter, a true nature lover and expert. He preferred to spend his holidays in the Pyrenees, lying on his back on a mountain slope, peering at the lammergeiers (a rare, very large vulture) circling above, one of the few places where they were still to be found.

Luckily he and his Board were open to my suggestions, and after some time a business-trained young man was taken on, who could occupy himself with fundraising.

Before he got married, Winfried was living with his parents in their large house in Vienna, and I always stayed with them during my visits, which meant an intensive and very necessary exercise of my German. I had clearly suffered from the fact that because of the war and the German occupation of the Netherlands, I had only had three years of German at High School.

WWF Italy was a well-intentioned chaos – what else? – and so it also became one of my 'patients'. I was able to get my usual procedure accepted: appoint a full-time manager to join the willing amateurs, who regarded the WWF more as a hobby.

Together with one of their Board members, Alessandro (Alex) Muzi Falconi, I interviewed a number of candidates, of which one, Maria Christina Carradini, was our final choice. Later on I wondered what Alex's choice had actually been based on, because some years later he and Christina got married.

The wedding was in 1987, and I had already left the WWF, but some contact remained, especially with the Italian colleagues and friends, and so Alex asked me to be best man at his wedding. This took place at the town hall in Lerici, and was followed by a festive lunch at the golf club. It was an unforgettable occasion, and Toni and I thoroughly enjoyed that typical Italian atmosphere: warm, gay and slightly chaotic, but in such a way that everything turned out very well nevertheless. We had once done an Italian language course, but my mastery of that beautiful language was not such that I was confident of properly fulfilling my role as best man before the Mayor of Lerici, who was performing the ceremony himself. (the Muzi Falconis are an old aristocratic family). But I had learnt a few necessary sentences by heart, and everything went well.

All our Italian friends spoke fluent English and /or French. Alex even had an English mother, the same as Robert Lasagna, the Vice President of WWF Italia. Robert and his charming wife Francesca, who taught chemistry at the University of Milan, also became good friends, and I always stayed with them during my many visits to Milan. Robert originally worked for the international advertising firm Ogilvy and Mathers, then later on, started his own company, and ultimately became PR man for the Italian television magnate Berlusconi during his first campaign for prime minister. Later Robert became a Senator in the Italian Parliament.

Alex's mother, Mary, was a very special person. She had married an Italian diplomat, who was representing his country in Ethiopia when she gave birth to their first child in a tent whilst on safari in the desert. She told us fascinating stories about her experiences as the wife of a diplomat. When her husband was ambassador in Djarkarta, Indonesia, it often happened that through seniority, she had to sit next to President Soekarno at a gala dinner. It was generally known that the President was very interested in attractive young women, and sometimes she was diplomatically able to change places with younger women to do him a favour.

With Toni, Niels Halbertsma, Director of WWF Netherlands, and the highly decorated Ambonese Indonesian Julius Tahija (RMWO) who fought with the Dutch against the Japanese), at the 'WWF Awards Dinner' given by HRH Prince Philip in Château d'Aigle, Switzerland.

After her husband retired, they had to look for a place to live. Once when they were staying at Lerici on the Bay of La Spezia, she was walking near Montemarcello, a picturesque old fishing village dating back to the Middle Ages, like so many along the coast of Italy. Her attention was drawn to an old ruin in the hills. It was a lookout tower, many of which used to be built along the coast in former times to warn the inhabitants if pirates or other undesirable folk were approaching. Then all the inhabitants on the coast would quickly withdraw to the village high up in the hills, in this case Montemarcello. And all of a sudden she visualised it: their new home had to be built around this old tower.

A well known architect from Rome was contracted, and he created a really wonderful house, in which the old ruin was cleverly assimilated. Then it was time for Montemarcello itself.

Mary managed to persuade a number of friends and acquaintances from Milan (including her three sons and the Lasagnas) to buy some uninhabited dilapidated buildings and have them completely restored as holiday homes, all the time maintaining the original style and features of the historic village. At the same time Mary had running water, electricity and telephone supplied to the village. The result was amazing, and we have had many enjoyable times there with our Italian friends.

When Mary died a few years ago, the village square was renamed Baronessa Muzi Falconi.

Back to WWF. The Secretary-General of WWF Italia was Arturo Osio, a rather surly and reticent bachelor, who as usual knew all about nature conservation, but practically nothing about fundraising. This was more or less solved when Christina was given an office in Milan, the business centre of Italy, while Arturo remained at the Headquarters of WWF Italia in Rome to maintain his contacts with the Government and nature protection organisations.

To my surprise I actually got on well with Arturo, and one day he invited Toni and me to spend a weekend with him at his property on the magnificent peninsula of Argentaria. When I mentioned this invitation to the President of WWF Italia, Fulco Pratesi, he burst out: 'What? From Osio? Nobody has ever had as much as an espresso from him!'

Arturo fetched us from 'Leonardo da Vinci' Airport, Rome, and showed us the city by night. The atmosphere in that ancient city with its magnificent squares, fountains and romantic alleyways, is indescribable.

Early the next morning Arturo drove us to Argentaria. His house apparently formed part of a large property belonging to his uncle, a banker, where members of the Osio family each had their own place. We arrived at his house through wrought-iron gates and a long driveway through a beautiful park and olive groves. The first thing we noticed was the delicious smell of a barbecue, and his housekeeper soon put a large dorado fish on the grill for lunch. We drank wine from his own vineyards and the salad was prepared with olive oil from his own groves. After a siesta, we walked over the property to the sea for a refreshing swim.

La dolce vita …

The northern NOs were a separate story. Because they always used to stick together – they also speak each other's languages; even most Finns speak Swedish – they were called the 'Scandinavian Mafia'. They also fell under my special attention, and I paid many visits to their respective offices in Oslo, Copenhagen, Stockholm and Helsinki. I usually combined this with their own annual 'Nordic Meeting', which was organised in turn by one of them.

I always received an invitation beforehand together with the agenda, in addition to a special reminder to not forget to bring the 'duty free' drinks (alcohol was very highly taxed in Scandinavia).

I shall never forget one special experience, when I travelled to Helsinki in the middle of the winter. As usual I stayed with my Finnish colleague, Mauri Rautkari, Director of WWF Finland, on the outskirts of Helsinki. After the meeting, I and the complete 'mafia' went off to the back garden of the Rautkaris, where a real, original sauna was built, partly underground. We did have to clear the snow away first, though, but, warmed up by my 'duty free', that was quickly done. After each 'cooking', we rolled naked in the snow – as etiquette requires – until I asked Mauri suddenly:

'Where are all those virgins who are supposed to beat us with birch branches?'

To which he promptly retaliated: 'They refused to come when they heard a wild Dutchman would be here!'

The personal contacts and often friendships with people of different nationalities are among the most pleasant memories of my WWF time.

One of my reorganisations concerned WWF Spain, or the 'Asociaciòn para la Defensa de la Naturaleza' (ADENA). With the help of a head hunter, I found (again) a woman, Cristina Garcia-Orcoyen, who was subsequently appointed as Secretary-General by the Spanish WWF Board. Her father was the gynaecologist of the Royal Household, so perhaps that had some influence on the choice.

King Juan Carlos was Honorary President of ADENA, and when it was decided under Cristina's management to launch a large fundraising project, she was able to persuade the King through the President of ADENA, the Duke of Calabria (the King's cousin) to lend his support. It was said that this support consisted in picking up the telephone and calling a great number of influential and wealthy people personally to ask for their support.

Success guaranteed!

Furthermore, Prince Philip, The Duke of Edinburgh, who had succeeded Prince Bernhard as President of WWF-International, and Luc Hoffman, the Vice President, were also invited to add extra lustre to the whole affair.

My most important contact in Spain was Don José ('Pepe') Mayorga, a wealthy businessman, who was also a member of the international Executive Committee of the WWF. Pepe had become a dear friend, so when Toni was also invited for the opening of the fundraising project in Madrid in the Spring of 1983, he invited us both to stay with him at his home, together with Luc Hoffman.

One of the events on the programme was a visit by Prince Philip to the Coto Doñana, a very important wetland nature reserve on the Atlantic Coast, and Don Gonzalez Byass, the producer and owner of the well known sherry, was acting as host. I travelled the day before to Jerez de la Frontera (the name 'sherry' is derived from 'Jerez', the town where this wine originates) to make the necessary preparations, and I stayed with the Gonzalez Byass family.

It was interesting that, although they were obviously Spanish, you could still detect the centuries old English blood in the Byass family. The Don was a tall, very distinguished figure, who spoke perfect English, and even breakfast the next morning could not have been more British: a choice of fried kidneys, bacon, sausages, fried eggs, kippers and toast.

After Prince Philip and his party had arrived by air, we first visited the 'Bodega', where Prince Philip was presented with a dozen bottles of sherry of the year of his birth. The lid of the cask from which the sherry had been drawn for Prince Philip, was hung on the wall with his name on it, next to other famous names like Winston Churchill and Dwight D. Eisenhower.

I and the others were given a handsome wooden case, decorated with the Gonzalez Byass arms, and containing three different bottles of vintage sherry.

The highlight of the busy programme, which also included a lunch given by the British Ambassador, was a colourful reception and dinner given at the Palace by King Juan Carlos and Queen Sofia.

Soldiers arrayed in shining sixteenth-century cuirass, plumed helmets, and armed with halberds, were lining both sides of the wide staircase leading from the giant hall to the reception rooms.

'El Rey', King Juan Carlos, Honorary President of WWF Spain.

All the prominent people who had contributed to the project had been invited. During the apéritif, Prince Philip was standing talking to the King, and there was an enormous elephant's foot made into a little table standing next to them for their glasses. I happened to walk by, and apparently Prince Philip noticed me glancing sideways at the elephant's foot because he suddenly called me over and said: 'Juanito, I don't think our Director of Coordination approves of the President of ADENA using an elephant's foot as a table.' Luckily the King knew Philip's sense of humour, and laughed off my initial embarrassment.

The entire Royal Family was present at the gala dinner. The sister of the King was blind, as we had been told earlier, but this was not noticeable. We were amazed at how well she moved around with no apparent help from her husband, a doctor, who accompanied her. Later on at the dinner table, ex-King Simeon of Bulgaria, who sat next to Toni, told her that when the Infanta entertained at home, she poured the drinks herself for her guests: she could tell when the glass was full enough by holding a finger in it. Ex-King Simeon, who lived with his family in Madrid, said also that he had to work very hard for a living as a businessman: the days were long, there were no more siestas, and yet you didn't dine before ten o'clock in the evening. That made sense: our invitation was for 21.45 hours.

We had an interesting talk with Don Juan, the King's father, a very friendly gentleman. He told us that he had grown up in this palace, which is now exclusively used for ceremonial occasions. As a young child he used to ride his bicycle at top speed through the endless passages. However, what had given him the most satisfaction in his life, he said, was when he was promoted to Rear Admiral. A striking remark for the man who actually should have been the heir to the throne.

It should be emphasised here that all this pomp and splendour, in addition to the popularity of the Royal couple, greatly contributed to spreading the message of ADENA to the general public, aided by the press, who gave it full coverage, and that is what it was all about.

The Asiatic organisations, Pakistan, India and Thailand also fell under my responsibility. The involvement in Pakistan and India, following my standard procedure, led to the appointment of a retired Air Marshall and a retired Major General respectively. As was to be expected, this gave rise at Headquarters to some sarcastic comments: the Rear Admiral was in the process of militarising the WWF. But still, in those developing countries, it is often precisely the military who are able to bring some kind of order and discipline to an organisation, and as long as they are supported by others who are well versed in nature conservation, – and there is certainly no lack of those – it can only have a favourable effect on the result.

Although the WWF Directors of the Asiatic countries attended the annual meetings in Switzerland, a regular visit to those countries by the Director of National Organisations Development (in the meantime I had been 'promoted', and my title altered, after a new McKinsey report), was naturally not practical in view of the distance. But when in March 1984 it finally came about, I made it a combined visit, one week in each of the three countries, and at their special invitation, Toni went along too – after all she had entertained all of them at our home many times.

The first stop was Bangkok, where we were awaited at the airfield by a hostess, an acquaintance of our host, Pisit na Patalung. She apparently had access everywhere, and walked us through customs and all checks straight to where Pisit was waiting outside.

Pisit had reserved the bridal suite for us at the luxury hotel (at reduced price: the manager of the hotel was also somehow involved with the WWF) and we were enchanted to find several vases of beautiful orchids in our sitting room, in addition to bowls of exotic tropical fruit.

One of the highlights of our trip to Thailand was a visit to the nature reserve Khao Yai in the north of the country. During the long journey up there by car I noticed numerous eating stalls at the side of the road, which strongly reminded me of the 'warongs' in the East Indies in former times. On an impulse I suggested that we eat in one of those stalls since it was about time for lunch. Pisit, clearly surprised and amused, agreed, and we found a suitable one where we were served a delicious meal of Thai dishes that were as yet unknown to us. As far as Pisit was concerned, we could do no wrong: 'You are not visitors, it's like feeding the natives!'

There were still wild elephants and tigers roaming around in the reserve, but they hid themselves from us, as opposed to a band of Grey Gibbons, a protected ape species, who accompanied us for a while with their characteristic 'wow-wow' call.

At breakfast the next morning outside in the enclosure, a sambar buck, a large Asiatic deer, came begging for food.

The Sambar buck showing interest in Toni's breakfast.

Business activities consisted of various meetings with interested people with a view to setting up a worthy WWF Thailand in due course, and a well-attended talk for the Rotary Club Bangkok. At any rate, it provided plenty of publicity for the WWF.

One of the most interesting persons we met there was Mechai Viravaidya, a dynamic Thai (with a Scottish mother), who was occupied with population issues. He had already acquired an international reputation for his work in bringing the excessively high birth rate in Thailand down to acceptable proportions. He had achieved this by the introduction of condoms, which were unknown in Thailand (from then on they were called 'mechais'). He succeeded in getting condoms accepted by a people who were very prudish by nature, at least for the outside world, by turning it into a joke in a most original way: organising competitions between the various villages in blowing up condoms. Later on there was even a competition in the Olympic stadium between the Fire Brigade, the Police, the Military Forces etc. in the presence of King Bumiphol and Queen Sirikit. He was so successful that, as Secretary-General of the 'Population and Community Development Association', he created a special clinic for birth control, where representatives of various Asiatic countries could follow courses. I especially remember seeing there a large poster showing an Indonesian couple, she holding a baby in her arms, and he holding a toddler by the hand, and the words: 'Dua anak tjukup!' (two children are enough). He was rewarded for his initiatives with a special prize from the United Nations. Needless to say how much these initiatives touched me; at last someone was tackling the problem at the root.

The next stop was Bombay, India. We were awaited there by Major General (ret.) Eustace D'Souza; as his name already indicates, a Catholic Indian, born in the former Portuguese colony Goa, and a decorated veteran of the landing at Anzio, Italy, in 1944.

There too it was a succession of meetings and discussions, and it was often a rather exotic gathering. For instance, the President of WWF India was the ex-Maharajah of Baroda. Because titles had been abolished in India, he was now called Fatesinghrao Gaekwad (Jacky for his friends). He had had military training at Sandhurst, England, and liked to be addressed as 'Colonel'.

We travelled to Baroda from Bombay by air, and were taken first to the 'old' palace, which was now used for guests, where we refreshed ourselves, before being brought to the 'new' palace, where the family lived, for lunch. This palace also possessed a private museum containing among many other objects a magnificent collection of jade and precious gems of former Maharanees. *Sic transit gloria…*

Another interesting member of the Board of Trustees of WWF India was Godrej, a Parsee, and so a descendant of the Persians who, under Alexander the Great in the fourth century B.C., occupied parts of India. Parsees do not mix, or hardly so, with the local population, and have much paler skins. They are extremely enterprising, and therefore often wealthy. Godrej was a captain of industry, and he invited us to visit 'his' village near Bombay, complete with shops, schools and hospital, all belonging to Godrej, and populated by the workers in his factories and their families.

Often on this journey, I wondered as to how much the interest in nature conservation was sincere, or if it were a form of snobbishness because they could mix with VIPs such as Prince Bernhard and Prince Philip. Although, this perhaps also applied to many in the West, and that interest can naturally only be favourable for the ultimate goal: the conservation of nature. Slightly down the scale, there definitely were people who were genuinely interested in nature.

A good example of this last category was Dr. Khalid Hamid Sheikh, a biologist, and the honorary administrator of WWF Pakistan, who accompanied us during our visit to Lahore. He was a very kind and cultured man, and had an equally charming wife, who looked after Toni during our stay in Lahore. He told us that their marriage had not been arranged, but was of their own free choice, which, he said, was rather unusual in Pakistan.

Our visit coincided with the opening of a 'Plants Campaign' organised by WWF Pakistan, and we were both asked to take part, Toni to present prizes, and I for a talk in the Hilton Hotel.

Toni was first driven to the University where she was to fetch Mrs Khalid, who was a professor there. The driver went inside to get her while Toni waited outside in the car. All of a sudden, things seemed to get out of hand when she heard loud shots close by. A man hurried out of the building and signalled to Toni to stoop down with him behind the car, but luckily nothing else happened, and when Toni asked the man what it was, he simply brushed it off with the remark: 'It's probably fireworks!' Although Toni later commented to the Khalids that it had been the warmest reception she had had so far, no more was said about it.

A very special happening was the wedding of a nephew of Syed (meaning descendant of the prophet Mohammed) Babar Ali, the President of WWF Pakistan, a very wealthy businessman, and also a member of the international Board of Trustees of WWF. The marriage, arranged, of course, by the mutual families, was celebrated in an enormous tent, where the magnificently attired bridal couple were seated on a kind of raised throne, and the hundreds of guests were sitting strictly separated, the men on one side, and the women on the other side. Later on, everybody went to another part of the tent where a huge amount of delicacies and fruit juices were displayed. Then the two sexes were allowed to mingle again.

An amusing evening was spent at the invitation of the new Director of WWF Pakistan, Vice Air Marshall (ret.) Zafar Chaudhry, in the local Officers Club in Karachi, which was clearly still a remnant of British rule, complete with leather armchairs, and the guest book on a desk. You could fancy you were in England, except that all the faces around you were dark. Also at the bar: all the men were wearing a typical British tweed jacket or blazer with a double split, and spoke perfect 'Oxford' English.

We were asked what we would like to drink, and I looked hesitantly at the bottles lined up behind the bar, all colourful fruit juices of course.

'Would you like to leave it to the barman?', we were asked, and that seemed like an excellent idea. The barman got down to work behind the bar with his cocktail shaker, and produced an attractive looking, orange-coloured drink. But with the first big swallow – I was quite thirsty in that hot climate – I nearly fell over backwards: it must have been at least fifty percent alcohol. They all seemed to be enjoying the situation, asked if we liked the drink, and then (Muslims) merrily drank with us.

We had a very special experience during our visit to a WWF manifestation in Karachi. We were invited by a Pakistani WWF woman biologist to witness the yearly arrival of marine turtles, on the well known Turtle Beach on the Indian Ocean. They return at night to the beach where they were born to lay their eggs, a ritual that has been going on for millions of years . and this was the same beach where twenty years earlier we had spent a day relaxing with the two Neptune crews.

We arrived around midnight, when it was absolutely quiet except for the sound of breaking waves. We saw in the faint moonlight that the invasion was already in full swing, and we felt that we were watching a scene from primeval times, which in fact it was. Everywhere the immense turtles were coming on land to begin laboriously digging a hole in the sand with their rear legs. Then the eggs appeared like sticky, dinted ping-pong balls. As soon as the turtle, which we had been watching fascinated for hours, had finished laying her eggs, and began to cover them up with sand, the poor animal was unceremoniously picked up by two men, and put down next to the hole, so that the eggs could be removed. A rather disrespectful and abrupt treatment, which we didn't like: they could have waited until the animal had finished and gone back to sea. The eggs were then taken to an enclosed area, guarded by WWF personnel, where they were buried in the sand to be further hatched by the sun, safe from people, sea gulls and rats who all like to help themselves to the yearly treat.

We went back the next morning to watch the hatching of an earlier brood. As a gesture to their guests, they gave us a bucket full of baby turtles to be put out, and it was very touching to pick up the floundering little animals and put them down close to the sea in the right direction, after which they made their way to the safe waves by rapid swimming motions with their little 'flippers'. It made up a bit for the rather rough treatment of the mother turtle the night before.

The last stop before leaving Pakistan was Islamabad for the final meetings. It was cold and misty, and my clearest memory is of the cannabis that was growing wild at the side of the road.

We left Pakistan to return to Switzerland from Karachi, where we were first treated to a fantastic Chinese festive dinner given in our honour by the owner of the restaurant, whose precise connection with the WWF was not clear to me. Unfortunately I could not thoroughly enjoy the meal, partly due to the fact that I was suffering from an acute stomach upset, caused by drinking a glass of sugar cane juice – from a vendor on the street, when I should have known better. Apparently I had lost the resistance of my youth in the East Indies.

With Prince Philip (left) and Thor Heyerdahl, at WWF 20th Anniversary in London.

All the National Organisations met once a year at the International Headquarters in Gland, and once a year in one of the participating countries, where at the same time the yearly meeting of the Executive Committee took place. In May 1984 it was the turn of WWF U.S.A in Washington, and as was to be expected from our American colleagues, they went all out. They had formed a 'Welcoming Committee' of about a hundred and twenty prominent people, of which the Vice President and Mrs. Bush were the Honorary Chairmen, and included the Chief Justice of the United States Warren E. Berger, Mr. And Mrs. Henry Kissinger, and Robert McNamara.

We were all accommodated in one of the best hotels in Washington, the 'Embassy Row' on Massachusetts Avenue, and we happened to arrive there at the same time as Prince Philip. As we entered, he pointed to the monogram of the hotel above the entrance, an intertwined E and R, and said: 'I think I'll feel at home here!'

Such luxury did not go down well with some of the N.O. representatives, although the typical American hospitality was well meant, and the required donations for expenses (except for the hotel) could easily be obtained.

Nevertheless this five star hotel was a bit too much for the representatives of India and Pakistan, Eustace d'Souza and Khalid Hamid respectively, and to my surprise and pleasure I discovered that the Major General (ret.) of the Indian Army, who had fought twice against the Pakistani Army, and the Doctor of Biology at the Pakistan University in Lahore, who should in fact have been arch-enemies, were actually sharing a room to save costs! I only found out when I saw the Catholic and the Muslim fraternally having breakfast together every morning. What a shared interest in nature conservation can do.

For me it obviously meant a series of meetings and presentations, but a special programme had been put together for the VIPs, which included Toni. For one of the events, a 'celebrity lunch' given by the Ambassador of Sweden and his wife, at which Prince Bernhard was guest of honour, Toni was asked by Charles de Haes to look after the wife of Syed Babar Ali, whom we already knew from our visit to Pakistan. Charles was afraid that Mrs. Babar Ali might perhaps not feel completely at ease in that Western gathering. But Toni soon came to a different conclusion: they were standing drinking a glass of orange juice together when Mrs. Babar Ali, who was in beautiful, colourful, silk Pakistan attire, suddenly exclaimed:

'That's James Stewart sitting over there. I'm going over to say hello to him, do you want to come with me?' (Mr. and Mrs. James Stewart were also on the Welcoming Committee).

So Toni meekly followed while Mrs Babar Ali explained that James Stewart was her favourite film actor. The ladies introduced themselves, and he was very friendly and communicative, as I also learned myself when I talked to him later on. Moreover, we also had something in common: we had both flown during the war, he as an air gunner in B17s over Germany. It happened to be Jimmy Stewart's eightieth birthday that day.

With film actor James Stewart on his eightieth birthday.

A 'cook out' at the home of Vice President George Bush was also on the programme. We were all fetched from the hotel by bus, and everybody had to identify themselves and show their invitation card to a Secret Service Agent before being allowed in the bus. We wondered if Prince Philip, who was also on the bus, also had to identify himself.

When I wandered off into the large garden, holding my glass, I got a shock when I nearly bumped into another Secret Service Agent, this time with an automatic weapon at the ready.

'An Evening with World Wildlife Fund' in the presence of Prince Philip and Sir Peter Scott, had been organised at the Smithsonian Institution, among the stuffed animals, including the largest African elephant ever shot. I was talking to Mechai Viravaidya, the Thai I had already met in Bangkok. Through my visit to Thailand he had become interested in the work of the WWF, and had been invited, partly also on my recommendation, to become a member of the WWF Board of Trustees, a result which gave me great satisfaction.

I asked him that evening if he was already a member of the Thousand and One Club, a very exclusive gathering of one thousand participants, who were personally chosen by Prince Bernhard, and invited to give a donation of ten thousand dollars (at that time) to the WWF, and so become a member of the Club.

Vice President Bush and Russel Train, President of WWF USA,
both good for a laugh.

The way this original idea came into being is rather amusing. Charles de Haes, who was then working for the Rothman Group, was once sitting in a car with his boss, Dr. Anton Rupert, who was also a member of the Executive Committee of WWF, when Rupert said that they had to find a way to set up a separate fund. If they could find a thousand people, who each deposited ten thousand dollars in a fund, they could pay all the administrative costs, such as salaries of personnel, with the interest on that capital of ten million dollars. Then they would be able to say that no donations to WWF International were used to finance the organisation, as is usually the case with donations to charity. Every cent would go to the goal it was intended for – nature conservation. Dr.Rupert then went on to say that he had discussed the idea with Prince Bernhard, who was the ideal person to preside over the Club of a Thousand; he could invite members to the Palace once a year, for instance – snob appeal!

'But we need someone to find those thousand members, and I think that is just something for you, Charles. And you can put me down as the first candidate.'

Charles answered spontaneously: 'Wonderful idea, and I'm the second!'

'Very generous of you, Charles', Rupert reacted, although Charles first had to borrow the money, as he told me later.

And so Charles de Haes became 'Special Assistant' to Prince Bernhard, and he was successful. Within three years he had his thousand members together, from forty-six different countries, of what was now called the 'The 1001 Nature Trust', the 'one' being Prince Bernhard, of course.

The interest of the members was kept going by organising exclusive excursions, naturally all paid for by themselves, to important nature areas, such as the Antarctic and the Galapagos Islands, which in the beginning were often led by Sir Peter Scott.

Furthermore, membership could not be passed on, so that when a member died, a new member would be selected from the waiting list, which meant a new contribution of ten thousand dollars every time. And as can be expected, most very wealthy people are quite elderly.

Mechai was immediately interested, pulled out his cheque book straight away, wrote out a cheque for ten thousand dollars, and said: 'Rudi, you can fix this, OK?'

How could I refuse? I went to look for Prince Bernhard, who luckily was also present, and took him aside to explain quickly what an exceptional man Mechai was. (Mechai had just clearly demonstrated this in Washington, when at the end of his presentation to the Board, he handed out to all those present a keyring with a brightly coloured condom encased in plastic.)

Prince Bernhard, known for being quick to make a decision, did not disappoint me and said:

'OK Rudi, I trust your judgement, we'll let him precede.'

Back in Switzerland a curious event occurred. One of the most threatened larger animals is the tiger, which was once found all over Asia, up to and including even the Middle East, and in Siberia. From the very beginning the WWF had conducted an intensive campaign to protect the tiger, and within the framework of that campaign, research had ascertained that various sub-species of Felix Tigris were already extinct. One of these sub-species was the Balinese tiger, of which not a single photo could be found for the photo library at WWF Headquarters.

Prince Bernhard receiving the Directors of the National Organisations at Soestdijk Palace.

During a discussion with Peter Jackson, who was very knowledgeable about tigers, I suddenly remembered that among the many hunting photographs which I had inherited from my father, there was one of him, posing with his trophy, a tiger he had just shot in Bali. The skin of this tiger, with a 'B'mark between the ears, used to lie on the floor of my father's study. When I mentioned this, Peter enthusiastically asked me for a copy, I promised him one on condition that my father's name would not be mentioned with it, although naturally at the time the photo was taken,1924, tigers were plentiful everywhere, and were even considered to be very dangerous and harmful. I was assured that I would keep the copyright of the photo, the only one in the whole world. In the course of time, it appeared that there was quite a bit of interest worldwide for this very rare photo (see photo on page 12), typically from the National Geographic Society, so that now and again a few hundred Swiss francs came in. I had arranged with Peter Jackson, who had meanwhile been appointed Chairman of the Cat Specialist Group of IUCN, that this money would be put into the bank account of my father's granddaughter, Françoise, with the conviction that this would undoubtedly have had his full approval

Peter's fascination with tigers also appears from a story he once told me. He was walking alone in daytime through a forest in a nature reserve in India. As always, he was unarmed, although he had been warned about the presence of tigers.

Suddenly he saw a huge tiger lying asleep on the path ahead. Peter stiffened, and stood motionless, taking heart from the knowledge (or hope?) that tigers will seldom attack an upright person, unless it is a man-eater of course. The tiger opened one eye, and slowly stretched itself and yawned. Then with an agile movement, the tiger got up, gave Peter a look, and withdrew in a calm and stately manner, as befits the King of the Jungle.

Both Peter and I were moved when he told this story.

My final task at the WWF was introducing formal contracts between the International WWF and the different National Organisations. In my new function as Director of National Organisations Development, I and our lawyer, the Australian Barry Cocks, were charged with the task of discussing with all the NOs the obligations and rights *vis à vis* WWF International, in order to come to an agreement. This ultimately resulted in a formal signing of the agreement by the President of the WWF, Prince Philip, and the chairmen of the different National Organisations.

After that was done, the end of my WWF time was approaching fast because we had decided definitely to retire at the end of the year, and live in the South of France. After almost ten years with the WWF, I had now turned sixty-one, and had in fact fulfilled my task of putting the weaker brothers on their feet, and I felt that I should leave at a high point. When I informed my boss, Director-General Charles de Haes, of my intention, his first reaction was: 'Why?'. And that is exactly what I wanted to hear.

Prince Philip presented me with a handsome 'coffee table book' with a flattering inscription, and the farewell party given by Charles and Elizabeth de Haes at their home in November 1984 was a great success. Vice President Luc Hoffman said some kind words and gave us a standing invitation to stay with him in the Camargue.

*Prince Philip, President of WWF International, and his cousin the Duke of
Calabria, President of WWF Spain, signing the contract under the supervision
of Barry Cocks and myself. On the left of Prince Philip the Director-General
of WWF-International Charles de Haes.*

This farewell had a special significance for me. In the first place it
meant the end of a period which I had spent with a very special and
varied group of people – a greater contrast with the 'uniform' Royal
Navy with its relatively level-headed and sober personnel is not
conceivable – and in the second place because at the same time my
'productive' life was coming to an end.

Looking back on those inspiring; sometimes adventurous years, I
look upon my entry into the Royal Navy and the outbreak of the war
against Japan in 1941 as a turning point, a kind of point of reference:
the abrupt end of a carefree youth in my beloved East Indies, and the
sudden confrontation with dramatic events. But I suppose that this is
the case for most of the youth of my generation, who were so
abruptly catapulted into adulthood.

For the rest, I can also see a certain symmetry. In my youth I was
fascinated from a very early age by nature, and by animals in
particular. So when I ultimately arrived at the World Wildlife Fund,
the circle was complete.

Epilogue

One evening a few years later in the South of France the telephone rang. It was someone from the television programme 'Missing Without a Trace', who told me during the live transmission that there was a married couple in the studio who were looking for the helicopter pilot who had rescued them in Oude Tonge during the Great Flood in 1953. From the description of the rescue, I remembered the event very well, and I was very sorry that I was not able to meet them at that moment (see photo on page 142).

Shortly afterwards I received a letter from Johan Los in Oude Tonge, who described in detail what had happened between the Saturday night of the first of January 1953 and the rescue on the following Monday afternoon.

He and his wife, Sara, had seen their four-year-old daughter, and the father and sister of Johan, slip off the roof one by one, and drown before their eyes. His pregnant wife, their three-year-old daughter and he himself were eventually rescued by Taco and me on the Monday afternoon.

He ended his letter with an invitation to visit him and his wife in Oude Tonge.

A bit later I received another letter, this time from his daughter Willie, who was born three weeks after the rescue. She wrote that her parents were still suffering from trauma after all that had happened, especially around 1st February every year. However, that first contact by letter with me had done them a lot of good, so that they were now better able to talk about it together. She further wondered if it would be possible for me to arrange a helicopter flight sometime for her parents over Oude Tonge. I wrote back that I was no longer in a position to organise such an event, but that I would do my best.

The occasion indeed arose at the seventy-fifth Jubilee of the Naval Air Service in 1992. Through the mediation of the Flag Officer of the Naval Air Service, Commodore Rein Zeijlemaker, a helicopter was made available for a trip to Oude Tonge. It was arranged that daughter Willie and I would fly with the crew of the helicopter from the Naval Air Base Valkenburg for the visit, which had to be a complete surprise for the Los family. On the way there in the helicopter, the excited Willie sighed that being in a helicopter for the first time was a bit scary, so I gently pointed out that it was not *really* the first time for her ...

The helicopter landed behind the restored farm. The meeting with Sara and Johan Los was quite emotional, but later it appeared that this whole happening had had a very positive effect, and they were able to cope better with their trauma afterwards.

Later on we visited each other in our homes, and we still write to each other at Christmas.

Meeting with the Los Family in 1992. Daughter Willie Los is on the right.